Just The facts101 Textbook Key Facts

Kuwait Customs, Trade Regulations and Procedures Handbook: Strategic and Practical Information

by cram101
Texbook NOT Included

Table of Contents

Just The Facts101

Exam Prep for

Kuwait Customs, Trade Regulations and Procedures Handbook: Strategic and Practical Information

Just The Facts101 Exam Prep

eAIN 464180

Foundations of Business

A business, also known as an enterprise, agency or a firm, is an entity involved in the provision of goods and/or services to consumers. Businesses are prevalent in capitalist economies, where most of them are privately owned and provide goods and services to customers in exchange for other goods, services, or money.

:: Casting (manufacturing) ::

A _________ is a regularity in the world, man-made design, or abstract ideas. As such, the elements of a _________ repeat in a predictable manner. A geometric _________ is a kind of _________ formed of geometric shapes and typically repeated like a wallpaper design.

Exam Probability: **High**

1. *Answer choices:*

(see index for correct answer)

- a. Directional solidification
- b. Foundry sand testing
- c. Full-mold casting
- d. Tundish

Guidance: level 1

:: Telecommunication theory ::

In reliability theory and reliability engineering, the term _________ has the following meanings.

Exam Probability: **Medium**

2. *Answer choices:*

(see index for correct answer)

- a. Electrical length
- b. Root-raised-cosine filter
- c. Availability
- d. Intersymbol interference

Guidance: level 1

:: Stochastic processes ::

_________ in its modern meaning is a "new idea, creative thoughts, new imaginations in form of device or method". _________ is often also viewed as the application of better solutions that meet new requirements, unarticulated needs, or existing market needs. Such _________ takes place through the provision of more-effective products, processes, services, technologies, or business models that are made available to markets, governments and society. An _________ is something original and more effective and, as a consequence, new, that "breaks into" the market or society. _________ is related to, but not the same as, invention, as _________ is more apt to involve the practical implementation of an invention to make a meaningful impact in the market or society, and not all _________ s require an invention. _________ often manifests itself via the engineering process, when the problem being solved is of a technical or scientific nature. The opposite of _________ is exnovation.

Exam Probability: **Low**

3. *Answer choices:*

(see index for correct answer)

- a. Innovation
- b. Gaussian process
- c. Heston model
- d. Continuous stochastic process

Guidance: level 1

:: Marketing ::

_________ is the percentage of a market accounted for by a specific entity. In a survey of nearly 200 senior marketing managers, 67% responded that they found the revenue- "dollar _________ " metric very useful, while 61% found "unit _________ " very useful.

Exam Probability: **Low**

4. *Answer choices:*

(see index for correct answer)

- a. Field marketing
- b. Multicultural marketing
- c. National brand
- d. Consumer culture theory

Guidance: level 1

:: Basic financial concepts ::

_________ is a sustained increase in the general price level of goods and services in an economy over a period of time.When the general price level rises, each unit of currency buys fewer goods and services; consequently, _________ reflects a reduction in the purchasing power per unit of money a loss of real value in the medium of exchange and unit of account within the economy. The measure of _________ is the _________ rate, the annualized percentage change in a general price index, usually the consumer price index, over time. The opposite of _________ is deflation.

Exam Probability: **Low**

5. *Answer choices:*

(see index for correct answer)

- a. Eurodollar
- b. Inflation
- c. Base effect
- d. Financial transaction

Guidance: level 1

:: Management occupations ::

_________ ship is the process of designing, launching and running a new business, which is often initially a small business. The people who create these businesses are called _________ s.

Exam Probability: **Low**

6. *Answer choices:*

(see index for correct answer)

- a. Arts administration
- b. Female entrepreneur
- c. City manager
- d. Manager without portfolio

Guidance: level 1

:: Commercial item transport and distribution ::

A _________ is a commitment or expectation to perform some action in general or if certain circumstances arise. A _________ may arise from a system of ethics or morality, especially in an honor culture. Many duties are created by law, sometimes including a codified punishment or liability for non-performance. Performing one`s _________ may require some sacrifice of self-interest.

Exam Probability: **Medium**

7. *Answer choices:*

(see index for correct answer)

- a. Duty
- b. Counter-to-counter package
- c. International Road Transport Union
- d. Consignor

Guidance: level 1

:: Human resource management ::

__________ are the people who make up the workforce of an organization, business sector, or economy. "Human capital" is sometimes used synonymously with " __________ ", although human capital typically refers to a narrower effect . Likewise, other terms sometimes used include manpower, talent, labor, personnel, or simply people.

Exam Probability: **High**

8. *Answer choices:*

(see index for correct answer)

- a. Competency-based management
- b. Human resources
- c. Dr. Marri Channa Reddy Human Resource Development Institute of Andhra Pradesh
- d. Professional employer organization

Guidance: level 1

:: Credit cards ::

The __________ Company, also known as Amex, is an American multinational financial services corporation headquartered in Three World Financial Center in New York City. The company was founded in 1850 and is one of the 30 components of the Dow Jones Industrial Average. The company is best known for its charge card, credit card, and traveler`s cheque businesses.

Exam Probability: **Low**

9. *Answer choices:*

(see index for correct answer)

- a. Revolution Money
- b. Accolades Card
- c. American Express
- d. Wireless identity theft

Guidance: level 1

:: ::

_________ is a means of protection from financial loss. It is a form of risk management, primarily used to hedge against the risk of a contingent or uncertain loss

Exam Probability: **Medium**

10. *Answer choices:*

(see index for correct answer)

- a. information systems assessment
- b. open system
- c. cultural
- d. process perspective

Guidance: level 1

:: Supply chain management terms ::

In business and finance, _________ is a system of organizations, people, activities, information, and resources involved inmoving a product or service from supplier to customer. _________ activities involve the transformation of natural resources, raw materials, and components into a finished product that is delivered to the end customer. In sophisticated _________ systems, used products may re-enter the _________ at any point where residual value is recyclable. _________ s link value chains.

Exam Probability: **Low**

11. *Answer choices:*

(see index for correct answer)

- a. Supply chain
- b. Final assembly schedule
- c. Will call
- d. Widget

Guidance: level 1

:: Market research ::

__________ , an acronym for Information through Disguised Experimentation is an annual market research fair conducted by the students of IIM-Lucknow. Students create games and use various other simulated environments to capture consumers' subconscious thoughts. This innovative method of market research removes the sensitization effect that might bias peoples answers to questions. This ensures that the most truthful answers are captured to research questions. The games are designed in such a way that the observers can elicit all the required information just by observing and noting down the behaviour and the responses of the participants.

Exam Probability: **High**

12. *Answer choices:*
(see index for correct answer)

- a. Multistage sampling
- b. Demographic marketer
- c. BrandZ
- d. INDEX

Guidance: level 1

:: Legal terms ::

__________ , a form of alternative dispute resolution , is a way to resolve disputes outside the courts. The dispute will be decided by one or more persons , which renders the " __________ award". An __________ award is legally binding on both sides and enforceable in the courts.

Exam Probability: **Medium**

13. *Answer choices:*
(see index for correct answer)

- a. Adjustment
- b. Arbitration
- c. Holding
- d. Collateral estoppel

Guidance: level 1

:: Materials ::

A _________ , also known as a feedstock, unprocessed material, or primary commodity, is a basic material that is used to produce goods, finished products, energy, or intermediate materials which are feedstock for future finished products. As feedstock, the term connotes these materials are bottleneck assets and are highly important with regard to producing other products. An example of this is crude oil, which is a _________ and a feedstock used in the production of industrial chemicals, fuels, plastics, and pharmaceutical goods; lumber is a _________ used to produce a variety of products including all types of furniture. The term " _________ " denotes materials in minimally processed or unprocessed in states; e.g., raw latex, crude oil, cotton, coal, raw biomass, iron ore, air, logs, or water i.e. "...any product of agriculture, forestry, fishing and any other mineral that is in its natural form or which has undergone the transformation required to prepare it for internationally marketing in substantial volumes."

Exam Probability: **Low**

14. *Answer choices:*

(see index for correct answer)

- a. Raw material
- b. Lute
- c. Ion Gel
- d. LRPu

Guidance: level 1

:: Strategic management ::

_________ is a strategic planning technique used to help a person or organization identify strengths, weaknesses, opportunities, and threats related to business competition or project planning. It is intended to specify the objectives of the business venture or project and identify the internal and external factors that are favorable and unfavorable to achieving those objectives. Users of a _________ often ask and answer questions to generate meaningful information for each category to make the tool useful and identify their competitive advantage. SWOT has been described as the tried-and-true tool of strategic analysis.

Exam Probability: **High**

15. *Answer choices:*

(see index for correct answer)

- a. Strategic early warning system
- b. SWOT analysis
- c. Operating model
- d. Outsights

Guidance: level 1

:: Infographics ::

A _________ is a symbolic representation of information according to visualization technique. _________ s have been used since ancient times, but became more prevalent during the Enlightenment. Sometimes, the technique uses a three-dimensional visualization which is then projected onto a two-dimensional surface. The word graph is sometimes used as a synonym for _________ .

Exam Probability: **Medium**

16. *Answer choices:*

(see index for correct answer)

- a. Webdings
- b. Cave5D
- c. Diagram
- d. Sparkline

Guidance: level 1

:: Identity management ::

_________ is the ability of an individual or group to seclude themselves, or information about themselves, and thereby express themselves selectively. The boundaries and content of what is considered private differ among cultures and individuals, but share common themes. When something is private to a person, it usually means that something is inherently special or sensitive to them. The domain of _________ partially overlaps with security , which can include the concepts of appropriate use, as well as protection of information. _________ may also take the form of bodily integrity.

Exam Probability: **High**

17. *Answer choices:*

(see index for correct answer)

- a. Identity assurance
- b. Privacy
- c. Password manager
- d. Mobile Signature Roaming

Guidance: level 1

:: Consumer theory ::

A _________ is a technical term in psychology, economics and philosophy usually used in relation to choosing between alternatives. For example, someone prefers A over B if they would rather choose A than B.

Exam Probability: **Low**

18. *Answer choices:*

(see index for correct answer)

- a. Lexicographic preferences
- b. Cross elasticity of demand
- c. Consumer sovereignty
- d. Preference

Guidance: level 1

:: Fraud ::

In law, _________ is intentional deception to secure unfair or unlawful gain, or to deprive a victim of a legal right. _________ can violate civil law , a criminal law , or it may cause no loss of money, property or legal right but still be an element of another civil or criminal wrong. The purpose of _________ may be monetary gain or other benefits, for example by obtaining a passport, travel document, or driver`s license, or mortgage _________ , where the perpetrator may attempt to qualify for a mortgage by way of false statements.

Exam Probability: **Low**

19. *Answer choices:*

(see index for correct answer)

- a. Pious fraud

- b. Corporate scandal
- c. Missing trader fraud
- d. Regummed stamp

Guidance: level 1

:: Loans ::

In finance, a _________ is the lending of money by one or more individuals, organizations, or other entities to other individuals, organizations etc. The recipient incurs a debt, and is usually liable to pay interest on that debt until it is repaid, and also to repay the principal amount borrowed.

Exam Probability: **Medium**

20. *Answer choices:*

(see index for correct answer)

- a. Section 502 loans
- b. Loan waiver
- c. Secured loan
- d. Loan

Guidance: level 1

:: Generally Accepted Accounting Principles ::

In business and accounting, _________ is an entity`s income minus cost of goods sold, expenses and taxes for an accounting period. It is computed as the residual of all revenues and gains over all expenses and losses for the period, and has also been defined as the net increase in shareholders` equity that results from a company`s operations. In the context of the presentation of financial statements, the IFRS Foundation defines _________ as synonymous with profit and loss. The difference between revenue and the cost of making a product or providing a service, before deducting overheads, payroll, taxation, and interest payments. This is different from operating income .

Exam Probability: **Low**

21. *Answer choices:*

(see index for correct answer)

- a. Fin 48
- b. Depreciation

- c. Completed-contract method
- d. Net income

Guidance: level 1

:: Economic globalization ::

__________ is an agreement in which one company hires another company to be responsible for a planned or existing activity that is or could be done internally,and sometimes involves transferring employees and assets from one firm to another.

Exam Probability: **Low**

22. *Answer choices:*

(see index for correct answer)

- a. reshoring
- b. global financial

Guidance: level 1

:: Employment ::

The __________ is an individual`s metaphorical "journey" through learning, work and other aspects of life. There are a number of ways to define __________ and the term is used in a variety of ways.

Exam Probability: **Low**

23. *Answer choices:*

(see index for correct answer)

- a. Career
- b. Taleo
- c. Effective altruism
- d. AMCAT

Guidance: level 1

:: Euthenics ::

__________ is an ethical framework and suggests that an entity, be it an organization or individual, has an obligation to act for the benefit of society at large. __________ is a duty every individual has to perform so as to maintain a balance between the economy and the ecosystems. A trade-off may exist between economic development, in the material sense, and the welfare of the society and environment, though this has been challenged by many reports over the past decade. __________ means sustaining the equilibrium between the two. It pertains not only to business organizations but also to everyone whose any action impacts the environment. This responsibility can be passive, by avoiding engaging in socially harmful acts, or active, by performing activities that directly advance social goals. __________ must be intergenerational since the actions of one generation have consequences on those following.

Exam Probability: **Low**

24. *Answer choices:*

(see index for correct answer)

- a. Social responsibility
- b. Family and consumer science
- c. Euthenics
- d. Minnie Cumnock Blodgett

Guidance: level 1

:: Monopoly (economics) ::

A __________ is a form of intellectual property that gives its owner the legal right to exclude others from making, using, selling, and importing an invention for a limited period of years, in exchange for publishing an enabling public disclosure of the invention. In most countries __________ rights fall under civil law and the __________ holder needs to sue someone infringing the __________ in order to enforce his or her rights. In some industries __________ s are an essential form of competitive advantage; in others they are irrelevant.

Exam Probability: **High**

25. *Answer choices:*

(see index for correct answer)

- a. Municipalization
- b. Patent

- c. Contestable market
- d. Average cost pricing

Guidance: level 1

:: Human resource management ::

__________ encompasses values and behaviors that contribute to the unique social and psychological environment of a business. The __________ influences the way people interact, the context within which knowledge is created, the resistance they will have towards certain changes, and ultimately the way they share knowledge. __________ represents the collective values, beliefs and principles of organizational members and is a product of factors such as history, product, market, technology, strategy, type of employees, management style, and national culture; culture includes the organization`s vision, values, norms, systems, symbols, language, assumptions, environment, location, beliefs and habits.

Exam Probability: **Low**

26. *Answer choices:*

(see index for correct answer)

- a. Organizational culture
- b. Public service motivation
- c. Expense management
- d. Flextime

Guidance: level 1

:: Data management ::

__________ is a form of intellectual property that grants the creator of an original creative work an exclusive legal right to determine whether and under what conditions this original work may be copied and used by others, usually for a limited term of years. The exclusive rights are not absolute but limited by limitations and exceptions to __________ law, including fair use. A major limitation on __________ on ideas is that __________ protects only the original expression of ideas, and not the underlying ideas themselves.

Exam Probability: **Medium**

27. *Answer choices:*

(see index for correct answer)

- a. Core data integration
- b. PerformancePoint
- c. Data room
- d. Copyright

Guidance: level 1

:: Poker strategy ::

_________ is any measure taken to guard a thing against damage caused by outside forces. _________ can be provided to physical objects, including organisms, to systems, and to intangible things like civil and political rights. Although the mechanisms for providing _________ vary widely, the basic meaning of the term remains the same. This is illustrated by an explanation found in a manual on electrical wiring.

Exam Probability: **Low**

28. *Answer choices:*

(see index for correct answer)

- a. Position
- b. Q-ratio
- c. Steal
- d. Fundamental theorem of poker

Guidance: level 1

:: Cash flow ::

_________ s are narrowly interconnected with the concepts of value, interest rate and liquidity.A _________ that shall happen on a future day tN can be transformed into a _________ of the same value in t0.

Exam Probability: **Medium**

29. *Answer choices:*

(see index for correct answer)

- a. Cash flow
- b. Cash flow loan
- c. Discounted payback period
- d. First Chicago Method

Guidance: level 1

:: Project management ::

In political science, an _________ is a means by which a petition signed by a certain minimum number of registered voters can force a government to choose to either enact a law or hold a public vote in parliament in what is called indirect _________ , or under direct _________ , the proposition is immediately put to a plebiscite or referendum, in what is called a Popular initiated Referendum or citizen-initiated referendum).

Exam Probability: **Medium**

30. *Answer choices:*

(see index for correct answer)

- a. Decision table
- b. Budgeted cost of work performed
- c. Grandfather principle
- d. Initiative

Guidance: level 1

:: Macroeconomics ::

_________ is the increase in the inflation-adjusted market value of the goods and services produced by an economy over time. It is conventionally measured as the percent rate of increase in real gross domestic product, or real GDP.

Exam Probability: **Medium**

31. *Answer choices:*

(see index for correct answer)

- a. Sudden stop
- b. Real gross domestic product
- c. Lucas islands model
- d. Classical dichotomy

Guidance: level 1

:: Business models ::

A _________ is "an autonomous association of persons united voluntarily to meet their common economic, social, and cultural needs and aspirations through a jointly-owned and democratically-controlled enterprise". _________ s may include.

Exam Probability: **Low**

32. *Answer choices:*

(see index for correct answer)

- a. Low-cost carrier
- b. Freemium
- c. Meta learning
- d. Cooperative

Guidance: level 1

:: Project management ::

Some scenarios associate "this kind of planning" with learning "life skills". _________ s are necessary, or at least useful, in situations where individuals need to know what time they must be at a specific location to receive a specific service, and where people need to accomplish a set of goals within a set time period.

Exam Probability: **Medium**

33. *Answer choices:*

(see index for correct answer)

- a. PM Declaration of Interdependence
- b. Project cancellation
- c. project triangle
- d. Schedule

Guidance: level 1

:: Marketing techniques ::

__________ is the activity of dividing a broad consumer or business market, normally consisting of existing and potential customers, into sub-groups of consumers based on some type of shared characteristics. In dividing or segmenting markets, researchers typically look for common characteristics such as shared needs, common interests, similar lifestyles or even similar demographic profiles. The overall aim of segmentation is to identify high yield segments – that is, those segments that are likely to be the most profitable or that have growth potential – so that these can be selected for special attention .

Exam Probability: **High**

34. *Answer choices:*

(see index for correct answer)

- a. AIDA
- b. Blackout dates
- c. Shopped
- d. Market segmentation

Guidance: level 1

:: Credit cards ::

A __________ is a payment card issued to users to enable the cardholder to pay a merchant for goods and services based on the cardholder's promise to the card issuer to pay them for the amounts plus the other agreed charges. The card issuer creates a revolving account and grants a line of credit to the cardholder, from which the cardholder can borrow money for payment to a merchant or as a cash advance.

Exam Probability: **Low**

35. *Answer choices:*

(see index for correct answer)

- a. Revolution Money
- b. The Everything Card
- c. Card scheme
- d. Credit card

Guidance: level 1

:: Energy and fuel journals ::

In physics, energy is the quantitative property that must be transferred to an object in order to perform work on, or to heat, the object. Energy is a conserved quantity; the law of conservation of energy states that energy can be converted in form, but not created or destroyed. The SI unit of energy is the joule, which is the energy transferred to an object by the work of moving it a distance of 1 metre against a force of 1 newton.

Exam Probability: **High**

36. *Answer choices:*

(see index for correct answer)

- a. Energies
- b. Solar Energy Materials and Solar Cells
- c. Fuel Cells
- d. The Energy Journal

Guidance: level 1

:: Production and manufacturing ::

__________ is a set of techniques and tools for process improvement. Though as a shortened form it may be found written as 6S, it should not be confused with the methodology known as 6S .

Exam Probability: **Medium**

37. *Answer choices:*

(see index for correct answer)

- a. Six Sigma
- b. Contract manufacturer
- c. Queueing theory
- d. Joint product

Guidance: level 1

:: International relations ::

A _________ is any event that is going to lead to an unstable and dangerous situation affecting an individual, group, community, or whole society. Crises are deemed to be negative changes in the security, economic, political, societal, or environmental affairs, especially when they occur abruptly, with little or no warning. More loosely, it is a term meaning "a testing time" or an "emergency event".

Exam Probability: **High**

38. *Answer choices:*

(see index for correct answer)

- a. Policy of deliberate ambiguity
- b. Annexationism
- c. National interest
- d. EECCA

Guidance: level 1

:: Money ::

In economics, _________ is money in the physical form of currency, such as banknotes and coins. In bookkeeping and finance, _________ is current assets comprising currency or currency equivalents that can be accessed immediately or near-immediately . _________ is seen either as a reserve for payments, in case of a structural or incidental negative _________ flow or as a way to avoid a downturn on financial markets.

Exam Probability: **High**

39. *Answer choices:*

(see index for correct answer)

- a. Cash
- b. Chained dollars
- c. Ideal money
- d. Money creation

Guidance: level 1

:: Health promotion ::

_________ , as defined by the World _________ Organization , is "a state of complete physical, mental and social well-being and not merely the absence of disease or infirmity." This definition has been subject to controversy, as it may have limited value for implementation. _________ may be defined as the ability to adapt and manage physical, mental and social challenges throughout life.

Exam Probability: **Low**

40. *Answer choices:*

(see index for correct answer)

- a. The Gordie Foundation
- b. Centre for Research on Inner City Health
- c. Health
- d. Health advocacy

Guidance: level 1

:: Business ::

A _________ is a mathematical object used to count, measure, and label. The original examples are the natural _________ s 1, 2, 3, 4, and so forth. A written symbol like "5" that represents a _________ is called a numeral. A numeral system is an organized way to write and manipulate this type of symbol, for example the Hindu–Arabic numeral system allows combinations of numerical digits like "5" and "0" to represent larger _________ s like 50. A numeral in linguistics can refer to a symbol like 5, the words or phrase that names a _________ , like "five hundred", or other words that mean a specific _________ , like "dozen". In addition to their use in counting and measuring, numerals are often used for labels , for ordering , and for codes . In common usage, _________ may refer to a symbol, a word or phrase, or the mathematical object.

Exam Probability: **Medium**

41. *Answer choices:*

(see index for correct answer)

- a. Relationship Science
- b. Business interaction networks
- c. First party leads
- d. Number

Guidance: level 1

:: Marketing ::

A __________ is the quantity of payment or compensation given by one party to another in return for one unit of goods or services.. A __________ is influenced by both production costs and demand for the product. A __________ may be determined by a monopolist or may be imposed on the firm by market conditions.

Exam Probability: **Medium**

42. *Answer choices:*

(see index for correct answer)

- a. Experiential marketing
- b. Price
- c. Medical science liaison
- d. Demonstrator model

Guidance: level 1

:: ::

Competition arises whenever at least two parties strive for a goal which cannot be shared: where one`s gain is the other`s loss .

Exam Probability: **Low**

43. *Answer choices:*

(see index for correct answer)

- a. levels of analysis
- b. personal values
- c. Competitor
- d. process perspective

Guidance: level 1

:: Management ::

A __________ is when two or more people come together to discuss one or more topics, often in a formal or business setting, but __________ s also occur in a variety of other environments. Many various types of __________ s exist.

Exam Probability: **High**

44. *Answer choices:*

(see index for correct answer)

- a. Productive efficiency
- b. Context analysis
- c. Core competency
- d. Radical transparency

Guidance: level 1

:: Competition (economics) ::

__________ arises whenever at least two parties strive for a goal which cannot be shared: where one`s gain is the other`s loss .

Exam Probability: **Medium**

45. *Answer choices:*

(see index for correct answer)

- a. Currency competition
- b. National Competitiveness Report of Armenia
- c. Competition
- d. School choice

Guidance: level 1

:: Stock market ::

A __________ , equity market or share market is the aggregation of buyers and sellers of stocks , which represent ownership claims on businesses; these may include securities listed on a public stock exchange, as well as stock that is only traded privately. Examples of the latter include shares of private companies which are sold to investors through equity crowdfunding platforms. Stock exchanges list shares of common equity as well as other security types, e.g. corporate bonds and convertible bonds.

Exam Probability: **High**

46. *Answer choices:*

(see index for correct answer)

- a. Stockjobber
- b. London Stock Exchange Group
- c. Earnings call
- d. Stock market

Guidance: level 1

:: Project management ::

Contemporary business and science treat as a _________ any undertaking, carried out individually or collaboratively and possibly involving research or design, that is carefully planned to achieve a particular aim.

Exam Probability: **High**

47. *Answer choices:*

(see index for correct answer)

- a. Project
- b. Schedule
- c. Fast-track construction
- d. Graphical path method

Guidance: level 1

:: Logistics ::

_________ is generally the detailed organization and implementation of a complex operation. In a general business sense, _________ is the management of the flow of things between the point of origin and the point of consumption in order to meet requirements of customers or corporations. The resources managed in _________ may include tangible goods such as materials, equipment, and supplies, as well as food and other consumable items. The _________ of physical items usually involves the integration of information flow, materials handling, production, packaging, inventory, transportation, warehousing, and often security.

Exam Probability: **Low**

48. *Answer choices:*

(see index for correct answer)

- a. StarShipIt
- b. Trailer tracking
- c. Logistics
- d. Bucket brigade

Guidance: level 1

:: Human resource management ::

_________ is the corporate management term for the act of reorganizing the legal, ownership, operational, or other structures of a company for the purpose of making it more profitable, or better organized for its present needs. Other reasons for _________ include a change of ownership or ownership structure, demerger, or a response to a crisis or major change in the business such as bankruptcy, repositioning, or buyout. _________ may also be described as corporate _________ , debt _________ and financial _________ .

Exam Probability: **Low**

49. *Answer choices:*

(see index for correct answer)

- a. Organization chart
- b. Restructuring
- c. Induction programme
- d. Idea portal

Guidance: level 1

:: Income ::

_________ is a ratio between the net profit and cost of investment resulting from an investment of some resources. A high ROI means the investment`s gains favorably to its cost. As a performance measure, ROI is used to evaluate the efficiency of an investment or to compare the efficiencies of several different investments. In purely economic terms, it is one way of relating profits to capital invested. _________ is a performance measure used by businesses to identify the efficiency of an investment or number of different investments.

Exam Probability: **Medium**

50. *Answer choices:*

(see index for correct answer)

- a. Independent income
- b. Implied level of government service
- c. Private income
- d. Per capita income

Guidance: level 1

:: Mathematical finance ::

In economics and finance, _________ , also known as present discounted value, is the value of an expected income stream determined as of the date of valuation. The _________ is always less than or equal to the future value because money has interest-earning potential, a characteristic referred to as the time value of money, except during times of negative interest rates, when the _________ will be more than the future value. Time value can be described with the simplified phrase, "A dollar today is worth more than a dollar tomorrow". Here, `worth more` means that its value is greater. A dollar today is worth more than a dollar tomorrow because the dollar can be invested and earn a day`s worth of interest, making the total accumulate to a value more than a dollar by tomorrow. Interest can be compared to rent. Just as rent is paid to a landlord by a tenant without the ownership of the asset being transferred, interest is paid to a lender by a borrower who gains access to the money for a time before paying it back. By letting the borrower have access to the money, the lender has sacrificed the exchange value of this money, and is compensated for it in the form of interest. The initial amount of the borrowed funds is less than the total amount of money paid to the lender.

Exam Probability: **High**

51. *Answer choices:*

(see index for correct answer)

- a. Weighted average cost of capital
- b. Constant elasticity of variance model
- c. No-arbitrage bounds
- d. Perpetuity

Guidance: level 1

:: Marketing ::

The __________ is a foundation model for businesses. The __________ has been defined as the "set of marketing tools that the firm uses to pursue its marketing objectives in the target market". Thus the __________ refers to four broad levels of marketing decision, namely: product, price, place, and promotion. Marketing practice has been occurring for millennia, but marketing theory emerged in the early twentieth century. The contemporary __________, or the 4 Ps, which has become the dominant framework for marketing management decisions, was first published in 1960. In services marketing, an extended __________ is used, typically comprising 7 Ps, made up of the original 4 Ps extended by process, people, and physical evidence. Occasionally service marketers will refer to 8 Ps, comprising these 7 Ps plus performance.

Exam Probability: **Low**

52. *Answer choices:*

(see index for correct answer)

- a. Franchise fee
- b. The Cellar
- c. Cannibalization
- d. Marketing mix

Guidance: level 1

:: Derivatives (finance) ::

__________ is any bodily activity that enhances or maintains physical fitness and overall health and wellness. It is performed for various reasons, to aid growth and improve strength, preventing aging, developing muscles and the cardiovascular system, honing athletic skills, weight loss or maintenance, improving health and also for enjoyment. Many individuals choose to __________ outdoors where they can congregate in groups, socialize, and enhance well-being.

Exam Probability: **High**

53. *Answer choices:*

(see index for correct answer)

- a. John J. Ensminger
- b. Foreign exchange derivative
- c. STIRT
- d. Structured note

Guidance: level 1

:: Decision theory ::

A _________ is a deliberate system of principles to guide decisions and achieve rational outcomes. A _________ is a statement of intent, and is implemented as a procedure or protocol. Policies are generally adopted by a governance body within an organization. Policies can assist in both subjective and objective decision making. Policies to assist in subjective decision making usually assist senior management with decisions that must be based on the relative merits of a number of factors, and as a result are often hard to test objectively, e.g. work-life balance _________ . In contrast policies to assist in objective decision making are usually operational in nature and can be objectively tested, e.g. password _________ .

Exam Probability: **Medium**

54. *Answer choices:*

(see index for correct answer)

- a. Flipism
- b. ERulemaking
- c. Sure-thing principle
- d. Choquet integral

Guidance: level 1

:: Finance ::

_________ is a field that is concerned with the allocation of assets and liabilities over space and time, often under conditions of risk or uncertainty. _________ can also be defined as the art of money management. Participants in the market aim to price assets based on their risk level, fundamental value, and their expected rate of return. _________ can be split into three sub-categories: public _________ , corporate _________ and personal _________ .

Exam Probability: **Medium**

55. *Answer choices:*

(see index for correct answer)

- a. Financial Education Instructor of the Year

- b. Ohlson o-score
- c. Turnkey Asset Management Program
- d. Security agreement

Guidance: level 1

:: Real estate ::

_________s serve several societal needs – primarily as shelter from weather, security, living space, privacy, to store belongings, and to comfortably live and work. A _________ as a shelter represents a physical division of the human habitat and the outside .

Exam Probability: **High**

56. *Answer choices:*

(see index for correct answer)

- a. Land description
- b. Building
- c. Exchanging contracts
- d. Commercial property

Guidance: level 1

:: International trade ::

The law or principle of _________ holds that under free trade, an agent will produce more of and consume less of a good for which they have a _________ . _________ is the economic reality describing the work gains from trade for individuals, firms, or nations, which arise from differences in their factor endowments or technological progress. In an economic model, agents have a _________ over others in producing a particular good if they can produce that good at a lower relative opportunity cost or autarky price, i.e. at a lower relative marginal cost prior to trade. One shouldn`t compare the monetary costs of production or even the resource costs of production. Instead, one must compare the opportunity costs of producing goods across countries.

Exam Probability: **High**

57. *Answer choices:*

(see index for correct answer)

- a. Reciprocity

- b. DataArt
- c. Comparative advantage
- d. Trade

Guidance: level 1

:: Management ::

_________ is the practice of initiating, planning, executing, controlling, and closing the work of a team to achieve specific goals and meet specific success criteria at the specified time.

Exam Probability: **Medium**

58. *Answer choices:*

(see index for correct answer)

- a. Double linking
- b. Personal offshoring
- c. Industrial democracy
- d. Completed Staff Work

Guidance: level 1

:: Manufacturing ::

A _________ is an object used to extend the ability of an individual to modify features of the surrounding environment. Although many animals use simple _________ s, only human beings, whose use of stone _________ s dates back hundreds of millennia, use _________ s to make other _________ s. The set of _________ s needed to perform different tasks that are part of the same activity is called gear or equipment.

Exam Probability: **Medium**

59. *Answer choices:*

(see index for correct answer)

- a. Kit-of-parts
- b. International Manufacturing Technology Show
- c. Agri-Fab, Inc.
- d. Tool

Guidance: level 1

Management

Management is the administration of an organization, whether it is a business, a not-for-profit organization, or government body. Management includes the activities of setting the strategy of an organization and coordinating the efforts of its employees (or of volunteers) to accomplish its objectives through the application of available resources, such as financial, natural, technological, and human resources.

:: Organizational behavior ::

In organizational behavior and industrial and organizational psychology, _________ is an individual`s psychological attachment to the organization. The basis behind many of these studies was to find ways to improve how workers feel about their jobs so that these workers would become more committed to their organizations. _________ predicts work variables such as turnover, organizational citizenship behavior, and job performance. Some of the factors such as role stress, empowerment, job insecurity and employability, and distribution of leadership have been shown to be connected to a worker`s sense of _________ .

Exam Probability: **Medium**

1. *Answer choices:*

(see index for correct answer)

- a. Counterproductive norms
- b. Nut Island effect
- c. Achievement Motivation Inventory
- d. Organizational Expedience

Guidance: level 1

:: Management ::

A _________ is an idea of the future or desired result that a person or a group of people envisions, plans and commits to achieve. People endeavor to reach _________ s within a finite time by setting deadlines.

Exam Probability: **High**

2. *Answer choices:*

(see index for correct answer)

- a. Goal
- b. Vasa syndrome
- c. Quality, cost, delivery
- d. Porter five forces analysis

Guidance: level 1

:: Leadership ::

_________ is a theory of leadership where a leader works with teams to identify needed change, creating a vision to guide the change through inspiration, and executing the change in tandem with committed members of a group; it is an integral part of the Full Range Leadership Model. _________ serves to enhance the motivation, morale, and job performance of followers through a variety of mechanisms; these include connecting the follower`s sense of identity and self to a project and to the collective identity of the organization; being a role model for followers in order to inspire them and to raise their interest in the project; challenging followers to take greater ownership for their work, and understanding the strengths and weaknesses of followers, allowing the leader to align followers with tasks that enhance their performance.

Exam Probability: **Medium**

3. *Answer choices:*

(see index for correct answer)

- a. Transformational leadership
- b. European Center for Leadership Development
- c. Motivational Leadership
- d. Outstanding leadership theory

Guidance: level 1

:: Management ::

A __________ is a formal written document containing business goals, the methods on how these goals can be attained, and the time frame within which these goals need to be achieved. It also describes the nature of the business, background information on the organization, the organization`s financial projections, and the strategies it intends to implement to achieve the stated targets. In its entirety, this document serves as a road map that provides direction to the business.

Exam Probability: **Medium**

4. *Answer choices:*

(see index for correct answer)

- a. Kata
- b. Business plan
- c. Management buyout
- d. Records manager

Guidance: level 1

:: Reputation management ::

__________ or image of a social entity is an opinion about that entity, typically as a result of social evaluation on a set of criteria.

Exam Probability: **High**

5. *Answer choices:*

(see index for correct answer)

- a. Reputation
- b. Conversocial
- c. Slashdot
- d. Sybil attack

Guidance: level 1

:: Management occupations ::

__________ ship is the process of designing, launching and running a new business, which is often initially a small business. The people who create these businesses are called __________ s.

Exam Probability: **High**

6. *Answer choices:*
(see index for correct answer)

- a. General counsel
- b. Entrepreneur
- c. Deputy mayor
- d. Legislator

Guidance: level 1

:: Outsourcing ::

__________ is the relocation of a business process from one country to another—typically an operational process, such as manufacturing, or supporting processes, such as accounting. Typically this refers to a company business, although state governments may also employ __________ . More recently, technical and administrative services have been offshored.

Exam Probability: **High**

7. *Answer choices:*
(see index for correct answer)

- a. Offshoring
- b. Cyient
- c. Global sourcing
- d. Managed VoIP Service

Guidance: level 1

:: Quality management ::

_________ ensures that an organization, product or service is consistent. It has four main components: quality planning, quality assurance, quality control and quality improvement. _________ is focused not only on product and service quality, but also on the means to achieve it. _________ , therefore, uses quality assurance and control of processes as well as products to achieve more consistent quality. What a customer wants and is willing to pay for it determines quality. It is written or unwritten commitment to a known or unknown consumer in the market . Thus, quality can be defined as fitness for intended use or, in other words, how well the product performs its intended function

Exam Probability: **Medium**

8. *Answer choices:*

(see index for correct answer)

- a. EFQM
- b. Det Norske Veritas
- c. Common Assessment Framework
- d. Quality management

Guidance: level 1

:: Systems thinking ::

In business management, a _________ is a company that facilitates the learning of its members and continuously transforms itself. The concept was coined through the work and research of Peter Senge and his colleagues.

Exam Probability: **Medium**

9. *Answer choices:*

(see index for correct answer)

- a. The Arlington Institute
- b. Learning organization
- c. Thought leader
- d. IBZL

Guidance: level 1

:: ::

In logic and philosophy, an _________ is a series of statements , called the premises or premisses , intended to determine the degree of truth of another statement, the conclusion. The logical form of an _________ in a natural language can be represented in a symbolic formal language, and independently of natural language formally defined " _________ s" can be made in math and computer science.

Exam Probability: **Medium**

10. *Answer choices:*

(see index for correct answer)

- a. cultural
- b. imperative
- c. Character
- d. process perspective

Guidance: level 1

:: Logistics ::

_________ is generally the detailed organization and implementation of a complex operation. In a general business sense, _________ is the management of the flow of things between the point of origin and the point of consumption in order to meet requirements of customers or corporations. The resources managed in _________ may include tangible goods such as materials, equipment, and supplies, as well as food and other consumable items. The _________ of physical items usually involves the integration of information flow, materials handling, production, packaging, inventory, transportation, warehousing, and often security.

Exam Probability: **Medium**

11. *Answer choices:*

(see index for correct answer)

- a. Merge in transit
- b. Transport and logistics centre
- c. International Society of Logistics
- d. Logistics

Guidance: level 1

:: Data collection ::

A _________ is an utterance which typically functions as a request for information. _________ s can thus be understood as a kind of illocutionary act in the field of pragmatics or as special kinds of propositions in frameworks of formal semantics such as alternative semantics or inquisitive semantics. The information requested is expected to be provided in the form of an answer. _________ s are often conflated with interrogatives, which are the grammatical forms typically used to achieve them. Rhetorical _________ s, for example, are interrogative in form but may not be considered true _________ s as they are not expected to be answered. Conversely, non-interrogative grammatical structures may be considered _________ s as in the case of the imperative sentence "tell me your name".

Exam Probability: **Low**

12. *Answer choices:*

(see index for correct answer)

- a. PISCES
- b. North Atlantic Population Project
- c. Question
- d. European Social Survey

Guidance: level 1

:: Labor ::

The workforce or labour force is the labour pool in employment. It is generally used to describe those working for a single company or industry, but can also apply to a geographic region like a city, state, or country. Within a company, its value can be labelled as its "Workforce in Place". The workforce of a country includes both the employed and the unemployed. The labour force participation rate, LFPR , is the ratio between the labour force and the overall size of their cohort . The term generally excludes the employers or management, and can imply those involved in manual labour. It may also mean all those who are available for work.

Exam Probability: **Medium**

13. *Answer choices:*

(see index for correct answer)

- a. Social division of labor
- b. Labor force
- c. Working Saturday
- d. Universal validity of collective labour agreements

Guidance: level 1

:: ::

__________ is the moral stance, political philosophy, ideology, or social outlook that emphasizes the moral worth of the individual. Individualists promote the exercise of one`s goals and desires and so value independence and self-reliance and advocate that interests of the individual should achieve precedence over the state or a social group, while opposing external interference upon one`s own interests by society or institutions such as the government. __________ is often defined in contrast to totalitarianism, collectivism, and more corporate social forms.

Exam Probability: **Medium**

14. *Answer choices:*

(see index for correct answer)

- a. open system
- b. hierarchical
- c. deep-level diversity
- d. personal values

Guidance: level 1

:: ::

A __________ is a type of job aid used to reduce failure by compensating for potential limits of human memory and attention. It helps to ensure consistency and completeness in carrying out a task. A basic example is the "to do list". A more advanced __________ would be a schedule, which lays out tasks to be done according to time of day or other factors. A primary task in __________ is documentation of the task and auditing against the documentation.

Exam Probability: **High**

15. *Answer choices:*

(see index for correct answer)

- a. surface-level diversity
- b. co-culture
- c. hierarchical perspective
- d. Checklist

Guidance: level 1

:: Critical thinking ::

An _________ is someone who has a prolonged or intense experience through practice and education in a particular field. Informally, an _________ is someone widely recognized as a reliable source of technique or skill whose faculty for judging or deciding rightly, justly, or wisely is accorded authority and status by peers or the public in a specific well-distinguished domain. An _________ , more generally, is a person with extensive knowledge or ability based on research, experience, or occupation and in a particular area of study. _________ s are called in for advice on their respective subject, but they do not always agree on the particulars of a field of study. An _________ can be believed, by virtue of credential, training, education, profession, publication or experience, to have special knowledge of a subject beyond that of the average person, sufficient that others may officially rely upon the individual`s opinion. Historically, an _________ was referred to as a sage . The individual was usually a profound thinker distinguished for wisdom and sound judgment.

Exam Probability: **Medium**

16. *Answer choices:*
(see index for correct answer)

- a. Argument by example
- b. False equivalence
- c. Association for Informal Logic and Critical Thinking
- d. TregoED

Guidance: level 1

:: Information science ::

_________ is the resolution of uncertainty; it is that which answers the question of "what an entity is" and thus defines both its essence and nature of its characteristics. _________ relates to both data and knowledge, as data is meaningful _________ representing values attributed to parameters, and knowledge signifies understanding of a concept. _________ is uncoupled from an observer, which is an entity that can access _________ and thus discern what it specifies; _________ exists beyond an event horizon for example. In the case of knowledge, the _________ itself requires a cognitive observer to be obtained.

Exam Probability: **High**

17. *Answer choices:*

(see index for correct answer)

- a. Ontology alignment
- b. Actionable information logistics
- c. Information
- d. Scientific communication

Guidance: level 1

:: Production and manufacturing ::

An _________ is a manufacturing process in which parts are added as the semi-finished assembly moves from workstation to workstation where the parts are added in sequence until the final assembly is produced. By mechanically moving the parts to the assembly work and moving the semi-finished assembly from work station to work station, a finished product can be assembled faster and with less labor than by having workers carry parts to a stationary piece for assembly.

Exam Probability: **Low**

18. *Answer choices:*

(see index for correct answer)

- a. Mockup
- b. Rolled throughput yield
- c. Assembly line
- d. Profibus

Guidance: level 1

:: Product design ::

__________ as a verb is to create a new product to be sold by a business to its customers. A very broad coefficient and effective generation and development of ideas through a process that leads to new products. Thus, it is a major aspect of new product development.

Exam Probability: **Medium**

19. *Answer choices:*

(see index for correct answer)

- a. Rubbot
- b. Marcus Notley
- c. Crippleware
- d. Andrea Fogli

Guidance: level 1

:: Income ::

__________ is a ratio between the net profit and cost of investment resulting from an investment of some resources. A high ROI means the investment's gains favorably to its cost. As a performance measure, ROI is used to evaluate the efficiency of an investment or to compare the efficiencies of several different investments. In purely economic terms, it is one way of relating profits to capital invested. __________ is a performance measure used by businesses to identify the efficiency of an investment or number of different investments.

Exam Probability: **Medium**

20. *Answer choices:*

(see index for correct answer)

- a. Income Per User
- b. Return on investment
- c. Implied level of government service
- d. Income earner

Guidance: level 1

:: Internet privacy ::

An _________ is a private network accessible only to an organization`s staff. Often, a wide range of information and services are available on an organization`s internal _________ that are unavailable to the public, unlike the Internet. A company-wide _________ can constitute an important focal point of internal communication and collaboration, and provide a single starting point to access internal and external resources. In its simplest form, an _________ is established with the technologies for local area networks and wide area networks . Many modern _________ s have search engines, user profiles, blogs, mobile apps with notifications, and events planning within their infrastructure.

Exam Probability: **High**

21. *Answer choices:*

(see index for correct answer)

- a. Intranet
- b. Digitalcourage
- c. Right to be forgotten
- d. Secure messaging

Guidance: level 1

:: ::

A _________ is an organization, usually a group of people or a company, authorized to act as a single entity and recognized as such in law. Early incorporated entities were established by charter . Most jurisdictions now allow the creation of new _________ s through registration.

Exam Probability: **Medium**

22. *Answer choices:*

(see index for correct answer)

- a. Corporation
- b. corporate values
- c. empathy
- d. cultural

Guidance: level 1

:: Business process ::

A __________ or business method is a collection of related, structured activities or tasks by people or equipment which in a specific sequence produce a service or product for a particular customer or customers. __________ es occur at all organizational levels and may or may not be visible to the customers. A __________ may often be visualized as a flowchart of a sequence of activities with interleaving decision points or as a process matrix of a sequence of activities with relevance rules based on data in the process. The benefits of using __________ es include improved customer satisfaction and improved agility for reacting to rapid market change. Process-oriented organizations break down the barriers of structural departments and try to avoid functional silos.

Exam Probability: **High**

23. *Answer choices:*

(see index for correct answer)

- a. Business process
- b. Dynamic business process management
- c. IDS Scheer
- d. Business logic

Guidance: level 1

:: ::

__________ is the assignment of any responsibility or authority to another person to carry out specific activities. It is one of the core concepts of management leadership. However, the person who delegated the work remains accountable for the outcome of the delegated work. __________ empowers a subordinate to make decisions, i.e. it is a shifting of decision-making authority from one organizational level to a lower one. __________ , if properly done, is not fabrication. The opposite of effective __________ is micromanagement, where a manager provides too much input, direction, and review of delegated work. In general, __________ is good and can save money and time, help in building skills, and motivate people. On the other hand, poor __________ might cause frustration and confusion to all the involved parties. Some agents, however, do not favour a __________ and consider the power of making a decision rather burdensome.

Exam Probability: **High**

24. *Answer choices:*

(see index for correct answer)

- a. levels of analysis
- b. Delegation
- c. open system
- d. cultural

Guidance: level 1

:: Management occupations ::

_________ is the process of designing, launching and running a new business, which is often initially a small business. The people who create these businesses are called entrepreneurs.

Exam Probability: **High**

25. *Answer choices:*

(see index for correct answer)

- a. Business magnate
- b. Chief gaming officer
- c. Apparatchik
- d. Business manager

Guidance: level 1

:: Training ::

_________ is action or inaction that is regulated to be in accordance with a particular system of governance. _________ is commonly applied to regulating human and animal behavior, and furthermore, it is applied to each activity-branch in all branches of organized activity, knowledge, and other fields of study and observation. _________ can be a set of expectations that are required by any governing entity including the self, groups, classes, fields, industries, or societies.

Exam Probability: **Medium**

26. *Answer choices:*

(see index for correct answer)

- a. American Council on Exercise
- b. Discipline

- c. Fartlek
- d. Officer training

Guidance: level 1

:: ::

A _________ is a leader`s method of providing direction, implementing plans, and motivating people. Various authors have proposed identifying many different _________ s as exhibited by leaders in the political, business or other fields. Studies on _________ are conducted in the military field, expressing an approach that stresses a holistic view of leadership, including how a leader`s physical presence determines how others perceive that leader. The factors of physical presence in this context include military bearing, physical fitness, confidence, and resilience. The leader`s intellectual capacity helps to conceptualize solutions and to acquire knowledge to do the job. A leader`s conceptual abilities apply agility, judgment, innovation, interpersonal tact, and domain knowledge. Domain knowledge encompasses tactical and technical knowledge as well as cultural and geopolitical awareness. Daniel Goleman in his article "Leadership that Gets Results" talks about six styles of leadership.

Exam Probability: **Low**

27. *Answer choices:*

(see index for correct answer)

- a. co-culture
- b. open system
- c. information systems assessment
- d. Leadership style

Guidance: level 1

:: ::

__________ is a kind of action that occur as two or more objects have an effect upon one another. The idea of a two-way effect is essential in the concept of __________ , as opposed to a one-way causal effect. A closely related term is interconnectivity, which deals with the __________ s of __________ s within systems: combinations of many simple __________ s can lead to surprising emergent phenomena. __________ has different tailored meanings in various sciences. Changes can also involve __________ .

Exam Probability: **Medium**

28. *Answer choices:*
(see index for correct answer)

- a. Interaction
- b. process perspective
- c. similarity-attraction theory
- d. personal values

Guidance: level 1

:: Power (social and political) ::

__________ is a form of reverence gained by a leader who has strong interpersonal relationship skills. __________ , as an aspect of personal power, becomes particularly important as organizational leadership becomes increasingly about collaboration and influence, rather than command and control.

Exam Probability: **Low**

29. *Answer choices:*
(see index for correct answer)

- a. need for power
- b. Hard power
- c. Referent power

Guidance: level 1

:: Classification systems ::

__________ is the practice of comparing business processes and performance metrics to industry bests and best practices from other companies. Dimensions typically measured are quality, time and cost.

Exam Probability: **Low**

30. *Answer choices:*
(see index for correct answer)

- a. Transformed cladistics
- b. Crime Classification Manual
- c. PANOSE
- d. Benchmarking

Guidance: level 1

:: Financial risk ::

__________ is a type of risk faced by investors, corporations, and governments that political decisions, events, or conditions will significantly affect the profitability of a business actor or the expected value of a given economic action. __________ can be understood and managed with reasoned foresight and investment.

Exam Probability: **Low**

31. *Answer choices:*
(see index for correct answer)

- a. Political risk
- b. Discounted maximum loss
- c. Spectral risk measure
- d. Student Investment Advisory Service

Guidance: level 1

:: Evaluation ::

_________ is the practice of being honest and showing a consistent and uncompromising adherence to strong moral and ethical principles and values.In ethics, _________ is regarded as the honesty and truthfulness or accuracy of one`s actions. _________ can stand in opposition to hypocrisy, in that judging with the standards of _________ involves regarding internal consistency as a virtue, and suggests that parties holding within themselves apparently conflicting values should account for the discrepancy or alter their beliefs. The word _________ evolved from the Latin adjective integer, meaning whole or complete. In this context, _________ is the inner sense of "wholeness" deriving from qualities such as honesty and consistency of character. As such, one may judge that others "have _________ " to the extent that they act according to the values, beliefs and principles they claim to hold.

Exam Probability: **Medium**

32. *Answer choices:*

(see index for correct answer)

- a. Academic equivalency evaluation
- b. Appraisal
- c. Knowledge survey
- d. Integrity

Guidance: level 1

:: Time management ::

_________ is the process of planning and exercising conscious control of time spent on specific activities, especially to increase effectiveness, efficiency, and productivity. It involves a juggling act of various demands upon a person relating to work, social life, family, hobbies, personal interests and commitments with the finiteness of time. Using time effectively gives the person "choice" on spending/managing activities at their own time and expediency.

Exam Probability: **Low**

33. *Answer choices:*

(see index for correct answer)

- a. waiting room
- b. Time Trek

- c. Time management
- d. Sufficient unto the day is the evil thereof

Guidance: level 1

:: Organizational theory ::

__________ refers to both a body of non-elective government officials and an administrative policy-making group. Historically, a __________ was a government administration managed by departments staffed with non-elected officials. Today, __________ is the administrative system governing any large institution, whether publicly owned or privately owned. The public administration in many countries is an example of a __________ , but so is the centralized hierarchical structure of a business firm.

Exam Probability: **Low**

34. *Answer choices:*

(see index for correct answer)

- a. Mutual aid
- b. Decentralization
- c. Bureaucracy
- d. Conflict

Guidance: level 1

:: Workplace ::

__________ is asystematic determination of a subject`s merit, worth and significance, using criteria governed by a set of standards. It can assist an organization, program, design, project or any other intervention or initiative to assess any aim, realisable concept/proposal, or any alternative, to help in decision-making; or to ascertain the degree of achievement or value in regard to the aim and objectives and results of any such action that has been completed. The primary purpose of __________ , in addition to gaining insight into prior or existing initiatives, is to enable reflection and assist in the identification of future change.

Exam Probability: **High**

35. *Answer choices:*

(see index for correct answer)

- a. Staff turnover
- b. Evaluation
- c. Workplace conflict
- d. Occupational stress

Guidance: level 1

:: International trade ::

_________ involves the transfer of goods or services from one person or entity to another, often in exchange for money. A system or network that allows _________ is called a market.

Exam Probability: **High**

36. *Answer choices:*

(see index for correct answer)

- a. Common external tariff
- b. The Product Space
- c. International Coffee Agreement
- d. Trade

Guidance: level 1

:: ::

A _________ or sample _________ is a single measure of some attribute of a sample . It is calculated by applying a function to the values of the items of the sample, which are known together as a set of data.

Exam Probability: **High**

37. *Answer choices:*

(see index for correct answer)

- a. surface-level diversity
- b. co-culture
- c. Statistic
- d. hierarchical

Guidance: level 1

:: Organizational theory ::

Decentralisation is the process by which the activities of an organization, particularly those regarding planning and decision making, are distributed or delegated away from a central, authoritative location or group. Concepts of _________ have been applied to group dynamics and management science in private businesses and organizations, political science, law and public administration, economics, money and technology.

Exam Probability: **Low**

38. *Answer choices:*

(see index for correct answer)

- a. Participatory organization
- b. Linking pin model
- c. resource dependence
- d. Mimetic isomorphism

Guidance: level 1

:: Human resource management ::

_________ is the strategic approach to the effective management of people in an organization so that they help the business to gain a competitive advantage. It is designed to maximize employee performance in service of an employer`s strategic objectives. HR is primarily concerned with the management of people within organizations, focusing on policies and on systems. HR departments are responsible for overseeing employee-benefits design, employee recruitment, training and development, performance appraisal, and Reward management . HR also concerns itself with organizational change and industrial relations, that is, the balancing of organizational practices with requirements arising from collective bargaining and from governmental laws.

Exam Probability: **Low**

39. *Answer choices:*

(see index for correct answer)

- a. Organizational culture
- b. Idea portal
- c. ABC Consultants
- d. Human resource management

Guidance: level 1

:: Supply chain management ::

_________ is the process of finding and agreeing to terms, and acquiring goods, services, or works from an external source, often via a tendering or competitive bidding process. _________ is used to ensure the buyer receives goods, services, or works at the best possible price when aspects such as quality, quantity, time, and location are compared. Corporations and public bodies often define processes intended to promote fair and open competition for their business while minimizing risks such as exposure to fraud and collusion.

Exam Probability: **Medium**

40. *Answer choices:*

(see index for correct answer)

- a. Supply chain management software
- b. RFTrax
- c. Application service provider
- d. Supply chain cyber security

Guidance: level 1

:: ::

A _________ is a professional who provides expert advice in a particular area such as security , management, education, accountancy, law, human resources, marketing , finance, engineering, science or any of many other specialized fields.

Exam Probability: **Low**

41. *Answer choices:*

(see index for correct answer)

- a. empathy
- b. open system
- c. functional perspective
- d. Consultant

Guidance: level 1

:: Human resource management ::

__________ is a family of procedures to identify the content of a job in terms of activities involved and attributes or job requirements needed to perform the activities. __________ provides information of organizations which helps to determine which employees are best fit for specific jobs. Through __________ , the analyst needs to understand what the important tasks of the job are, how they are carried out, and the necessary human qualities needed to complete the job successfully.

Exam Probability: **High**

42. *Answer choices:*

(see index for correct answer)

- a. Joint Personnel Administration
- b. Job enlargement
- c. Management development
- d. Behavioral Competencies

Guidance: level 1

:: Project management ::

__________ is the right to exercise power, which can be formalized by a state and exercised by way of judges, appointed executives of government, or the ecclesiastical or priestly appointed representatives of a God or other deities.

Exam Probability: **Low**

43. *Answer choices:*

(see index for correct answer)

- a. Authority
- b. Scope statement
- c. Gantt chart
- d. Project risk management

Guidance: level 1

:: ::

A _________ is the ability to carry out a task with determined results often within a given amount of time, energy, or both. _________ s can often be divided into domain-general and domain-specific _________ s. For example, in the domain of work, some general _________ s would include time management, teamwork and leadership, self-motivation and others, whereas domain-specific _________ s would be used only for a certain job. _________ usually requires certain environmental stimuli and situations to assess the level of _________ being shown and used.

Exam Probability: **Medium**

44. *Answer choices:*

(see index for correct answer)

- a. Skill
- b. empathy
- c. functional perspective
- d. information systems assessment

Guidance: level 1

:: Management ::

In business, a _________ is the attribute that allows an organization to outperform its competitors. A _________ may include access to natural resources, such as high-grade ores or a low-cost power source, highly skilled labor, geographic location, high entry barriers, and access to new technology.

Exam Probability: **Medium**

45. *Answer choices:*

(see index for correct answer)

- a. Managerialism
- b. Process capability
- c. Competitive advantage
- d. Strategic management

Guidance: level 1

:: Strategic management ::

__________ is a strategic planning technique used to help a person or organization identify strengths, weaknesses, opportunities, and threats related to business competition or project planning. It is intended to specify the objectives of the business venture or project and identify the internal and external factors that are favorable and unfavorable to achieving those objectives. Users of a __________ often ask and answer questions to generate meaningful information for each category to make the tool useful and identify their competitive advantage. SWOT has been described as the tried-and-true tool of strategic analysis.

Exam Probability: **High**

46. *Answer choices:*
(see index for correct answer)

- a. Bellwether Services
- b. SWOT analysis
- c. Operating model
- d. E-learning Maturity Model

Guidance: level 1

:: Survey methodology ::

An __________ is a conversation where questions are asked and answers are given. In common parlance, the word " __________ " refers to a one-on-one conversation between an __________ er and an __________ ee. The __________ er asks questions to which the __________ ee responds, usually so information may be transferred from __________ ee to __________ er . Sometimes, information can be transferred in both directions. It is a communication, unlike a speech, which produces a one-way flow of information.

Exam Probability: **Medium**

47. *Answer choices:*
(see index for correct answer)

- a. Group concept mapping
- b. Interview
- c. Computer-assisted survey information collection
- d. Scale analysis

Guidance: level 1

:: Management ::

A _________ is someone who engages in facilitation—any activity that makes a social process easy or easier. A _________ often helps a group of people to understand their common objectives and assists them to plan how to achieve these objectives; in doing so, the _________ remains "neutral", meaning he/she does not take a particular position in the discussion. Some _________ tools will try to assist the group in achieving a consensus on any disagreements that preexist or emerge in the meeting so that it has a strong basis for future action.

Exam Probability: **High**

48. *Answer choices:*

(see index for correct answer)

- a. Coworking
- b. Change advisory board
- c. middle manager
- d. Facilitator

Guidance: level 1

:: Income ::

In business and accounting, net income is an entity`s income minus cost of goods sold, expenses and taxes for an accounting period. It is computed as the residual of all revenues and gains over all expenses and losses for the period, and has also been defined as the net increase in shareholders` equity that results from a company`s operations. In the context of the presentation of financial statements, the IFRS Foundation defines net income as synonymous with profit and loss. The difference between revenue and the cost of making a product or providing a service, before deducting overheads, payroll, taxation, and interest payments. This is different from operating income .

Exam Probability: **Medium**

49. *Answer choices:*

(see index for correct answer)

- a. Net national income
- b. Per capita income
- c. Bottom line
- d. Passive income

Guidance: level 1

:: Marketing ::

__________ is the percentage of a market accounted for by a specific entity. In a survey of nearly 200 senior marketing managers, 67% responded that they found the revenue- "dollar __________ " metric very useful, while 61% found "unit __________ " very useful.

Exam Probability: **High**

50. *Answer choices:*

(see index for correct answer)

- a. Demonstrator model
- b. Customer value proposition
- c. Blind taste test
- d. Market share

Guidance: level 1

:: Management ::

The term __________ refers to measures designed to increase the degree of autonomy and self-determination in people and in communities in order to enable them to represent their interests in a responsible and self-determined way, acting on their own authority. It is the process of becoming stronger and more confident, especially in controlling one`s life and claiming one`s rights. __________ as action refers both to the process of self- __________ and to professional support of people, which enables them to overcome their sense of powerlessness and lack of influence, and to recognize and use their resources. To do work with power.

Exam Probability: **Medium**

51. *Answer choices:*

(see index for correct answer)

- a. Radical transparency
- b. Corporate transparency
- c. Certified Energy Manager
- d. Empowerment

Guidance: level 1

:: Data analysis ::

In statistics, the _________ is a measure that is used to quantify the amount of variation or dispersion of a set of data values. A low _________ indicates that the data points tend to be close to the mean of the set, while a high _________ indicates that the data points are spread out over a wider range of values.

Exam Probability: **Low**

52. *Answer choices:*

(see index for correct answer)

- a. Photoanalysis
- b. Standard deviation
- c. Evolutionary data mining
- d. Stationary subspace analysis

Guidance: level 1

:: Asset ::

In financial accounting, an _________ is any resource owned by the business. Anything tangible or intangible that can be owned or controlled to produce value and that is held by a company to produce positive economic value is an _________. Simply stated, _________ s represent value of ownership that can be converted into cash . The balance sheet of a firm records the monetary value of the _________ s owned by that firm. It covers money and other valuables belonging to an individual or to a business.

Exam Probability: **Low**

53. *Answer choices:*

(see index for correct answer)

- a. Current asset
- b. Asset

Guidance: level 1

:: Human resource management ::

_________ is the corporate management term for the act of reorganizing the legal, ownership, operational, or other structures of a company for the purpose of making it more profitable, or better organized for its present needs. Other reasons for _________ include a change of ownership or ownership structure, demerger, or a response to a crisis or major change in the business such as bankruptcy, repositioning, or buyout. _________ may also be described as corporate _________ , debt _________ and financial _________ .

Exam Probability: **High**

54. *Answer choices:*

(see index for correct answer)

- a. Flextime
- b. Workforce modeling
- c. Herrmann Brain Dominance Instrument
- d. Restructuring

Guidance: level 1

:: Human resource management ::

_________ , also known as management by results , was first popularized by Peter Drucker in his 1954 book The Practice of Management. _________ is the process of defining specific objectives within an organization that management can convey to organization members, then deciding on how to achieve each objective in sequence. This process allows managers to take work that needs to be done one step at a time to allow for a calm, yet productive work environment. This process also helps organization members to see their accomplishments as they achieve each objective, which reinforces a positive work environment and a sense of achievement. An important part of MBO is the measurement and comparison of an employee`s actual performance with the standards set. Ideally, when employees themselves have been involved with the goal-setting and choosing the course of action to be followed by them, they are more likely to fulfill their responsibilities.According to George S. Odiorne, the system of _________ can be described as a process whereby the superior and subordinate jointly identify common goals, define each individual`s major areas of responsibility in terms of the results expected of him or her, and use these measures as guides for operating the unit and assessing the contribution of each of its members.

Exam Probability: **Medium**

55. *Answer choices:*

(see index for correct answer)

- a. Kelly Services
- b. Open-book management
- c. Management by objectives
- d. The Giving of Orders

Guidance: level 1

:: Decision theory ::

A __________ is a decision support tool that uses a tree-like model of decisions and their possible consequences, including chance event outcomes, resource costs, and utility. It is one way to display an algorithm that only contains conditional control statements.

Exam Probability: **Low**

56. *Answer choices:*

(see index for correct answer)

- a. Polychotomous key
- b. Homothetic preferences
- c. Decision tree
- d. VIKOR method

Guidance: level 1

:: Decision theory ::

Within economics the concept of __________ is used to model worth or value, but its usage has evolved significantly over time. The term was introduced initially as a measure of pleasure or satisfaction within the theory of utilitarianism by moral philosophers such as Jeremy Bentham and John Stuart Mill. But the term has been adapted and reapplied within neoclassical economics, which dominates modern economic theory, as a __________ function that represents a consumer`s preference ordering over a choice set. As such, it is devoid of its original interpretation as a measurement of the pleasure or satisfaction obtained by the consumer from that choice.

Exam Probability: **Medium**

57. *Answer choices:*
(see index for correct answer)

- a. Feasible region
- b. Utility
- c. Statistical murder
- d. Wild card

Guidance: level 1

:: ::

An _________ is the production of goods or related services within an economy. The major source of revenue of a group or company is the indicator of its relevant _________. When a large group has multiple sources of revenue generation, it is considered to be working in different industries. Manufacturing _________ became a key sector of production and labour in European and North American countries during the Industrial Revolution, upsetting previous mercantile and feudal economies. This came through many successive rapid advances in technology, such as the production of steel and coal.

Exam Probability: **Low**

58. *Answer choices:*
(see index for correct answer)

- a. deep-level diversity
- b. hierarchical perspective
- c. similarity-attraction theory
- d. Character

Guidance: level 1

:: ::

_________ is the capacity of consciously making sense of things, establishing and verifying facts, applying logic, and changing or justifying practices, institutions, and beliefs based on new or existing information. It is closely associated with such characteristically human activities as philosophy, science, language, mathematics and art, and is normally considered to be a distinguishing ability possessed by humans. _________, or an aspect of it, is sometimes referred to as rationality.

Exam Probability: **High**

59. *Answer choices:*

(see index for correct answer)

- a. corporate values
- b. information systems assessment
- c. hierarchical
- d. deep-level diversity

Guidance: level 1

Business law

Corporate law (also known as business law) is the body of law governing the rights, relations, and conduct of persons, companies, organizations and businesses. It refers to the legal practice relating to, or the theory of corporations. Corporate law often describes the law relating to matters which derive directly from the life-cycle of a corporation. It thus encompasses the formation, funding, governance, and death of a corporation.

:: Contract law ::

An _________ is a contract, the terms of which have been agreed by spoken communication. This is in contrast to a written contract, where the contract is a written document. There may be written, or other physical evidence, of an _________ – for example where the parties write down what they have agreed – but the contract itself is not a written one.

Exam Probability: **Medium**

1. *Answer choices:*

(see index for correct answer)

- a. Oral contract
- b. Unconscionability
- c. Undue influence
- d. Contract B

Guidance: level 1

:: Insolvency ::

_________ is the state of being unable to pay the money owed, by a person or company, on time; those in a state of _________ are said to be insolvent. There are two forms: cash-flow _________ and balance-sheet _________ .

Exam Probability: **High**

2. *Answer choices:*

(see index for correct answer)

- a. Insolvency
- b. Preferential creditor
- c. Personal Insolvency Arrangement
- d. United Kingdom insolvency law

Guidance: level 1

:: Manufactured goods ::

A _________ or final good is any commodity that is produced or consumed by the consumer to satisfy current wants or needs. _________ s are ultimately consumed, rather than used in the production of another good. For example, a microwave oven or a bicycle that is sold to a consumer is a final good or _________ , but the components that are sold to be used in those goods are intermediate goods. For example, textiles or transistors can be used to make some further goods.

Exam Probability: **Low**

3. *Answer choices:*

(see index for correct answer)

- a. Household goods
- b. Bespoke
- c. Tarpaulin
- d. Final good

Guidance: level 1

:: Financial regulatory authorities of the United States ::

The _________ is the revenue service of the United States federal government. The government agency is a bureau of the Department of the Treasury, and is under the immediate direction of the Commissioner of Internal Revenue, who is appointed to a five-year term by the President of the United States. The IRS is responsible for collecting taxes and administering the Internal Revenue Code, the main body of federal statutory tax law of the United States. The duties of the IRS include providing tax assistance to taxpayers and pursuing and resolving instances of erroneous or fraudulent tax filings. The IRS has also overseen various benefits programs, and enforces portions of the Affordable Care Act.

Exam Probability: **Low**

4. *Answer choices:*

(see index for correct answer)

- a. Securities Investor Protection Corporation
- b. Internal Revenue Service
- c. Consumer Financial Protection Bureau
- d. National Futures Association

Guidance: level 1

:: Statutory law ::

_________ or statute law is written law set down by a body of legislature or by a singular legislator . This is as opposed to oral or customary law; or regulatory law promulgated by the executive or common law of the judiciary. Statutes may originate with national, state legislatures or local municipalities.

Exam Probability: **Medium**

5. *Answer choices:*

(see index for correct answer)

- a. statute law
- b. Statutory Law
- c. Statute of repose
- d. incorporation by reference

Guidance: level 1

:: Types of business entity ::

A _________ , the basic form of partnership under common law, is in most countries an association of persons or an unincorporated company with the following major features.

Exam Probability: **Low**

6. *Answer choices:*

(see index for correct answer)

- a. Non-profit distributing organisation
- b. General partnership
- c. Kommanditselskab
- d. Unlimited liability corporation

Guidance: level 1

:: Criminal procedure ::

In law, a verdict is the formal finding of fact made by a jury on matters or questions submitted to the jury by a judge. In a bench trial, the judge`s decision near the end of the trial is simply referred to as a finding. In England and Wales, a coroner`s findings are called verdicts .

Exam Probability: **High**

7. *Answer choices:*

(see index for correct answer)

- a. Exoneration
- b. Directed verdict

Guidance: level 1

:: Contract law ::

In contract law, a _________ is a promise which is not a condition of the contract or an innominate term: it is a term "not going to the root of the contract", and which only entitles the innocent party to damages if it is breached: i.e. the _________ is not true or the defaulting party does not perform the contract in accordance with the terms of the _________ . A _________ is not guarantee. It is a mere promise. It may be enforced if it is breached by an award for the legal remedy of damages.

Exam Probability: **Low**

8. *Answer choices:*

(see index for correct answer)

- a. Handshake deal
- b. Retainer agreement
- c. Warranty
- d. Pact ink

Guidance: level 1

:: Intention ::

_________ is the mental element of a person`s intention to commit a crime; or knowledge that one`s action or lack of action would cause a crime to be committed. It is a necessary element of many crimes.

Exam Probability: **Low**

9. *Answer choices:*
(see index for correct answer)

- a. bona fide
- b. Letter of Intent

Guidance: level 1

:: Negotiable instrument law ::

In the United States, The Preservation of Consumers' Claims and Defenses [_________ Rule], formally known as the "Trade Regulation Rule Concerning Preservation of Consumers` Claims and Defenses," protects consumers when merchants sell a consumer`s credit contracts to other lenders. Specifically, it preserves consumers` right to assert the same legal claims and defenses against anyone who purchases the credit contract, as they would have against the seller who originally provided the credit. [16 Code of Federal Regulations Part 433]

Exam Probability: **Low**

10. *Answer choices:*
(see index for correct answer)

- a. Swift v. Tyson
- b. Regulation CC
- c. Holder in due course
- d. Real defense

Guidance: level 1

:: Consumer theory ::

A _________ is a technical term in psychology, economics and philosophy usually used in relation to choosing between alternatives. For example, someone prefers A over B if they would rather choose A than B.

Exam Probability: **High**

11. *Answer choices:*
(see index for correct answer)

- a. Preference
- b. Time-based pricing
- c. Demand vacuum
- d. Expenditure function

Guidance: level 1

:: Project management ::

_________ is the right to exercise power, which can be formalized by a state and exercised by way of judges, appointed executives of government, or the ecclesiastical or priestly appointed representatives of a God or other deities.

Exam Probability: **High**

12. *Answer choices:*
(see index for correct answer)

- a. Site survey
- b. Transport Initiatives Edinburgh
- c. Market requirements document
- d. Burn down chart

Guidance: level 1

:: Abuse of the legal system ::

_________ occurs when a person is restricted in their personal movement within any area without justification or consent. Actual physical restraint is not necessary for _________ to occur. A _________ claim may be made based upon private acts, or upon wrongful governmental detention. For detention by the police, proof of _________ provides a basis to obtain a writ of habeas corpus.

Exam Probability: **High**

13. *Answer choices:*
(see index for correct answer)

- a. Forum shopping
- b. Obstruction of Justice
- c. False imprisonment

Guidance: level 1

:: ::

__________ is the assignment of any responsibility or authority to another person to carry out specific activities. It is one of the core concepts of management leadership. However, the person who delegated the work remains accountable for the outcome of the delegated work. __________ empowers a subordinate to make decisions, i.e. it is a shifting of decision-making authority from one organizational level to a lower one. __________, if properly done, is not fabrication. The opposite of effective __________ is micromanagement, where a manager provides too much input, direction, and review of delegated work. In general, __________ is good and can save money and time, help in building skills, and motivate people. On the other hand, poor __________ might cause frustration and confusion to all the involved parties. Some agents, however, do not favour a __________ and consider the power of making a decision rather burdensome.

Exam Probability: **Low**

14. *Answer choices:*

(see index for correct answer)

- a. similarity-attraction theory
- b. corporate values
- c. Character
- d. information systems assessment

Guidance: level 1

:: Anti-competitive behaviour ::

Restraints of trade is a common law doctrine relating to the enforceability of contractual restrictions on freedom to conduct business. It is a precursor of modern competition law. In an old leading case of Mitchel v Reynolds Lord Smith LC said,

Exam Probability: **High**

15. *Answer choices:*

(see index for correct answer)

- a. Strategic entry deterrence
- b. Restraint of trade
- c. SK Hynix
- d. Exclusive dealing

Guidance: level 1

:: Mereology ::

__________ , in the abstract, is what belongs to or with something, whether as an attribute or as a component of said thing. In the context of this article, it is one or more components , whether physical or incorporeal, of a person's estate; or so belonging to, as in being owned by, a person or jointly a group of people or a legal entity like a corporation or even a society. Depending on the nature of the __________ , an owner of __________ has the right to consume, alter, share, redefine, rent, mortgage, pawn, sell, exchange, transfer, give away or destroy it, or to exclude others from doing these things, as well as to perhaps abandon it; whereas regardless of the nature of the __________ , the owner thereof has the right to properly use it , or at the very least exclusively keep it.

Exam Probability: **Medium**

16. *Answer choices:*

(see index for correct answer)

- a. Gunk
- b. Mereological nihilism
- c. Property
- d. Meronomy

Guidance: level 1

:: ::

A _________ , in law, is a set of facts sufficient to justify a right to sue to obtain money, property, or the enforcement of a right against another party. The term also refers to the legal theory upon which a plaintiff brings suit . The legal document which carries a claim is often called a `statement of claim` in English law, or a `complaint` in U.S. federal practice and in many U.S. states. It can be any communication notifying the party to whom it is addressed of an alleged fault which resulted in damages, often expressed in amount of money the receiving party should pay/reimburse.

Exam Probability: **Low**

17. *Answer choices:*

(see index for correct answer)

- a. corporate values
- b. hierarchical perspective
- c. similarity-attraction theory
- d. deep-level diversity

Guidance: level 1

:: Product liability ::

_________ is the area of law in which manufacturers, distributors, suppliers, retailers, and others who make products available to the public are held responsible for the injuries those products cause. Although the word "product" has broad connotations, _________ as an area of law is traditionally limited to products in the form of tangible personal property.

Exam Probability: **Low**

18. *Answer choices:*

(see index for correct answer)

- a. Product liability
- b. Chinese drywall
- c. Market share liability
- d. Consumer Protection Act 1987

Guidance: level 1

:: ::

In law, an _________ is the process in which cases are reviewed, where parties request a formal change to an official decision. _________ s function both as a process for error correction as well as a process of clarifying and interpreting law. Although appellate courts have existed for thousands of years, common law countries did not incorporate an affirmative right to _________ into their jurisprudence until the 19th century.

Exam Probability: **Low**

19. *Answer choices:*

(see index for correct answer)

- a. empathy
- b. Appeal
- c. imperative
- d. levels of analysis

Guidance: level 1

:: Personal property law ::

Bailment describes a legal relationship in common law where physical possession of personal property, or a chattel, is transferred from one person to another person who subsequently has possession of the property. It arises when a person gives property to someone else for safekeeping, and is a cause of action independent of contract or tort.

Exam Probability: **Low**

20. *Answer choices:*

(see index for correct answer)

- a. Bailee
- b. bailment

Guidance: level 1

:: Commercial crimes ::

__________ is the process of concealing the origins of money obtained illegally by passing it through a complex sequence of banking transfers or commercial transactions. The overall scheme of this process returns the money to the launderer in an obscure and indirect way.

Exam Probability: **Medium**

21. *Answer choices:*

(see index for correct answer)

- a. Legal abuse
- b. Price gouging
- c. Warehouse bank
- d. False advertising

Guidance: level 1

:: ::

An __________ is a contingent motivator. Traditional __________ s are extrinsic motivators which reward actions to yield a desired outcome. The effectiveness of traditional __________ s has changed as the needs of Western society have evolved. While the traditional __________ model is effective when there is a defined procedure and goal for a task, Western society started to require a higher volume of critical thinkers, so the traditional model became less effective. Institutions are now following a trend in implementing strategies that rely on intrinsic motivations rather than the extrinsic motivations that the traditional __________ s foster.

Exam Probability: **High**

22. *Answer choices:*

(see index for correct answer)

- a. surface-level diversity
- b. functional perspective
- c. co-culture
- d. open system

Guidance: level 1

:: Business law ::

The _________ , first published in 1952, is one of a number of Uniform Acts that have been established as law with the goal of harmonizing the laws of sales and other commercial transactions across the United States of America through UCC adoption by all 50 states, the District of Columbia, and the Territories of the United States.

Exam Probability: **Low**

23. *Answer choices:*

(see index for correct answer)

- a. Uniform Commercial Code
- b. Principal
- c. Novated lease
- d. Free agent

Guidance: level 1

:: Monopoly (economics) ::

_________ is a category of property that includes intangible creations of the human intellect. _________ encompasses two types of rights: industrial property rights and copyright. It was not until the 19th century that the term " _________ " began to be used, and not until the late 20th century that it became commonplace in the majority of the world.

Exam Probability: **Medium**

24. *Answer choices:*

(see index for correct answer)

- a. Price-cap regulation
- b. Economies of scope
- c. Network effect
- d. Chamberlinian monopolistic competition

Guidance: level 1

:: Treaties ::

A _________ is an agreement under international law entered into by actors in international law, namely sovereign states and international organizations. A _________ may also be known as an agreement, protocol, covenant, convention, pact, or exchange of letters, among other terms. Regardless of terminology, all of these forms of agreements are, under international law, equally considered treaties and the rules are the same.

Exam Probability: **High**

25. *Answer choices:*

(see index for correct answer)

- a. Clausula rebus sic stantibus
- b. Treaty
- c. Guillotine clause
- d. Full Powers

Guidance: level 1

:: ::

_________ is a process under which executive or legislative actions are subject to review by the judiciary. A court with authority for _________ may invalidate laws, acts and governmental actions that are incompatible with a higher authority: an executive decision may be invalidated for being unlawful or a statute may be invalidated for violating the terms of a constitution. _________ is one of the checks and balances in the separation of powers: the power of the judiciary to supervise the legislative and executive branches when the latter exceed their authority. The doctrine varies between jurisdictions, so the procedure and scope of _________ may differ between and within countries.

Exam Probability: **High**

26. *Answer choices:*

(see index for correct answer)

- a. Sarbanes-Oxley act of 2002
- b. Judicial review
- c. hierarchical
- d. similarity-attraction theory

Guidance: level 1

:: Chemical industry ::

The _________ for the Protection of Literary and Artistic Works, usually known as the _________ , is an international agreement governing copyright, which was first accepted in Berne, Switzerland, in 1886.

Exam Probability: **Low**

27. *Answer choices:*

(see index for correct answer)

- a. Chemical leasing
- b. Middle German Chemical Triangle
- c. Regulation of chemicals
- d. Berne Convention

Guidance: level 1

:: ::

Credit is the trust which allows one party to provide money or resources to another party wherein the second party does not reimburse the first party immediately , but promises either to repay or return those resources at a later date. In other words, credit is a method of making reciprocity formal, legally enforceable, and extensible to a large group of unrelated people.

Exam Probability: **Low**

28. *Answer choices:*

(see index for correct answer)

- a. Sarbanes-Oxley act of 2002
- b. levels of analysis
- c. Consumer credit
- d. process perspective

Guidance: level 1

:: Writs ::

In common law, a _________ is a formal _________ ten order issued by a body with administrative or judicial jurisdiction; in modern usage, this body is generally a court. Warrants, prerogative _________ s, and subpoenas are common types of _________ , but many forms exist and have existed.

Exam Probability: **Low**

29. *Answer choices:*

(see index for correct answer)

- a. Qui tam
- b. Writ of assistance
- c. Writ

Guidance: level 1

:: Business law ::

A _________ is a group of people who jointly supervise the activities of an organization, which can be either a for-profit business, nonprofit organization, or a government agency. Such a board`s powers, duties, and responsibilities are determined by government regulations and the organization`s own constitution and bylaws. These authorities may specify the number of members of the board, how they are to be chosen, and how often they are to meet.

Exam Probability: **Low**

30. *Answer choices:*

(see index for correct answer)

- a. Finance lease
- b. Board of directors
- c. Consularization
- d. Lien

Guidance: level 1

:: ::

The __________ is one of the several United States Uniform Acts proposed by the National Conference of Commissioners on Uniform State Laws . Forty-seven states, the District of Columbia, and the U.S. Virgin Islands have adopted the UETA. Its purpose is to harmonize state laws concerning retention of paper records and the validity of electronic signatures.

Exam Probability: **High**

31. *Answer choices:*

(see index for correct answer)

- a. hierarchical
- b. Uniform Electronic Transactions Act
- c. empathy
- d. open system

Guidance: level 1

:: Business law ::

An __________ is a clause in a contract that requires the parties to resolve their disputes through an arbitration process. Although such a clause may or may not specify that arbitration occur within a specific jurisdiction, it always binds the parties to a type of resolution outside the courts, and is therefore considered a kind of forum selection clause.

Exam Probability: **High**

32. *Answer choices:*

(see index for correct answer)

- a. Equity of redemption
- b. Arbitration clause
- c. Consularization
- d. Economic torts

Guidance: level 1

:: Competition law ::

In competition law, a _________ is a market in which a particular product or service is sold. It is the intersection of a relevant product market and a relevant geographic market. The European Commission defines a _________ and its product and geographic components as follows.

Exam Probability: **Low**

33. *Answer choices:*

(see index for correct answer)

- a. Competition law theory
- b. Illegal per se
- c. Small but significant and non-transitory increase in price
- d. Relevant market

Guidance: level 1

:: Finance ::

A _________, in the law of the United States, is a contract that governs the relationship between the parties to a kind of financial transaction known as a secured transaction. In a secured transaction, the Grantor assigns, grants and pledges to the grantee a security interest in personal property which is referred to as the collateral. Examples of typical collateral are shares of stock, livestock, and vehicles. A _________ is not used to transfer any interest in real property , only personal property. The document used by lenders to obtain a lien on real property is a mortgage or deed of trust.

Exam Probability: **High**

34. *Answer choices:*

(see index for correct answer)

- a. Stock buyback
- b. Swap rate
- c. Style investing
- d. Security agreement

Guidance: level 1

:: ::

An _________ is the production of goods or related services within an economy. The major source of revenue of a group or company is the indicator of its relevant _________ . When a large group has multiple sources of revenue generation, it is considered to be working in different industries. Manufacturing _________ became a key sector of production and labour in European and North American countries during the Industrial Revolution, upsetting previous mercantile and feudal economies. This came through many successive rapid advances in technology, such as the production of steel and coal.

Exam Probability: **Low**

35. *Answer choices:*

(see index for correct answer)

- a. Industry
- b. open system
- c. Character
- d. functional perspective

Guidance: level 1

:: Investment ::

In finance, the benefit from an _________ is called a return. The return may consist of a gain realised from the sale of property or an _________ , unrealised capital appreciation , or _________ income such as dividends, interest, rental income etc., or a combination of capital gain and income. The return may also include currency gains or losses due to changes in foreign currency exchange rates.

Exam Probability: **Medium**

36. *Answer choices:*

(see index for correct answer)

- a. Low Exercise Price Option
- b. Security characteristic line
- c. Investment
- d. Master-feeder

Guidance: level 1

:: Clauses of the United States Constitution ::

The _________ describes an enumerated power listed in the United States Constitution . The clause states that the United States Congress shall have power "To regulate Commerce with foreign Nations, and among the several States, and with the Indian Tribes." Courts and commentators have tended to discuss each of these three areas of commerce as a separate power granted to Congress. It is common to see the individual components of the _________ referred to under specific terms: the Foreign _________ , the Interstate _________ , and the Indian _________ .

Exam Probability: **High**

37. *Answer choices:*

(see index for correct answer)

- a. Full faith and credit
- b. Full Faith and Credit Clause
- c. Double Jeopardy Clause

Guidance: level 1

:: Business ethics ::

_________ is a type of harassment technique that relates to a sexual nature and the unwelcome or inappropriate promise of rewards in exchange for sexual favors. _________ includes a range of actions from mild transgressions to sexual abuse or assault. Harassment can occur in many different social settings such as the workplace, the home, school, churches, etc. Harassers or victims may be of any gender.

Exam Probability: **Low**

38. *Answer choices:*

(see index for correct answer)

- a. Institute of Business Ethics
- b. Product stewardship
- c. Sexual harassment
- d. Precarious work

Guidance: level 1

:: ::

__________ is the study and management of exchange relationships. __________ is the business process of creating relationships with and satisfying customers. With its focus on the customer, __________ is one of the premier components of business management.

Exam Probability: **Medium**

39. *Answer choices:*
(see index for correct answer)

- a. open system
- b. Marketing
- c. personal values
- d. corporate values

Guidance: level 1

:: Real estate ::

__________, real estate, realty, or immovable property In English common law refers to landed properties belonging to some person. It include all structures, crops, buildings, machinery, wells, dams, ponds, mines, canals, and roads, among other things. The term is historic, arising from the now-discontinued form of action, which distinguish between __________ disputes and personal property disputes. Personal property was, and continues to refer to all properties that are not real properties.

Exam Probability: **High**

40. *Answer choices:*
(see index for correct answer)

- a. Dominant estate
- b. Privately owned public space
- c. Property Information Questionnaire
- d. Real property

Guidance: level 1

:: Sureties ::

In finance, a _________ , _________ bond or guaranty involves a promise by one party to assume responsibility for the debt obligation of a borrower if that borrower defaults. The person or company providing the promise is also known as a " _________ " or as a "guarantor".

Exam Probability: **Low**

41. *Answer choices:*

(see index for correct answer)

- a. Surety
- b. Parole bond
- c. Estreature
- d. Miller Act

Guidance: level 1

:: ::

The _________ is the highest court within the hierarchy of courts in many legal jurisdictions. Other descriptions for such courts include court of last resort, apex court, and high court of appeal. Broadly speaking, the decisions of a _________ are not subject to further review by any other court. _________ s typically function primarily as appellate courts, hearing appeals from decisions of lower trial courts, or from intermediate-level appellate courts.

Exam Probability: **Medium**

42. *Answer choices:*

(see index for correct answer)

- a. interpersonal communication
- b. Supreme Court
- c. Character
- d. levels of analysis

Guidance: level 1

:: ::

A _________ is a person or firm who arranges transactions between a buyer and a seller for a commission when the deal is executed. A _________ who also acts as a seller or as a buyer becomes a principal party to the deal. Neither role should be confused with that of an agent—one who acts on behalf of a principal party in a deal.

Exam Probability: **High**

43. *Answer choices:*

(see index for correct answer)

- a. Character
- b. Sarbanes-Oxley act of 2002
- c. information systems assessment
- d. Broker

Guidance: level 1

:: Contract law ::

_________ is a doctrine in contract law that describes terms that are so extremely unjust, or overwhelmingly one-sided in favor of the party who has the superior bargaining power, that they are contrary to good conscience. Typically, an unconscionable contract is held to be unenforceable because no reasonable or informed person would otherwise agree to it. The perpetrator of the conduct is not allowed to benefit, because the consideration offered is lacking, or is so obviously inadequate, that to enforce the contract would be unfair to the party seeking to escape the contract.

Exam Probability: **High**

44. *Answer choices:*

(see index for correct answer)

- a. Franchisor
- b. Pre-existing duty rule
- c. Principles of International Commercial Contracts
- d. Unconscionability

Guidance: level 1

:: Business law ::

An _________ is a natural person, business, or corporation that provides goods or services to another entity under terms specified in a contract or within a verbal agreement. Unlike an employee, an _________ does not work regularly for an employer but works as and when required, during which time they may be subject to law of agency. _________ s are usually paid on a freelance basis. Contractors often work through a limited company or franchise, which they themselves own, or may work through an umbrella company.

Exam Probability: **Medium**

45. *Answer choices:*

(see index for correct answer)

- a. Holder
- b. Negative option billing
- c. Fraud deterrence
- d. Independent contractor

Guidance: level 1

:: ::

_________ is an insurance that covers the whole or a part of the risk of a person incurring medical expenses, spreading the risk over a large number of persons. By estimating the overall risk of health care and health system expenses over the risk pool, an insurer can develop a routine finance structure, such as a monthly premium or payroll tax, to provide the money to pay for the health care benefits specified in the insurance agreement. The benefit is administered by a central organization such as a government agency, private business, or not-for-profit entity.

Exam Probability: **Low**

46. *Answer choices:*

(see index for correct answer)

- a. Health insurance
- b. Character
- c. hierarchical perspective
- d. similarity-attraction theory

Guidance: level 1

:: Stock market ::

The _________ of a corporation is all of the shares into which ownership of the corporation is divided. In American English, the shares are commonly known as " _________ s". A single share of the _________ represents fractional ownership of the corporation in proportion to the total number of shares. This typically entitles the _________ holder to that fraction of the company's earnings, proceeds from liquidation of assets , or voting power, often dividing these up in proportion to the amount of money each _________ holder has invested. Not all _________ is necessarily equal, as certain classes of _________ may be issued for example without voting rights, with enhanced voting rights, or with a certain priority to receive profits or liquidation proceeds before or after other classes of shareholders.

Exam Probability: **High**

47. *Answer choices:*

(see index for correct answer)

- a. London Stock Exchange Group
- b. Program trading
- c. Green sheet
- d. Stock

Guidance: level 1

:: Legal doctrines and principles ::

_________ is a doctrine that a party is responsible for acts of their agents. For example, in the United States, there are circumstances when an employer is liable for acts of employees performed within the course of their employment. This rule is also called the master-servant rule, recognized in both common law and civil law jurisdictions.

Exam Probability: **Medium**

48. *Answer choices:*

(see index for correct answer)

- a. unconscionable contract
- b. Res ipsa
- c. Act of state doctrine
- d. Respondeat superior

Guidance: level 1

:: Decision theory ::

Within economics the concept of _________ is used to model worth or value, but its usage has evolved significantly over time. The term was introduced initially as a measure of pleasure or satisfaction within the theory of utilitarianism by moral philosophers such as Jeremy Bentham and John Stuart Mill. But the term has been adapted and reapplied within neoclassical economics, which dominates modern economic theory, as a _________ function that represents a consumer`s preference ordering over a choice set. As such, it is devoid of its original interpretation as a measurement of the pleasure or satisfaction obtained by the consumer from that choice.

Exam Probability: **High**

49. *Answer choices:*

(see index for correct answer)

- a. Applied information economics
- b. Outcome primacy
- c. Action axiom
- d. Decisional balance sheet

Guidance: level 1

:: ::

The _________ Act of 1890 was a United States antitrust law that regulates competition among enterprises, which was passed by Congress under the presidency of Benjamin Harrison.

Exam Probability: **Medium**

50. *Answer choices:*

(see index for correct answer)

- a. empathy
- b. deep-level diversity
- c. information systems assessment
- d. hierarchical

Guidance: level 1

:: Legal terms ::

_________ is the set of laws that governs how members of a society are to behave. It is contrasted with procedural law, which is the set of procedures for making, administering, and enforcing _________ . _________ defines rights and responsibilities in civil law, and crimes and punishments in criminal law. It may be codified in statutes or exist through precedent in common law.

Exam Probability: **Medium**

51. *Answer choices:*

(see index for correct answer)

- a. Enacted law
- b. False pretenses
- c. Carnal knowledge
- d. Prejudice

Guidance: level 1

:: Services management and marketing ::

A _________ or servicemark is a trademark used in the United States and several other countries to identify a service rather than a product.

Exam Probability: **High**

52. *Answer choices:*

(see index for correct answer)

- a. Reverse bounty
- b. Industrialization of services business model
- c. Services marketing
- d. Service mark

Guidance: level 1

:: ::

__________ refers to a business or organization attempting to acquire goods or services to accomplish its goals. Although there are several organizations that attempt to set standards in the __________ process, processes can vary greatly between organizations. Typically the word " __________ " is not used interchangeably with the word "procurement", since procurement typically includes expediting, supplier quality, and transportation and logistics in addition to __________ .

Exam Probability: **Low**

53. *Answer choices:*

(see index for correct answer)

- a. process perspective
- b. co-culture
- c. Purchasing
- d. hierarchical

Guidance: level 1

:: Business law ::

A __________ is an arrangement where parties, known as partners, agree to cooperate to advance their mutual interests. The partners in a __________ may be individuals, businesses, interest-based organizations, schools, governments or combinations. Organizations may partner to increase the likelihood of each achieving their mission and to amplify their reach. A __________ may result in issuing and holding equity or may be only governed by a contract.

Exam Probability: **High**

54. *Answer choices:*

(see index for correct answer)

- a. OHADA
- b. Partnership
- c. Oppression remedy
- d. Corporation by estoppel

Guidance: level 1

:: Business ::

An __________ is a key document used by limited liability companies to outline the business` financial and functional decisions including rules, regulations and provisions. The purpose of the document is to govern the internal operations of the business in a way that suits the specific needs of the business owners. Once the document is signed by the members of the limited liability company, it acts as an official contract binding them to its terms. __________ is mandatory as per laws only in 5 states - California, Delaware, Maine, Missouri, and New York LLCs operating without an __________ are governed by the state`s default rules contained in the relevant statute and developed through state court decisions. An __________ is similar in function to corporate by-laws, or analogous to a partnership agreement in multi-member LLCs. In single-member LLCs, an __________ is a declaration of the structure that the member has chosen for the company and sometimes used to prove in court that the LLC structure is separate from that of the individual owner and thus necessary so that the owner has documentation to prove that he or she is indeed separate from the entity itself.

Exam Probability: **Medium**

55. *Answer choices:*

(see index for correct answer)

- a. Door-to-door
- b. Operating agreement
- c. Signed number
- d. 24/7 service

Guidance: level 1

:: ::

__________ is widespread, interconnected digital technology. The term entered the popular culture from science fiction and the arts but is now used by technology strategists, security professionals, government, military and industry leaders and entrepreneurs to describe the domain of the global technology environment. Others consider __________ to be just a notional environment in which communication over computer networks occurs. The word became popular in the 1990s when the uses of the Internet, networking, and digital communication were all growing dramatically and the term " __________ " was able to represent the many new ideas and phenomena that were emerging. It has been called the largest unregulated and uncontrolled domain in the history of mankind, and is also unique because it is a domain created by people vice the traditional physical domains.

Exam Probability: **Low**

56. *Answer choices:*

(see index for correct answer)

- a. Cyberspace
- b. surface-level diversity
- c. personal values
- d. hierarchical

Guidance: level 1

:: Business law ::

In the United States, the United Kingdom, Australia, Canada and South Africa, __________ relates to the doctrines of the law of agency. It is relevant particularly in corporate law and constitutional law. __________ refers to a situation where a reasonable third party would understand that an agent had authority to act. This means a principal is bound by the agent`s actions, even if the agent had no actual authority, whether express or implied. It raises an estoppel because the third party is given an assurance, which he relies on and would be inequitable for the principal to deny the authority given. __________ can legally be found, even if actual authority has not been given.

Exam Probability: **Medium**

57. *Answer choices:*

(see index for correct answer)

- a. Limited partnership
- b. Fraudulent trading
- c. Forward-looking statement
- d. Undervalue transaction

Guidance: level 1

:: Money market instruments ::

_________ , in the global financial market, is an unsecured promissory note with a fixed maturity of not more than 270 days.

Exam Probability: **Medium**

58. *Answer choices:*

(see index for correct answer)

- a. Commercial Paper
- b. Banker's acceptance

Guidance: level 1

:: Meetings ::

A _________ is a body of one or more persons that is subordinate to a deliberative assembly. Usually, the assembly sends matters into a _________ as a way to explore them more fully than would be possible if the assembly itself were considering them. _________ s may have different functions and their type of work differ depending on the type of the organization and its needs.

Exam Probability: **Medium**

59. *Answer choices:*

(see index for correct answer)

- a. Committee
- b. European Architecture Students Assembly
- c. Program book
- d. Over the Air

Guidance: level 1

Finance

Finance is a field that is concerned with the allocation (investment) of assets and liabilities over space and time, often under conditions of risk or uncertainty. Finance can also be defined as the science of money management. Participants in the market aim to price assets based on their risk level, fundamental value, and their expected rate of return. Finance can be split into three sub-categories: public finance, corporate finance and personal finance.

:: Financial crises ::

A _________ is any of a broad variety of situations in which some financial assets suddenly lose a large part of their nominal value. In the 19th and early 20th centuries, many financial crises were associated with banking panics, and many recessions coincided with these panics. Other situations that are often called financial crises include stock market crashes and the bursting of other financial bubbles, currency crises, and sovereign defaults. Financial crises directly result in a loss of paper wealth but do not necessarily result in significant changes in the real economy .

Exam Probability: **High**

1. *Answer choices:*

(see index for correct answer)

- a. The Vienna Initiative
- b. United States credit default
- c. Wreck of the Tennessee Gravy Train
- d. Financial crisis

Guidance: level 1

:: Financial ratios ::

The __________ shows the percentage of how profitable a company`s assets are in generating revenue.

Exam Probability: **High**

2. *Answer choices:*

(see index for correct answer)

- a. Implied multiple
- b. Average accounting return
- c. Return on assets
- d. Total expense ratio

Guidance: level 1

:: Debt ::

__________ is the trust which allows one party to provide money or resources to another party wherein the second party does not reimburse the first party immediately , but promises either to repay or return those resources at a later date. In other words, __________ is a method of making reciprocity formal, legally enforceable, and extensible to a large group of unrelated people.

Exam Probability: **Low**

3. *Answer choices:*

(see index for correct answer)

- a. Debt relief
- b. Medical debt
- c. Credit crunch
- d. Credit

Guidance: level 1

:: Accounting journals and ledgers ::

The subledger, or _________ , provides details behind entries in the general ledger used in accounting. The subledger shows detail for part of the accounting records such as property and equipment, prepaid expenses, etc. The detail would include such items as date the item was purchased or expense incurred, a description of the item, the original balance, and the net book value. The total of the subledger would match the line item amount on the general ledger. This corresponding line item in the general ledger is referred to as the controlling account. The _________ balance is compared with its controlling account balance as part of the process of preparing a trial balance.

Exam Probability: **Low**

4. *Answer choices:*

(see index for correct answer)

- a. Subledger
- b. General journal
- c. Check register
- d. Sales journal

Guidance: level 1

:: ::

An _________ is a contingent motivator. Traditional _________ s are extrinsic motivators which reward actions to yield a desired outcome. The effectiveness of traditional _________ s has changed as the needs of Western society have evolved. While the traditional _________ model is effective when there is a defined procedure and goal for a task, Western society started to require a higher volume of critical thinkers, so the traditional model became less effective. Institutions are now following a trend in implementing strategies that rely on intrinsic motivations rather than the extrinsic motivations that the traditional _________ s foster.

Exam Probability: **Low**

5. *Answer choices:*

(see index for correct answer)

- a. Sarbanes-Oxley act of 2002
- b. Incentive
- c. personal values

- d. levels of analysis

Guidance: level 1

:: Margin policy ::

In finance, a __________ is a standardized forward contract, a legal agreement to buy or sell something at a predetermined price at a specified time in the future, between parties not known to each other. The asset transacted is usually a commodity or financial instrument. The predetermined price the parties agree to buy and sell the asset for is known as the forward price. The specified time in the future—which is when delivery and payment occur—is known as the delivery date. Because it is a function of an underlying asset, a __________ is a derivative product.

Exam Probability: **High**

6. *Answer choices:*

(see index for correct answer)

- a. Futures contract
- b. Regulation T

Guidance: level 1

:: Stock market ::

__________ is a form of stock which may have any combination of features not possessed by common stock including properties of both an equity and a debt instrument, and is generally considered a hybrid instrument. __________ s are senior to common stock, but subordinate to bonds in terms of claim and may have priority over common stock in the payment of dividends and upon liquidation. Terms of the __________ are described in the issuing company`s articles of association or articles of incorporation.

Exam Probability: **High**

7. *Answer choices:*

(see index for correct answer)

- a. Block premium
- b. Green sheet
- c. Preferred stock
- d. Foolish Four

Guidance: level 1

:: United States Generally Accepted Accounting Principles ::

In a companies` financial reporting, _________ "includes all changes in equity during a period except those resulting from investments by owners and distributions to owners". Because that use excludes the effects of changing ownership interest, an economic measure of _________ is necessary for financial analysis from the shareholders` point of view

Exam Probability: **High**

8. *Answer choices:*

(see index for correct answer)

- a. Cost segregation study
- b. Permanent fund
- c. FIN 46
- d. Comprehensive income

Guidance: level 1

:: Insolvency ::

_________ is a legal process through which people or other entities who cannot repay debts to creditors may seek relief from some or all of their debts. In most jurisdictions, _________ is imposed by a court order, often initiated by the debtor.

Exam Probability: **High**

9. *Answer choices:*

(see index for correct answer)

- a. Official Committee of Equity Security Holders
- b. Bankruptcy
- c. Conservatorship
- d. Preferential creditor

Guidance: level 1

:: Management accounting ::

In economics, _________ s, indirect costs or overheads are business expenses that are not dependent on the level of goods or services produced by the business. They tend to be time-related, such as interest or rents being paid per month, and are often referred to as overhead costs. This is in contrast to variable costs, which are volume-related and unknown at the beginning of the accounting year. For a simple example, such as a bakery, the monthly rent for the baking facilities, and the monthly payments for the security system and basic phone line are _________ s, as they do not change according to how much bread the bakery produces and sells. On the other hand, the wage costs of the bakery are variable, as the bakery will have to hire more workers if the production of bread increases. Economists reckon _________ as a entry barrier for new entrepreneurs.

Exam Probability: **Medium**

10. *Answer choices:*

(see index for correct answer)

- a. Grenzplankostenrechnung
- b. Financial statement analysis
- c. Certified Management Accountant
- d. Fixed cost

Guidance: level 1

:: Fraud ::

In law, _________ is intentional deception to secure unfair or unlawful gain, or to deprive a victim of a legal right. _________ can violate civil law , a criminal law , or it may cause no loss of money, property or legal right but still be an element of another civil or criminal wrong. The purpose of _________ may be monetary gain or other benefits, for example by obtaining a passport, travel document, or driver's license, or mortgage _________ , where the perpetrator may attempt to qualify for a mortgage by way of false statements.

Exam Probability: **Low**

11. *Answer choices:*

(see index for correct answer)

- a. Telephone numbers in the Dominican Republic
- b. World Luxury Association

- c. Wangiri
- d. Fraud

Guidance: level 1

:: Business law ::

__________ is where a person's financial liability is limited to a fixed sum, most commonly the value of a person's investment in a company or partnership. If a company with __________ is sued, then the claimants are suing the company, not its owners or investors. A shareholder in a limited company is not personally liable for any of the debts of the company, other than for the amount already invested in the company and for any unpaid amount on the shares in the company, if any. The same is true for the members of a __________ partnership and the limited partners in a limited partnership. By contrast, sole proprietors and partners in general partnerships are each liable for all the debts of the business .

Exam Probability: **Medium**

12. *Answer choices:*

(see index for correct answer)

- a. Limited liability
- b. Facilitating payment
- c. Duty of fair representation
- d. Installment sale

Guidance: level 1

:: ::

An __________, for United States federal income tax, is a closely held corporation that makes a valid election to be taxed under Subchapter S of Chapter 1 of the Internal Revenue Code. In general, __________ s do not pay any income taxes. Instead, the corporation's income or losses are divided among and passed through to its shareholders. The shareholders must then report the income or loss on their own individual income tax returns.

Exam Probability: **High**

13. *Answer choices:*

(see index for correct answer)

- a. levels of analysis
- b. corporate values
- c. Character
- d. hierarchical perspective

Guidance: level 1

:: Generally Accepted Accounting Principles ::

The first published description of the process is found in Luca Pacioli`s 1494 work Summa de arithmetica, in the section titled Particularis de Computis et Scripturis. Although he did not use the term, he essentially prescribed a technique similar to a post-closing _________ .

Exam Probability: **Medium**

14. *Answer choices:*

(see index for correct answer)

- a. Gross profit
- b. Trial balance
- c. Net realizable value
- d. Earnings before interest, taxes and depreciation

Guidance: level 1

:: Options (finance) ::

In finance, a put or _________ is a stock market device which gives the owner the right, but not the obligation, to sell an asset , at a specified price , by a predetermined date to a given party . The purchase of a _________ is interpreted as a negative sentiment about the future value of theunderlying stock. The term "put" comes from the fact that the owner has the right to "put up for sale" the stock or index.

Exam Probability: **High**

15. *Answer choices:*

(see index for correct answer)

- a. Cash or share option
- b. Put option
- c. Interest rate guarantee
- d. Warrant

Guidance: level 1

:: ::

_________ involves decision making. It can include judging the merits of multiple options and selecting one or more of them. One can make a _________ between imagined options or between real options followed by the corresponding action. For example, a traveler might choose a route for a journey based on the preference of arriving at a given destination as soon as possible. The preferred route can then follow from information such as the length of each of the possible routes, traffic conditions, etc. The arrival at a _________ can include more complex motivators such as cognition, instinct, and feeling.

Exam Probability: **Low**

16. *Answer choices:*

(see index for correct answer)

- a. process perspective
- b. levels of analysis
- c. open system
- d. Choice

Guidance: level 1

:: Financial statements ::

In financial accounting, a _________ or statement of financial position or statement of financial condition is a summary of the financial balances of an individual or organization, whether it be a sole proprietorship, a business partnership, a corporation, private limited company or other organization such as Government or not-for-profit entity. Assets, liabilities and ownership equity are listed as of a specific date, such as the end of its financial year. A _________ is often described as a "snapshot of a company`s financial condition". Of the four basic financial statements, the _________ is the only statement which applies to a single point in time of a business` calendar year.

Exam Probability: **High**

17. *Answer choices:*

(see index for correct answer)

- a. Emphasis of matter
- b. Financial report
- c. Balance sheet
- d. Government financial statements

Guidance: level 1

:: Occupations ::

An __________ is a practitioner of accounting or accountancy, which is the measurement, disclosure or provision of assurance about financial information that helps managers, investors, tax authorities and others make decisions about allocating resource.

Exam Probability: **High**

18. *Answer choices:*

(see index for correct answer)

- a. Commissionaire
- b. Accountant
- c. Housebreaker
- d. Nuclear gypsy

Guidance: level 1

:: Asset ::

In accounting, a __________ is any asset which can reasonably be expected to be sold, consumed, or exhausted through the normal operations of a business within the current fiscal year or operating cycle . Typical __________ s include cash, cash equivalents, short-term investments , accounts receivable, stock inventory, supplies, and the portion of prepaid liabilities which will be paid within a year.In simple words, assets which are held for a short period are known as __________ s. Such assets are expected to be realised in cash or consumed during the normal operating cycle of the business.

Exam Probability: **High**

19. *Answer choices:*

(see index for correct answer)

- a. Fixed asset
- b. Asset

Guidance: level 1

:: ::

__________ is the concept of one topic being connected to another topic in a way that makes it useful to consider the second topic when considering the first. The concept of __________ is studied in many different fields, including cognitive sciences, logic, and library and information science. Most fundamentally, however, it is studied in epistemology . Different theories of knowledge have different implications for what is considered relevant and these fundamental views have implications for all other fields as well.

Exam Probability: **Medium**

20. *Answer choices:*

(see index for correct answer)

- a. empathy
- b. functional perspective
- c. personal values
- d. Character

Guidance: level 1

:: ::

__________ refers to a business or organization attempting to acquire goods or services to accomplish its goals. Although there are several organizations that attempt to set standards in the __________ process, processes can vary greatly between organizations. Typically the word " __________ " is not used interchangeably with the word "procurement", since procurement typically includes expediting, supplier quality, and transportation and logistics in addition to __________ .

Exam Probability: **Medium**

21. *Answer choices:*

(see index for correct answer)

- a. co-culture
- b. functional perspective
- c. Purchasing
- d. levels of analysis

Guidance: level 1

:: ::

_________ is the field of accounting concerned with the summary, analysis and reporting of financial transactions related to a business. This involves the preparation of financial statements available for public use. Stockholders, suppliers, banks, employees, government agencies, business owners, and other stakeholders are examples of people interested in receiving such information for decision making purposes.

Exam Probability: **High**

22. *Answer choices:*

(see index for correct answer)

- a. deep-level diversity
- b. hierarchical
- c. corporate values
- d. information systems assessment

Guidance: level 1

:: Interest ::

In finance, _________ is the interest on a bond or loan that has accumulated since the principal investment, or since the previous coupon payment if there has been one already.

Exam Probability: **Medium**

23. *Answer choices:*

(see index for correct answer)

- a. Capital and Interest
- b. Interest bearing
- c. Interest at maturity
- d. Abstinence theory of interest

Guidance: level 1

:: Inventory ::

__________ is the amount of inventory a company has in stock at the end of its fiscal year. It is closely related with __________ cost, which is the amount of money spent to get these goods in stock. It should be calculated at the lower of cost or market.

Exam Probability: **High**

24. *Answer choices:*

(see index for correct answer)

- a. Stock demands
- b. Ending inventory
- c. Lower of cost or market
- d. Spare part

Guidance: level 1

:: ::

A __________ is an entity that owes a debt to another entity. The entity may be an individual, a firm, a government, a company or other legal person. The counterparty is called a creditor. When the counterpart of this debt arrangement is a bank, the __________ is more often referred to as a borrower.

Exam Probability: **High**

25. *Answer choices:*

(see index for correct answer)

- a. Character
- b. personal values
- c. co-culture
- d. similarity-attraction theory

Guidance: level 1

:: Elementary geometry ::

The _________ is the front of an animal`s head that features three of the head`s sense organs, the eyes, nose, and mouth, and through which animals express many of their emotions. The _________ is crucial for human identity, and damage such as scarring or developmental deformities affects the psyche adversely.

Exam Probability: **Low**

26. *Answer choices:*

(see index for correct answer)

- a. Face
- b. Direction
- c. Crossed ladders problem
- d. Bicone

Guidance: level 1

:: Financial ratios ::

_________ or asset turns is a financial ratio that measures the efficiency of a company`s use of its assets in generating sales revenue or sales income to the company.

Exam Probability: **High**

27. *Answer choices:*

(see index for correct answer)

- a. Capital employed
- b. Asset turnover
- c. stock turnover
- d. Profit margin

Guidance: level 1

:: Public finance ::

_________ is the process by which the monetary authority of a country, typically the central bank or currency board, controls either the cost of very short-term borrowing or the money supply, often targeting inflation rate or interest rate to ensure price stability and general trust in the currency.

Exam Probability: **Medium**

28. *Answer choices:*

(see index for correct answer)

- a. Fiscal policy
- b. Grant-in-aid
- c. Great Lakes Higher Education Corporation
- d. Monetary policy

Guidance: level 1

:: Decision theory ::

Within economics the concept of _________ is used to model worth or value, but its usage has evolved significantly over time. The term was introduced initially as a measure of pleasure or satisfaction within the theory of utilitarianism by moral philosophers such as Jeremy Bentham and John Stuart Mill. But the term has been adapted and reapplied within neoclassical economics, which dominates modern economic theory, as a _________ function that represents a consumer`s preference ordering over a choice set. As such, it is devoid of its original interpretation as a measurement of the pleasure or satisfaction obtained by the consumer from that choice.

Exam Probability: **Medium**

29. *Answer choices:*

(see index for correct answer)

- a. Bulk Dispatch Lapse
- b. Utility
- c. Belief decision matrix
- d. Ophelimity

Guidance: level 1

:: Expense ::

A company`s _________, or As a result, the computation of the _________ is considerably more complex. Tax law may provide for different treatment of items of income and expenses as a result of tax policy. The differences may be of permanent or temporary nature. Permanent items are in the form of non taxable income and non taxable expenses. Things such as expenses considered not deductible by taxing authorities , the range of tax rates applicable to various levels of income, different tax rates in different jurisdictions, multiple layers of tax on income, and other issues.

Exam Probability: **Medium**

30. *Answer choices:*

(see index for correct answer)

- a. Expense account
- b. Stock option expensing
- c. Tax expense
- d. Interest expense

Guidance: level 1

:: ::

In marketing, a _________ is a ticket or document that can be redeemed for a financial discount or rebate when purchasing a product.

Exam Probability: **Low**

31. *Answer choices:*

(see index for correct answer)

- a. functional perspective
- b. process perspective
- c. Coupon
- d. imperative

Guidance: level 1

:: Marketing ::

A _________ is the quantity of payment or compensation given by one party to another in return for one unit of goods or services.. A _________ is influenced by both production costs and demand for the product. A _________ may be determined by a monopolist or may be imposed on the firm by market conditions.

Exam Probability: **Low**

32. *Answer choices:*

(see index for correct answer)

- a. Price
- b. Optimal discriminant analysis
- c. Online lead generation
- d. Point of difference

Guidance: level 1

:: Actuarial science ::

_________ is the addition of interest to the principal sum of a loan or deposit, or in other words, interest on interest. It is the result of reinvesting interest, rather than paying it out, so that interest in the next period is then earned on the principal sum plus previously accumulated interest. _________ is standard in finance and economics.

Exam Probability: **High**

33. *Answer choices:*

(see index for correct answer)

- a. Risk measure
- b. Compound interest
- c. Insurable risk
- d. Future interests

Guidance: level 1

:: Mutualism (movement) ::

A __________ is a professionally managed investment fund that pools money from many investors to purchase securities. These investors may be retail or institutional in nature.

Exam Probability: **High**

34. *Answer choices:*

(see index for correct answer)

- a. Ayni
- b. History of the cooperative movement
- c. Mutual fund
- d. ICA Group

Guidance: level 1

:: Accounting terminology ::

Accounts are typically defined by an identifier and a caption or header and are coded by account type. In computerized accounting systems with computable quantity accounting, the accounts can have a quantity measure definition.

Exam Probability: **Low**

35. *Answer choices:*

(see index for correct answer)

- a. Capital expenditure
- b. Chart of accounts
- c. profit and loss statement
- d. Share premium

Guidance: level 1

:: ::

__________ is the process whereby a business sets the price at which it will sell its products and services, and may be part of the business`s marketing plan. In setting prices, the business will take into account the price at which it could acquire the goods, the manufacturing cost, the market place, competition, market condition, brand, and quality of product.

Exam Probability: **High**

36. *Answer choices:*

(see index for correct answer)

- a. corporate values
- b. levels of analysis
- c. co-culture
- d. Pricing

Guidance: level 1

:: ::

__________ focuses on ratios, equities and debts. It is useful for portfolio management,distribution of dividend,capital raising,hedging and looking after fluctuations in foreign currency and product cycles.Financial managers are the people who will do research and based on the research, decide what sort of capital to obtain in order to fund the company`s assets as well as maximizing the value of the firm for all the stakeholders. It also refers to the efficient and effective management of money in such a manner as to accomplish the objectives of the organization. It is the specialized function directly associated with the top management. The significance of this function is not seen in the `Line` but also in the capacity of the `Staff` in overall of a company. It has been defined differently by different experts in the field.

Exam Probability: **High**

37. *Answer choices:*

(see index for correct answer)

- a. imperative
- b. similarity-attraction theory
- c. Financial management
- d. process perspective

Guidance: level 1

:: Debt ::

A _________ is a party that has a claim on the services of a second party. It is a person or institution to whom money is owed. The first party, in general, has provided some property or service to the second party under the assumption that the second party will return an equivalent property and service. The second party is frequently called a debtor or borrower. The first party is called the _________ , which is the lender of property, service, or money.

Exam Probability: **Medium**

38. *Answer choices:*

(see index for correct answer)

- a. Creditor
- b. Debt crisis
- c. Debt-lag
- d. Debt wall

Guidance: level 1

:: ::

A _________ is any person who contracts to acquire an asset in return for some form of consideration.

Exam Probability: **High**

39. *Answer choices:*

(see index for correct answer)

- a. corporate values
- b. Buyer
- c. cultural
- d. similarity-attraction theory

Guidance: level 1

:: Management accounting ::

__________ is a managerial accounting cost concept. Under this method, manufacturing overhead is incurred in the period that a product is produced. This addresses the issue of absorption costing that allows income to rise as production rises. Under an absorption cost method, management can push forward costs to the next period when products are sold. This artificially inflates profits in the period of production by incurring less cost than would be incurred under a __________ system. __________ is generally not used for external reporting purposes. Under the Tax Reform Act of 1986, income statements must use absorption costing to comply with GAAP.

Exam Probability: **High**

40. *Answer choices:*
(see index for correct answer)

- a. Holding cost
- b. Constraints accounting
- c. Variable Costing
- d. Resource consumption accounting

Guidance: level 1

:: Generally Accepted Accounting Principles ::

__________ is a small amount of discretionary funds in the form of cash used for expenditures where it is not sensible to make any disbursement by cheque, because of the inconvenience and costs of writing, signing, and then cashing the cheque.

Exam Probability: **Medium**

41. *Answer choices:*
(see index for correct answer)

- a. Standard Business Reporting
- b. AICPA Statements of Position
- c. Petty cash
- d. Insurance asset management

Guidance: level 1

:: Financial risk ::

_________ is any of various types of risk associated with financing, including financial transactions that include company loans in risk of default. Often it is understood to include only downside risk, meaning the potential for financial loss and uncertainty about its extent.

Exam Probability: **Medium**

42. *Answer choices:*

(see index for correct answer)

- a. Political risk
- b. Financial risk
- c. Settlement risk
- d. Consistent pricing process

Guidance: level 1

:: Portfolio theories ::

In finance, the _________ is a model used to determine a theoretically appropriate required rate of return of an asset, to make decisions about adding assets to a well-diversified portfolio.

Exam Probability: **Medium**

43. *Answer choices:*

(see index for correct answer)

- a. Intertemporal portfolio choice
- b. Capital asset pricing model
- c. Maslowian portfolio theory
- d. Post-modern portfolio theory

Guidance: level 1

:: Banking ::

A __________ is a financial account maintained by a bank for a customer. A __________ can be a deposit account, a credit card account, a current account, or any other type of account offered by a financial institution, and represents the funds that a customer has entrusted to the financial institution and from which the customer can make withdrawals. Alternatively, accounts may be loan accounts in which case the customer owes money to the financial institution.

Exam Probability: **High**

44. *Answer choices:*

(see index for correct answer)

- a. Managed account
- b. Bank account
- c. Double default
- d. Master transaction agreement

Guidance: level 1

:: Business law ::

A __________, also known as the sole trader, individual entrepreneurship or proprietorship, is a type of enterprise that is owned and run by one person and in which there is no legal distinction between the owner and the business entity. A sole trader does not necessarily work `alone`—it is possible for the sole trader to employ other people.

Exam Probability: **High**

45. *Answer choices:*

(see index for correct answer)

- a. Certificate of incorporation
- b. Limited liability limited partnership
- c. Business license
- d. Extraordinary resolution

Guidance: level 1

:: Costs ::

In microeconomic theory, the _________, or alternative cost, of making a particular choice is the value of the most valuable choice out of those that were not taken. In other words, opportunity that will require sacrifices.

Exam Probability: **High**

46. *Answer choices:*

(see index for correct answer)

- a. Cost reduction
- b. Joint cost
- c. Social cost
- d. Opportunity cost

Guidance: level 1

:: Accounting terminology ::

Total _________ is a method of Accounting cost which entails the full cost of manufacturing or providing a service. TAC includes not just the costs of materials and labour, but also of all manufacturing overheads . The cost of each cost center can be direct or indirect. The direct cost can be easily identified with individual cost centers. Whereas indirect cost cannot be easily identified with the cost center. The distribution of overhead among the departments is called apportionment.

Exam Probability: **Medium**

47. *Answer choices:*

(see index for correct answer)

- a. managerial accounting
- b. Absorption costing
- c. Mark-to-market
- d. double-entry bookkeeping

Guidance: level 1

:: ::

In financial markets, a share is a unit used as mutual funds, limited partnerships, and real estate investment trusts. The owner of _________ in the corporation/company is a shareholder of the corporation. A share is an indivisible unit of capital, expressing the ownership relationship between the company and the shareholder. The denominated value of a share is its face value, and the total of the face value of issued _________ represent the capital of a company, which may not reflect the market value of those _________ .

Exam Probability: **High**

48. *Answer choices:*

(see index for correct answer)

- a. hierarchical perspective
- b. interpersonal communication
- c. Shares
- d. process perspective

Guidance: level 1

:: Business law ::

The expression " _________ " is somewhat confusing as it has a different meaning based on the context that is under consideration.From a product characteristic stand point, this type of a lease, as distinguished from a finance lease, is one where the lessor takes residual risk. As such, the lease is non full payout. From an accounting stand point, this type of lease results in off balance sheet financing.

Exam Probability: **High**

49. *Answer choices:*

(see index for correct answer)

- a. Complex structured finance transactions
- b. Lien
- c. Operating lease
- d. Duty of fair representation

Guidance: level 1

:: Financial regulatory authorities of the United States ::

The __________ is the revenue service of the United States federal government. The government agency is a bureau of the Department of the Treasury, and is under the immediate direction of the Commissioner of Internal Revenue, who is appointed to a five-year term by the President of the United States. The IRS is responsible for collecting taxes and administering the Internal Revenue Code, the main body of federal statutory tax law of the United States. The duties of the IRS include providing tax assistance to taxpayers and pursuing and resolving instances of erroneous or fraudulent tax filings. The IRS has also overseen various benefits programs, and enforces portions of the Affordable Care Act.

Exam Probability: **Low**

50. *Answer choices:*

(see index for correct answer)

- a. Farm Credit Administration
- b. Commodity Futures Trading Commission
- c. National Credit Union Administration
- d. Internal Revenue Service

Guidance: level 1

:: Financial markets ::

The __________, also called the aftermarket and follow on public offering is the financial market in which previously issued financial instruments such as stock, bonds, options, and futures are bought and sold. Another frequent usage of " __________ " is to refer to loans which are sold by a mortgage bank to investors such as Fannie Mae and Freddie Mac.

Exam Probability: **Low**

51. *Answer choices:*

(see index for correct answer)

- a. Secondary market
- b. Time-weighted average price
- c. Odd lot
- d. Power Plus Pro

Guidance: level 1

:: Financial risk ::

_________ is the risk that arises for bond owners from fluctuating interest rates. How much _________ a bond has depends on how sensitive its price is to interest rate changes in the market. The sensitivity depends on two things, the bond`s time to maturity, and the coupon rate of the bond.

Exam Probability: **Low**

52. *Answer choices:*

(see index for correct answer)

- a. Over-the-counter
- b. Valuation risk
- c. Investment management
- d. Fuel price risk management

Guidance: level 1

:: Interest rates ::

An _________ is the amount of interest due per period, as a proportion of the amount lent, deposited or borrowed . The total interest on an amount lent or borrowed depends on the principal sum, the _________ , the compounding frequency, and the length of time over which it is lent, deposited or borrowed.

Exam Probability: **Medium**

53. *Answer choices:*

(see index for correct answer)

- a. Inflation derivative
- b. Interest rate
- c. Effective interest rate
- d. Foreign exchange swap

Guidance: level 1

:: Subprime mortgage crisis ::

The __________ Group, Inc., is an American multinational investment bank and financial services company headquartered in New York City. It offers services in investment management, securities, asset management, prime brokerage, and securities underwriting.

Exam Probability: **High**

54. *Answer choices:*

(see index for correct answer)

- a. Goldman Sachs
- b. Cramdown
- c. Subprime mortgage crisis solutions debate
- d. Foreclosure rescue

Guidance: level 1

:: Payments ::

A __________ is the trade of value from one party to another for goods, or services, or to fulfill a legal obligation.

Exam Probability: **Medium**

55. *Answer choices:*

(see index for correct answer)

- a. Subsidy
- b. County payments
- c. Payment
- d. Incentive payments

Guidance: level 1

:: Generally Accepted Accounting Principles ::

_________, or non-current liabilities, are liabilities that are due beyond a year or the normal operation period of the company. The normal operation period is the amount of time it takes for a company to turn inventory into cash. On a classified balance sheet, liabilities are separated between current and _________ to help users assess the company's financial standing in short-term and long-term periods. _________ give users more information about the long-term prosperity of the company, while current liabilities inform the user of debt that the company owes in the current period. On a balance sheet, accounts are listed in order of liquidity, so _________ come after current liabilities. In addition, the specific long-term liability accounts are listed on the balance sheet in order of liquidity. Therefore, an account due within eighteen months would be listed before an account due within twenty-four months. Examples of _________ are bonds payable, long-term loans, capital leases, pension liabilities, post-retirement healthcare liabilities, deferred compensation, deferred revenues, deferred income taxes, and derivative liabilities.

Exam Probability: **High**

56. *Answer choices:*

(see index for correct answer)

- a. Deprival value
- b. Insurance asset management
- c. Long-term liabilities
- d. Deferred income

Guidance: level 1

:: Management accounting ::

_________ is the process of recording, classifying, analyzing, summarizing, and allocating costs associated with a process,after that developing various courses of action to control the costs. Its goal is to advise the management on how to optimize business practices and processes based on cost efficiency and capability. _________ provides the detailed cost information that management needs to control current operations and plan for the future.

Exam Probability: **Low**

57. *Answer choices:*

(see index for correct answer)

- a. Pre-determined overhead rate
- b. RCA open-source application
- c. Construction accounting
- d. Target costing

Guidance: level 1

:: Auditing ::

_________ , as defined by accounting and auditing, is a process for assuring of an organization`s objectives in operational effectiveness and efficiency, reliable financial reporting, and compliance with laws, regulations and policies. A broad concept, _________ involves everything that controls risks to an organization.

Exam Probability: **Low**

58. *Answer choices:*
(see index for correct answer)

- a. International Federation of Audit Bureaux of Circulations
- b. Continuous auditing
- c. Internal control
- d. Audit working papers

Guidance: level 1

:: Competition (economics) ::

_________ arises whenever at least two parties strive for a goal which cannot be shared: where one`s gain is the other`s loss .

Exam Probability: **Low**

59. *Answer choices:*
(see index for correct answer)

- a. Level playing field
- b. Economic forces
- c. Self-competition
- d. Competition

Guidance: level 1

Human resource management

Human resource (HR) management is the strategic approach to the effective management of organization workers so that they help the business gain a competitive advantage. It is designed to maximize employee performance in service of an employer's strategic objectives. HR is primarily concerned with the management of people within organizations, focusing on policies and on systems. HR departments are responsible for overseeing employee-benefits design, employee recruitment, training and development, performance appraisal, and rewarding (e.g., managing pay and benefit systems). HR also concerns itself with organizational change and industrial relations, that is, the balancing of organizational practices with requirements arising from collective bargaining and from governmental laws.

:: Human resource management ::

__________ refers to the anticipation of required human capital for an organization and the planning to meet those needs. The field increased in popularity after McKinsey's 1997 research and the 2001 book on The War for Talent. _________ in this context does not refer to the management of entertainers.

Exam Probability: **Medium**

1. *Answer choices:*

(see index for correct answer)

- a. Salary
- b. Simultaneous recruiting of new graduates
- c. Four-day week
- d. Talent management

Guidance: level 1

:: Survey methodology ::

A _________ is the procedure of systematically acquiring and recording information about the members of a given population. The term is used mostly in connection with national population and housing _________ es; other common _________ es include agriculture, business, and traffic _________ es. The United Nations defines the essential features of population and housing _________ es as "individual enumeration, universality within a defined territory, simultaneity and defined periodicity", and recommends that population _________ es be taken at least every 10 years. United Nations recommendations also cover _________ topics to be collected, official definitions, classifications and other useful information to co-ordinate international practice.

Exam Probability: **High**

2. *Answer choices:*

(see index for correct answer)

- a. Scale analysis
- b. Total survey error
- c. World Association for Public Opinion Research
- d. Census

Guidance: level 1

:: Labor rights ::

The _________ is the concept that people have a human _________ , or engage in productive employment, and may not be prevented from doing so. The _________ is enshrined in the Universal Declaration of Human Rights and recognized in international human rights law through its inclusion in the International Covenant on Economic, Social and Cultural Rights, where the _________ emphasizes economic, social and cultural development.

Exam Probability: **High**

3. *Answer choices:*

(see index for correct answer)

- a. Swift raids
- b. Right to work
- c. Grievance
- d. Kate Mullany House

Guidance: level 1

:: Human resource management ::

__________ is the corporate management term for the act of reorganizing the legal, ownership, operational, or other structures of a company for the purpose of making it more profitable, or better organized for its present needs. Other reasons for __________ include a change of ownership or ownership structure, demerger, or a response to a crisis or major change in the business such as bankruptcy, repositioning, or buyout. __________ may also be described as corporate __________, debt __________ and financial __________.

Exam Probability: **High**

4. *Answer choices:*

(see index for correct answer)

- a. Workforce planning
- b. Human resource consulting
- c. Employee exit management
- d. Open-book management

Guidance: level 1

:: Management ::

The __________ is a strategy performance management tool – a semi-standard structured report, that can be used by managers to keep track of the execution of activities by the staff within their control and to monitor the consequences arising from these actions.

Exam Probability: **Low**

5. *Answer choices:*

(see index for correct answer)

- a. Balanced scorecard
- b. Advisory board
- c. Intelligent customer
- d. Top development

Guidance: level 1

:: Information systems ::

__________ is the process of creating, sharing, using and managing the knowledge and information of an organisation. It refers to a multidisciplinary approach to achieving organisational objectives by making the best use of knowledge.

Exam Probability: **Medium**

6. *Answer choices:*

(see index for correct answer)

- a. 3D city models
- b. G-Book
- c. Knowledge management
- d. German Emigrants Database

Guidance: level 1

:: ::

In business strategy, __________ is establishing a competitive advantage by having the lowest cost of operation in the industry. __________ is often driven by company efficiency, size, scale, scope and cumulative experience .A __________ strategy aims to exploit scale of production, well-defined scope and other economies , producing highly standardized products, using advanced technology.In recent years, more and more companies have chosen a strategic mix to achieve market leadership. These patterns consist of simultaneous __________ , superior customer service and product leadership. Walmart has succeeded across the world due to its __________ strategy. The company has cut down on exesses at every point of production and thus are able to provide the consumers with quality products at low prices.

Exam Probability: **Medium**

7. *Answer choices:*

(see index for correct answer)

- a. Cost leadership
- b. personal values
- c. surface-level diversity
- d. deep-level diversity

Guidance: level 1

:: Psychometrics ::

A __________ is a set of categories designed to elicit information about a quantitative or a qualitative attribute. In the social sciences, particularly psychology, common examples are the Likert response scale and 1-10 __________ s in which a person selects the number which is considered to reflect the perceived quality of a product.

Exam Probability: **Low**

8. *Answer choices:*

(see index for correct answer)

- a. Latent variable
- b. Rating scale
- c. House-Tree-Person test
- d. Linear-on-the-fly testing

Guidance: level 1

:: Financial statements ::

In financial accounting, a __________ or statement of financial position or statement of financial condition is a summary of the financial balances of an individual or organization, whether it be a sole proprietorship, a business partnership, a corporation, private limited company or other organization such as Government or not-for-profit entity. Assets, liabilities and ownership equity are listed as of a specific date, such as the end of its financial year. A __________ is often described as a "snapshot of a company`s financial condition". Of the four basic financial statements, the __________ is the only statement which applies to a single point in time of a business` calendar year.

Exam Probability: **Medium**

9. *Answer choices:*

(see index for correct answer)

- a. Statements on auditing standards
- b. Financial statement
- c. Balance sheet
- d. Quarterly finance report

Guidance: level 1

:: Human resource management ::

__________ is the strategic approach to the effective management of people in an organization so that they help the business to gain a competitive advantage. It is designed to maximize employee performance in service of an employer's strategic objectives. HR is primarily concerned with the management of people within organizations, focusing on policies and on systems. HR departments are responsible for overseeing employee-benefits design, employee recruitment, training and development, performance appraisal, and Reward management . HR also concerns itself with organizational change and industrial relations, that is, the balancing of organizational practices with requirements arising from collective bargaining and from governmental laws.

Exam Probability: **Low**

10. *Answer choices:*

(see index for correct answer)

- a. Salary
- b. Human resource management
- c. Parallel running
- d. Applicant tracking system

Guidance: level 1

:: Sexual harassment in the United States ::

In law, a __________, reasonable man, or the man on the Clapham omnibus is a hypothetical person of legal fiction crafted by the courts and communicated through case law and jury instructions.

Exam Probability: **Low**

11. *Answer choices:*

(see index for correct answer)

- a. Sandy Gallin
- b. Reasonable person
- c. Fitzgerald v. Barnstable School Committee
- d. Charol Shakeshaft

Guidance: level 1

:: Organizational behavior ::

__________ is the act of matching attitudes, beliefs, and behaviors to group norms or politics. Norms are implicit, specific rules, shared by a group of individuals, that guide their interactions with others. People often choose to conform to society rather than to pursue personal desires because it is often easier to follow the path others have made already, rather than creating a new one. This tendency to conform occurs in small groups and/or society as a whole, and may result from subtle unconscious influences , or direct and overt social pressure. __________ can occur in the presence of others, or when an individual is alone. For example, people tend to follow social norms when eating or watching television, even when alone.

Exam Probability: **High**

12. *Answer choices:*

(see index for correct answer)

- a. History of contingency theories of leadership
- b. Nut Island effect
- c. Informal organization
- d. Managerial grid model

Guidance: level 1

:: Organizational behavior ::

Greenberg introduced the concept of __________ with regard to how an employee judges the behaviour of the organization and the employee`s resulting attitude and behaviour. .

Exam Probability: **Medium**

13. *Answer choices:*

(see index for correct answer)

- a. Counterproductive norms
- b. Civic virtue
- c. Boreout
- d. Organizational justice

Guidance: level 1

:: Minimum wage ::

A _________ is the lowest remuneration that employers can legally pay their workers—the price floor below which workers may not sell their labor. Most countries had introduced _________ legislation by the end of the 20th century.

Exam Probability: **Medium**

14. *Answer choices:*

(see index for correct answer)

- a. Guaranteed minimum income
- b. National Anti-Sweating League
- c. Minimum wage in Taiwan
- d. Minimum wage

Guidance: level 1

:: Psychometrics ::

Electronic assessment, also known as e-assessment, _________ , computer assisted/mediated assessment and computer-based assessment, is the use of information technology in various forms of assessment such as educational assessment, health assessment, psychiatric assessment, and psychological assessment. This may utilize an online computer connected to a network. This definition embraces a wide range of student activity ranging from the use of a word processor to on-screen testing. Specific types of e-assessment include multiple choice, online/electronic submission, computerized adaptive testing and computerized classification testing.

Exam Probability: **Medium**

15. *Answer choices:*

(see index for correct answer)

- a. Psychometrics of racism
- b. Attribute Hierarchy Method
- c. Borderline intellectual functioning
- d. Computerized adaptive testing

Guidance: level 1

:: Developmental psychology ::

__________ behavior refers to behavior that enables a person to get along in his or her environment with greatest success and least conflict with others. This is a term used in the areas of psychology and special education. __________ behavior relates to every day skills or tasks that the average person is able to complete, similar to the term life skills.

Exam Probability: **High**

16. *Answer choices:*

(see index for correct answer)

- a. Cognitive development
- b. Adult development

Guidance: level 1

:: ::

Domestic violence is violence or other abuse by one person against another in a domestic setting, such as in marriage or cohabitation. It may be termed intimate partner violence when committed by a spouse or partner in an intimate relationship against the other spouse or partner, and can take place in heterosexual or same-sex relationships, or between former spouses or partners. Domestic violence can also involve violence against children, parents, or the elderly. It takes a number of forms, including physical, verbal, emotional, economic, religious, reproductive, and sexual abuse, which can range from subtle, coercive forms to marital rape and to violent physical abuse such as choking, beating, female genital mutilation, and acid throwing that results in disfigurement or death. Domestic murders include stoning, bride burning, honor killings, and dowry deaths.

Exam Probability: **High**

17. *Answer choices:*

(see index for correct answer)

- a. process perspective
- b. Family violence
- c. surface-level diversity
- d. open system

Guidance: level 1

:: ::

A _________ service is an online platform which people use to build social networks or social relationship with other people who share similar personal or career interests, activities, backgrounds or real-life connections.

Exam Probability: **High**

18. *Answer choices:*

(see index for correct answer)

- a. interpersonal communication
- b. imperative
- c. similarity-attraction theory
- d. levels of analysis

Guidance: level 1

:: Unemployment ::

In economics, a _________ is a business cycle contraction when there is a general decline in economic activity. Macroeconomic indicators such as GDP , investment spending, capacity utilization, household income, business profits, and inflation fall, while bankruptcies and the unemployment rate rise. In the United Kingdom, it is defined as a negative economic growth for two consecutive quarters.

Exam Probability: **High**

19. *Answer choices:*

(see index for correct answer)

- a. Male unemployment
- b. Waithood
- c. Recession
- d. Labour Force Survey

Guidance: level 1

:: Employment ::

_________ is the probability that an individual will keep his/her job; a job with a high level of _________ is such that a person with the job would have a small chance of losing it.

Exam Probability: **Low**

20. *Answer choices:*

(see index for correct answer)

- a. Virtual Student Foreign Service
- b. Workgang
- c. Fly-in fly-out
- d. Job security

Guidance: level 1

:: ::

_________ involves the development of an action plan designed to motivate and guide a person or group toward a goal. _________ can be guided by goal-setting criteria such as SMART criteria. _________ is a major component of personal-development and management literature.

Exam Probability: **High**

21. *Answer choices:*

(see index for correct answer)

- a. Goal setting
- b. co-culture
- c. hierarchical
- d. corporate values

Guidance: level 1

:: Workplace ::

_________ is asystematic determination of a subject`s merit, worth and significance, using criteria governed by a set of standards. It can assist an organization, program, design, project or any other intervention or initiative to assess any aim, realisable concept/proposal, or any alternative, to help in decision-making; or to ascertain the degree of achievement or value in regard to the aim and objectives and results of any such action that has been completed. The primary purpose of _________ , in addition to gaining insight into prior or existing initiatives, is to enable reflection and assist in the identification of future change.

Exam Probability: **Medium**

22. *Answer choices:*

(see index for correct answer)

- a. Toxic workplace
- b. Workplace romance
- c. Emotions in the workplace
- d. Work etiquette

Guidance: level 1

:: Office work ::

The _________ is a concept in management developed by Laurence J. Peter, which observes that people in a hierarchy tend to rise to their "level of incompetence". In other words, an employee is promoted based on their success in previous jobs until they reach a level at which they are no longer competent, as skills in one job do not necessarily translate to another. The concept was elucidated in the 1969 book The _________ by Peter and Raymond Hull.

Exam Probability: **High**

23. *Answer choices:*

(see index for correct answer)

- a. Office humor
- b. Pink-collar worker
- c. Career woman
- d. Paperless office

Guidance: level 1

:: Employment ::

A _________ , a concept developed in contemporary research by organizational scholar Denise Rousseau, represents the mutual beliefs, perceptions and informal obligations between an employer and an employee. It sets the dynamics for the relationship and defines the detailed practicality of the work to be done. It is distinguishable from the formal written contract of employment which, for the most part, only identifies mutual duties and responsibilities in a generalized form.

Exam Probability: **High**

24. *Answer choices:*

(see index for correct answer)

- a. EuroMayDay
- b. Career break
- c. Psychological contract
- d. Dead-end job

Guidance: level 1

:: International trade ::

_________ or globalisation is the process of interaction and integration among people, companies, and governments worldwide. As a complex and multifaceted phenomenon, _________ is considered by some as a form of capitalist expansion which entails the integration of local and national economies into a global, unregulated market economy. _________ has grown due to advances in transportation and communication technology. With the increased global interactions comes the growth of international trade, ideas, and culture. _________ is primarily an economic process of interaction and integration that`s associated with social and cultural aspects. However, conflicts and diplomacy are also large parts of the history of _________ , and modern _________ .

Exam Probability: **High**

25. *Answer choices:*

(see index for correct answer)

- a. financial account
- b. International Association for Technology Trade

- c. Certificate of origin
- d. Globalization

Guidance: level 1

:: ::

The _________ of 1938 29 U.S.C. § 203 is a United States labor law that creates the right to a minimum wage, and "time-and-a-half" overtime pay when people work over forty hours a week. It also prohibits most employment of minors in "oppressive child labor". It applies to employees engaged in interstate commerce or employed by an enterprise engaged in commerce or in the production of goods for commerce, unless the employer can claim an exemption from coverage.

Exam Probability: **High**

26. *Answer choices:*

(see index for correct answer)

- a. Sarbanes-Oxley act of 2002
- b. similarity-attraction theory
- c. process perspective
- d. information systems assessment

Guidance: level 1

:: Stress ::

_________ means beneficial stress—either psychological, physical , or biochemical/radiological .

Exam Probability: **Medium**

27. *Answer choices:*

(see index for correct answer)

- a. Breaking point
- b. John Henryism
- c. Cortisol
- d. Eustress

Guidance: level 1

:: Lean manufacturing ::

_________ is the Sino-Japanese word for "improvement". In business, _________ refers to activities that continuously improve all functions and involve all employees from the CEO to the assembly line workers. It also applies to processes, such as purchasing and logistics, that cross organizational boundaries into the supply chain. It has been applied in healthcare, psychotherapy, life-coaching, government, and banking.

Exam Probability: **Medium**

28. *Answer choices:*
(see index for correct answer)

- a. Lean Government
- b. Supply chain responsiveness matrix
- c. Kaizen
- d. Lean software development

Guidance: level 1

:: Management ::

In the field of management, _________ involves the formulation and implementation of the major goals and initiatives taken by an organization`s top management on behalf of owners, based on consideration of resources and an assessment of the internal and external environments in which the organization operates.

Exam Probability: **Low**

29. *Answer choices:*
(see index for correct answer)

- a. Third-generation balanced scorecard
- b. Inside job
- c. Strategic management
- d. Fleet management

Guidance: level 1

:: Unemployment ::

__________ is the support service provided by responsible organizations, keen to support individuals who are exiting the business – to help former employees transition to new jobs and help them re-orient themselves in the job market. A consultancy firm usually provides the __________ services which are paid for by the former employer and are achieved usually through practical advice, training materials and workshops. Some companies may offer psychological support.

Exam Probability: **Low**

30. *Answer choices:*

(see index for correct answer)

- a. Phillips curve
- b. Employment Promotion and Protection against Unemployment Convention, 1988
- c. Discouraged worker
- d. Outplacement

Guidance: level 1

:: Options (finance) ::

__________ is a contractual agreement between a corporation and recipients of phantom shares that bestow upon the grantee the right to a cash payment at a designated time or in association with a designated event in the future, which payment is to be in an amount tied to the market value of an equivalent number of shares of the corporation`s stock. Thus, the amount of the payout will increase as the stock price rises, and decrease if the stock falls, but without the recipient actually receiving any stock. Like other forms of stock-based compensation plans, __________ broadly serves to align the interests of recipients and shareholders, incent contribution to share value, and encourage the retention or continued participation of contributors. Recipients are typically employees, but may also be directors, third-party vendors, or others.

Exam Probability: **Medium**

31. *Answer choices:*

(see index for correct answer)

- a. Phantom stock
- b. Swaption
- c. Credit default option
- d. Warrant

Guidance: level 1

:: Human resource management ::

_________ involves improving the effectiveness of organizations and the individuals and teams within them. Training may be viewed as related to immediate changes in organizational effectiveness via organized instruction, while development is related to the progress of longer-term organizational and employee goals. While _________ technically have differing definitions, the two are oftentimes used interchangeably and/or together. _________ has historically been a topic within applied psychology but has within the last two decades become closely associated with human resources management, talent management, human resources development, instructional design, human factors, and knowledge management.

Exam Probability: **High**

32. *Answer choices:*

(see index for correct answer)

- a. Open-book management
- b. Corporate Equality Index
- c. Attendance management
- d. Broadbanding

Guidance: level 1

:: Design of experiments ::

In the design of experiments, treatments are applied to experimental units in the treatment group. In comparative experiments, members of the complementary group, the _________, receive either no treatment or a standard treatment.

Exam Probability: **High**

33. *Answer choices:*

(see index for correct answer)

- a. Control group
- b. Provocation test
- c. Randomized experiment
- d. Null hypothesis

Guidance: level 1

:: Offshoring ::

A _________ is the temporary suspension or permanent termination of employment of an employee or, more commonly, a group of employees for business reasons, such as personnel management or downsizing an organization. Originally, _________ referred exclusively to a temporary interruption in work, or employment but this has evolved to a permanent elimination of a position in both British and US English, requiring the addition of "temporary" to specify the original meaning of the word. A _________ is not to be confused with wrongful termination. Laid off workers or displaced workers are workers who have lost or left their jobs because their employer has closed or moved, there was insufficient work for them to do, or their position or shift was abolished . Downsizing in a company is defined to involve the reduction of employees in a workforce. Downsizing in companies became a popular practice in the 1980s and early 1990s as it was seen as a way to deliver better shareholder value as it helps to reduce the costs of employers . Indeed, recent research on downsizing in the U.S., UK, and Japan suggests that downsizing is being regarded by management as one of the preferred routes to help declining organizations, cutting unnecessary costs, and improve organizational performance. Usually a _________ occurs as a cost cutting measure.

Exam Probability: **Medium**

34. *Answer choices:*

(see index for correct answer)

- a. Antex
- b. Flag of convenience
- c. Body shopping
- d. Layoff

Guidance: level 1

:: Fundamental analysis ::

__________, also known as letter stock or restricted securities, is stock of a company that is not fully transferable until certain conditions have been met. Upon satisfaction of those conditions, the stock is no longer restricted, and becomes transferable to the person holding the award. __________ is often used as a form of employee compensation, in which case it typically becomes transferrable upon the satisfaction of certain conditions, such as continued employment for a period of time or the achievement of particular product-development milestones, earnings per share goals or other financial targets. __________ is a popular alternative to stock options, particularly for executives, due to favorable accounting rules and income tax treatment.

Exam Probability: **Medium**

35. *Answer choices:*

(see index for correct answer)

- a. Equity value
- b. Enterprise value
- c. Economic Value Added
- d. Fundamental analysis

Guidance: level 1

:: Hazard analysis ::

A __________ is an agent which has the potential to cause harm to a vulnerable target. The terms " __________ " and "risk" are often used interchangeably. However, in terms of risk assessment, they are two very distinct terms. A __________ is any agent that can cause harm or damage to humans, property, or the environment. Risk is defined as the probability that exposure to a __________ will lead to a negative consequence, or more simply, a __________ poses no risk if there is no exposure to that __________ .

Exam Probability: **Low**

36. *Answer choices:*

(see index for correct answer)

- a. Risk assessment
- b. Hazardous Materials Identification System
- c. Hazard identification
- d. Hazard

Guidance: level 1

:: ::

The _________ or labour force is the labour pool in employment. It is generally used to describe those working for a single company or industry, but can also apply to a geographic region like a city, state, or country. Within a company, its value can be labelled as its " _________ in Place". The _________ of a country includes both the employed and the unemployed. The labour force participation rate, LFPR , is the ratio between the labour force and the overall size of their cohort . The term generally excludes the employers or management, and can imply those involved in manual labour. It may also mean all those who are available for work.

Exam Probability: **Low**

37. *Answer choices:*

(see index for correct answer)

- a. Workforce
- b. information systems assessment
- c. similarity-attraction theory
- d. interpersonal communication

Guidance: level 1

:: ::

_________ is the process of collecting, analyzing and/or reporting information regarding the performance of an individual, group, organization, system or component. _________ is not a new concept, some of the earliest records of human activity relate to the counting or recording of activities.

Exam Probability: **Low**

38. *Answer choices:*

(see index for correct answer)

- a. similarity-attraction theory
- b. hierarchical perspective
- c. cultural
- d. Performance measurement

Guidance: level 1

:: Business ethics ::

A _________ is a person who exposes any kind of information or activity that is deemed illegal, unethical, or not correct within an organization that is either private or public. The information of alleged wrongdoing can be classified in many ways: violation of company policy/rules, law, regulation, or threat to public interest/national security, as well as fraud, and corruption. Those who become _________ s can choose to bring information or allegations to surface either internally or externally. Internally, a _________ can bring his/her accusations to the attention of other people within the accused organization such as an immediate supervisor. Externally, a _________ can bring allegations to light by contacting a third party outside of an accused organization such as the media, government, law enforcement, or those who are concerned. _________ s, however, take the risk of facing stiff reprisal and retaliation from those who are accused or alleged of wrongdoing.

Exam Probability: **Medium**

39. *Answer choices:*

(see index for correct answer)

- a. Whistleblower
- b. Corruption of Foreign Public Officials Act
- c. Corporate sustainability
- d. Contingent work

Guidance: level 1

:: Employment compensation ::

In government contracting, a _________ is defined as the hourly wage, usual benefits and overtime, paid to the majority of workers, laborers, and mechanics within a particular area. This is usually the union wage.

Exam Probability: **High**

40. *Answer choices:*

(see index for correct answer)

- a. Prevailing wage
- b. Annual leave
- c. Protection of Wages Convention, 1949
- d. The Theory of Wages

Guidance: level 1

:: Survey methodology ::

__________ is often used to assess thoughts, opinions, and feelings. Surveys can be specific and limited, or they can have more global, widespread goals. Psychologists and sociologists often use surveys to analyze behavior, while it is also used to meet the more pragmatic needs of the media, such as, in evaluating political candidates, public health officials, professional organizations, and advertising and marketing directors. A survey consists of a predetermined set of questions that is given to a sample. With a representative sample, that is, one that is representative of the larger population of interest, one can describe the attitudes of the population from which the sample was drawn. Further, one can compare the attitudes of different populations as well as look for changes in attitudes over time. A good sample selection is key as it allows one to generalize the findings from the sample to the population, which is the whole purpose of __________ .

Exam Probability: **Low**

41. *Answer choices:*

(see index for correct answer)

- a. Inverse probability weighting
- b. Administrative error
- c. Scale analysis
- d. Public opinion

Guidance: level 1

:: Training ::

__________ refers to practicing newly acquired skills beyond the point of initial mastery. The term is also often used to refer to the pedagogical theory that this form of practice leads to automaticity or other beneficial consequences.

Exam Probability: **Low**

42. *Answer choices:*

(see index for correct answer)

- a. Overlearning

- b. Training workshop
- c. Adobe Captivate
- d. Strength and conditioning coach

Guidance: level 1

:: Labour law ::

A _________ is a legal contract that is meant to limit the liability of an employer whose employees are romantically involved. An employer may choose to require a _________ when a romantic relationship within the company becomes known, in order to indemnify the company in case the employees` romantic relationship fails, primarily so that one party can`t bring a sexual harassment lawsuit against the company. To that end, the _________ states that the relationship is consensual, and both parties of the relationship must sign it. The _________ may also stipulate rules for acceptable romantic behavior in the workplace.

Exam Probability: **Low**

43. *Answer choices:*

(see index for correct answer)

- a. Maximum medical improvement
- b. Love contract
- c. Positive action
- d. Undue hardship

Guidance: level 1

:: Management ::

_________ is a technique used by some employers to rotate their employees` assigned jobs throughout their employment. Employers practice this technique for a number of reasons. It was designed to promote flexibility of employees and to keep employees interested into staying with the company/organization which employs them. There is also research that shows how _________ s help relieve the stress of employees who work in a job that requires manual labor.

Exam Probability: **Medium**

44. *Answer choices:*

(see index for correct answer)

- a. Job rotation
- b. Data Item Descriptions
- c. Public sector consulting
- d. Quality, cost, delivery

Guidance: level 1

:: Employment ::

A flat organization has an organizational structure with few or no levels of middle management between staff and executives. An organization`s structure refers to the nature of the distribution of the units and positions within it, also to the nature of the relationships among those units and positions. Tall and flat organizations differ based on how many levels of management are present in the organization, and how much control managers are endowed with.

Exam Probability: **High**

45. *Answer choices:*

(see index for correct answer)

- a. Job attitude
- b. Employment
- c. Service voucher
- d. Delayering

Guidance: level 1

:: Psychometrics ::

In statistics and research, _________ is typically a measure based on the correlations between different items on the same test . It measures whether several items that propose to measure the same general construct produce similar scores. For example, if a respondent expressed agreement with the statements "I like to ride bicycles" and "I`ve enjoyed riding bicycles in the past", and disagreement with the statement "I hate bicycles", this would be indicative of good _________ of the test.

Exam Probability: **High**

46. *Answer choices:*

(see index for correct answer)

- a. Differential item functioning

- b. Polynomial conjoint measurement
- c. Assessment day
- d. Test score

Guidance: level 1

:: Business law ::

A pre-entry _________ is a form of union security agreement under which the employer agrees to hire union members only, and employees must remain members of the union at all times in order to remain employed. This is different from a post-entry _________ , which is an agreement requiring all employees to join the union if they are not already members. In a union shop, the union must accept as a member any person hired by the employer.

Exam Probability: **Low**

47. *Answer choices:*

(see index for correct answer)

- a. Limited partnership
- b. Limited liability limited partnership
- c. Board of directors
- d. Closed shop

Guidance: level 1

:: Human resource management ::

_________ is a family of procedures to identify the content of a job in terms of activities involved and attributes or job requirements needed to perform the activities. _________ provides information of organizations which helps to determine which employees are best fit for specific jobs. Through _________ , the analyst needs to understand what the important tasks of the job are, how they are carried out, and the necessary human qualities needed to complete the job successfully.

Exam Probability: **High**

48. *Answer choices:*

(see index for correct answer)

- a. Job analysis
- b. SLT Human Capital Solutions

- c. Resource-based view
- d. The war for talent

Guidance: level 1

:: Organizational structure ::

An _________ defines how activities such as task allocation, coordination, and supervision are directed toward the achievement of organizational aims.

Exam Probability: **Low**

49. *Answer choices:*

(see index for correct answer)

- a. Organization of the New York City Police Department
- b. Organizational structure
- c. Automated Bureaucracy
- d. Followership

Guidance: level 1

:: Educational assessment and evaluation ::

An _________ is a component of a competence to do a certain kind of work at a certain level. Outstanding _________ can be considered "talent". An _________ may be physical or mental. _________ is inborn potential to do certain kinds of work whether developed or undeveloped. Ability is developed knowledge, understanding, learned or acquired abilities or attitude. The innate nature of _________ is in contrast to skills and achievement, which represent knowledge or ability that is gained through learning.

Exam Probability: **High**

50. *Answer choices:*

(see index for correct answer)

- a. Graduate Record Examinations
- b. Assam Higher Secondary Education Council
- c. Aptitude
- d. Armed Services Vocational Aptitude Battery

Guidance: level 1

:: Training ::

_________ is a phase of training needs analysis directed at identifying which individuals within an organization should receive training.

Exam Probability: **Medium**

51. *Answer choices:*

(see index for correct answer)

- a. Youth Training Scheme
- b. Endurance training
- c. Person Analysis
- d. Enforcement

Guidance: level 1

:: Occupational safety and health organizations ::

The _________ is the United States federal agency responsible for conducting research and making recommendations for the prevention of work-related injury and illness. NIOSH is part of the Centers for Disease Control and Prevention within the U.S. Department of Health and Human Services.

Exam Probability: **Low**

52. *Answer choices:*

(see index for correct answer)

- a. Michigan Occupational Safety and Health Administration
- b. National Institute for Occupational Safety and Health
- c. OSHCR
- d. GEOLibrary

Guidance: level 1

:: Job interview ::

A _________ is a job interview in which the applicant is presented with a challenging business scenario that he/she must investigate and propose a solution to. _________ s are designed to test the candidate`s analytical skills and "soft" skills within a realistic business context. The case is often a business situation or a business case that the interviewer has worked on in real life.

Exam Probability: **High**

53. *Answer choices:*

(see index for correct answer)

- a. Informational interview
- b. Microsoft interview
- c. SOARA
- d. Case interview

Guidance: level 1

:: Employment ::

_________ s are experiential learning opportunities, similar to internships but generally shorter, provided by partnerships between educational institutions and employers to give students short practical experiences in their field of study. In medicine it may refer to a visiting physician who is not part of the regular staff. In law, it usually refers to rigorous legal work opportunities undertaken by law students for law school credit and pay, similar to that of a junior attorney. It is derived from Latin externus and from English -ship.

Exam Probability: **Medium**

54. *Answer choices:*

(see index for correct answer)

- a. Externship
- b. Monster Employment Index
- c. Labor geography
- d. Location independence

Guidance: level 1

:: ::

__________ is a form of government characterized by strong central power and limited political freedoms. Individual freedoms are subordinate to the state and there is no constitutional accountability and rule of law under an authoritarian regime. Authoritarian regimes can be autocratic with power concentrated in one person or it can be more spread out between multiple officials and government institutions. Juan Linz`s influential 1964 description of __________ characterized authoritarian political systems by four qualities.

Exam Probability: **Medium**

55. *Answer choices:*

(see index for correct answer)

- a. surface-level diversity
- b. interpersonal communication
- c. Authoritarianism
- d. imperative

Guidance: level 1

:: Labour relations ::

A __________, also known as a post-entry closed shop, is a form of a union security clause. Under this, the employer agrees to either only hire labor union members or to require that any new employees who are not already union members become members within a certain amount of time. Use of the __________ varies widely from nation to nation, depending on the level of protection given trade unions in general.

Exam Probability: **High**

56. *Answer choices:*

(see index for correct answer)

- a. Inflatable rat
- b. Union Wallonne des Entreprises
- c. Delta Board Council
- d. Boulwarism

Guidance: level 1

:: Occupational safety and health ::

_________ is a set of six naturally occurring silicate minerals, which all have in common their asbestiform habit: i.e., long , thin fibrous crystals, with each visible fiber composed of millions of microscopic "fibrils" that can be released by abrasion and other processes. The minerals are chrysotile, amosite, crocidolite, tremolite, anthophyllite, and actinolite.

Exam Probability: **High**

57. *Answer choices:*
(see index for correct answer)

- a. Occupational fatality
- b. Asbestos
- c. Cadmium
- d. Kazutaka Kogi

Guidance: level 1

:: Parental leave ::

_________ is a type of employment discrimination that occurs when expectant women are fired, not hired, or otherwise discriminated against due to their pregnancy or intention to become pregnant. Common forms of _________ include not being hired due to visible pregnancy or likelihood of becoming pregnant, being fired after informing an employer of one`s pregnancy, being fired after maternity leave, and receiving a pay dock due to pregnancy. Convention on the Elimination of All Forms of Discrimination against Women prohibits dismissal on the grounds of maternity or pregnancy and ensures right to maternity leave or comparable social benefits. The Maternity Protection Convention C 183 proclaims adequate protection for pregnancy as well. Though women have some protection in the United States because of the _________ Act of 1978, it has not completely curbed the incidence of _________ . The Equal Rights Amendment could ensure more robust sex equality ensuring that women and men could both work and have children at the same time.

Exam Probability: **Medium**

58. *Answer choices:*
(see index for correct answer)

- a. Geduldig v. Aiello
- b. Pregnant Workers Directive
- c. Cleveland Board of Education v. LaFleur

- d. Maternity and Parental Leave, etc Regulations 1999

Guidance: level 1

:: Business ethics cases ::

__________ , 477 U.S. 57 , is a US labor law case, where the United States Supreme Court, in a 9-0 decision, recognized sexual harassment as a violation of Title VII of the Civil Rights Act of 1964. The case was the first of its kind to reach the Supreme Court and would redefine sexual harassment in the workplace.

Exam Probability: **Medium**

59. *Answer choices:*

(see index for correct answer)

- a. Times-Picayune Publishing Co. v. United States
- b. Libor scandal
- c. Airborne
- d. Meritor Savings Bank v. Vinson

Guidance: level 1

Information systems

Information systems (IS) are formal, sociotechnical, organizational systems designed to collect, process, store, and distribute information. In a sociotechnical perspective Information Systems are composed by four components: technology, process, people and organizational structure.

:: Product testing ::

_________ is a characteristic of a product or system, whose interfaces are completely understood, to work with other products or systems, at present or in the future, in either implementation or access, without any restrictions.

Exam Probability: **High**

1. *Answer choices:*
(see index for correct answer)

- a. Testing reliability
- b. Interoperability
- c. Whisky tasting
- d. Destructive testing

Guidance: level 1

:: Google services ::

_________ is a discontinued image organizer and image viewer for organizing and editing digital photos, plus an integrated photo-sharing website, originally created by a company named Lifescape in 2002. In July 2004, Google acquired _________ from Lifescape and began offering it as freeware. " _________ " is a blend of the name of Spanish painter Pablo Picasso, the phrase mi casa and "pic" for pictures.

Exam Probability: **Medium**

2. *Answer choices:*

(see index for correct answer)

- a. Google Insights for Search
- b. Google One Pass
- c. Google Books Library Project
- d. Google eBooks

Guidance: level 1

:: Knowledge engineering ::

The _________ is an extension of the World Wide Web through standards by the World Wide Web Consortium . The standards promote common data formats and exchange protocols on the Web, most fundamentally the Resource Description Framework . According to the W3C, "The _________ provides a common framework that allows data to be shared and reused across application, enterprise, and community boundaries". The _________ is therefore regarded as an integrator across different content, information applications and systems.

Exam Probability: **High**

3. *Answer choices:*

(see index for correct answer)

- a. Knowledge Collection from Volunteer Contributors
- b. Semantic Web
- c. International Journal of Software Engineering and Knowledge Engineering
- d. Knowledge engineer

Guidance: level 1

:: ::

_________ is software designed to provide a platform for other software. Examples of _________ include operating systems like macOS, Ubuntu and Microsoft Windows, computational science software, game engines, industrial automation, and software as a service applications.

Exam Probability: **Low**

4. *Answer choices:*

(see index for correct answer)

- a. hierarchical
- b. deep-level diversity
- c. similarity-attraction theory
- d. System software

Guidance: level 1

:: Game artificial intelligence ::

In computer science, _________ , sometimes called machine intelligence, is intelligence demonstrated by machines, in contrast to the natural intelligence displayed by humans and animals. Colloquially, the term " _________ " is used to describe machines that mimic "cognitive" functions that humans associate with other human minds, such as "learning" and "problem solving".

Exam Probability: **High**

5. *Answer choices:*
(see index for correct answer)

- a. Language Acquisition Device
- b. Artificial intelligence
- c. Pathfinding
- d. Negascout

Guidance: level 1

:: Costs ::

In economics, _________ is the total economic cost of production and is made up of variable cost, which varies according to the quantity of a good produced and includes inputs such as labour and raw materials, plus fixed cost, which is independent of the quantity of a good produced and includes inputs that cannot be varied in the short term: fixed costs such as buildings and machinery, including sunk costs if any. Since cost is measured per unit of time, it is a flow variable.

Exam Probability: **Medium**

6. *Answer choices:*
(see index for correct answer)

- a. Repugnancy costs
- b. Total cost
- c. Khozraschyot

- d. Cost curve

Guidance: level 1

:: Business planning ::

__________ is an organization`s process of defining its strategy, or direction, and making decisions on allocating its resources to pursue this strategy. It may also extend to control mechanisms for guiding the implementation of the strategy. __________ became prominent in corporations during the 1960s and remains an important aspect of strategic management. It is executed by strategic planners or strategists, who involve many parties and research sources in their analysis of the organization and its relationship to the environment in which it competes.

Exam Probability: **High**

7. *Answer choices:*

(see index for correct answer)

- a. operational planning
- b. Strategic planning
- c. Gap analysis
- d. Joint decision trap

Guidance: level 1

:: E-commerce ::

A __________ is a plastic payment card that can be used instead of cash when making purchases. It is similar to a credit card, but unlike a credit card, the money is immediately transferred directly from the cardholder`s bank account when performing a transaction.

Exam Probability: **High**

8. *Answer choices:*

(see index for correct answer)

- a. Affiliate
- b. Paid content
- c. Dark store
- d. Debit card

Guidance: level 1

:: Knowledge representation ::

__________ is the system in which users apply public tags to online items, typically to make those items easier for themselves or others to find later. Over time, this can give rise to a classification system based on those tags and how often they are applied or searched for, in contrast to a taxonomic classification designed by the owners of the content and specified when it is published. This practice is also known as collaborative tagging, social classification, social indexing, and social tagging. __________ was originally "the result of personal free tagging of information [...] for one`s own retrieval", but online sharing and interaction expanded it into collaborative forms. Social tagging is the application of tags in an open online environment where the tags of other users are available to others. Collaborative tagging is tagging performed by a group of users. This type of __________ is commonly used in cooperative and collaborative projects such as research, content repositories, and social bookmarking.

Exam Probability: **High**

9. *Answer choices:*

(see index for correct answer)

- a. VoiD
- b. Knowledge space
- c. Designated Community
- d. Geopolitical ontology

Guidance: level 1

:: Global Positioning System ::

A __________ is a mechanism for determining the location of an object in space. Technologies for this task exist ranging from worldwide coverage with meter accuracy to workspace coverage with sub-millimetre accuracy.

Exam Probability: **High**

10. *Answer choices:*

(see index for correct answer)

- a. SailTimer
- b. RailRider
- c. Positioning system

- d. GPS Tuner

Guidance: level 1

:: Internet privacy ::

An __________ is a private network accessible only to an organization`s staff. Often, a wide range of information and services are available on an organization`s internal __________ that are unavailable to the public, unlike the Internet. A company-wide __________ can constitute an important focal point of internal communication and collaboration, and provide a single starting point to access internal and external resources. In its simplest form, an __________ is established with the technologies for local area networks and wide area networks . Many modern __________ s have search engines, user profiles, blogs, mobile apps with notifications, and events planning within their infrastructure.

Exam Probability: **Low**

11. *Answer choices:*

(see index for correct answer)

- a. GlobalPOV
- b. Intranet
- c. 2010 Duke University faux sex thesis controversy
- d. Right to be forgotten

Guidance: level 1

:: Management ::

The __________ is a strategy performance management tool – a semi-standard structured report, that can be used by managers to keep track of the execution of activities by the staff within their control and to monitor the consequences arising from these actions.

Exam Probability: **Medium**

12. *Answer choices:*

(see index for correct answer)

- a. Vorstand
- b. Change advisory board
- c. Balanced scorecard

- d. Strategic lenses

Guidance: level 1

:: Reputation management ::

A _________ is an astronomical object consisting of a luminous spheroid of plasma held together by its own gravity. The nearest _________ to Earth is the Sun. Many other _________ s are visible to the naked eye from Earth during the night, appearing as a multitude of fixed luminous points in the sky due to their immense distance from Earth. Historically, the most prominent _________ s were grouped into constellations and asterisms, the brightest of which gained proper names. Astronomers have assembled _________ catalogues that identify the known _________ s and provide standardized stellar designations. However, most of the estimated 300 sextillion _________ s in the Universe are invisible to the naked eye from Earth, including all _________ s outside our galaxy, the Milky Way.

Exam Probability: **High**

13. *Answer choices:*

(see index for correct answer)

- a. Raph Levien
- b. Star
- c. Reputation system
- d. BrandYourself

Guidance: level 1

:: E-commerce ::

Electronic governance or e-governance is the application of information and communication technology for delivering government services, exchange of information, communication transactions, integration of various stand-alone systems and services between government-to-citizen , _________ , government-to-government , government-to-employees as well as back-office processes and interactions within the entire government framework. Through e-governance, government services are made available to citizens in a convenient, efficient, and transparent manner. The three main target groups that can be distinguished in governance concepts are government, citizens, andbusinesses/interest groups. In e-governance, there are no distinct boundaries.

Exam Probability: **Low**

14. *Answer choices:*

(see index for correct answer)

- a. Click Frenzy
- b. Government-to-business
- c. ORCA
- d. XBRL GL

Guidance: level 1

:: ::

_________ is software designed to perform a group of coordinated functions, tasks, or activities for the benefit of the user. Examples of an application include a word processor, a spreadsheet, an accounting application, a web browser, an email client,a media player, a file viewer, an aeronautical flight simulator, a console game or a photo editor. The collective noun _________ refers to all applications collectively. This contrasts with system software, which is mainly involved with running the computer.

Exam Probability: **High**

15. *Answer choices:*

(see index for correct answer)

- a. cultural
- b. imperative
- c. hierarchical
- d. personal values

Guidance: level 1

:: ::

__________ is a free email service developed by Google. Users can access __________ on the web and using third-party programs that synchronize email content through POP or IMAP protocols. __________ started as a limited beta release on April 1, 2004 and ended its testing phase on July 7, 2009.

Exam Probability: **Medium**

16. *Answer choices:*

(see index for correct answer)

- a. Gmail
- b. hierarchical
- c. surface-level diversity
- d. levels of analysis

Guidance: level 1

:: ::

In communications and information processing, __________ is a system of rules to convert information—such as a letter, word, sound, image, or gesture—into another form or representation, sometimes shortened or secret, for communication through a communication channel or storage in a storage medium. An early example is the invention of language, which enabled a person, through speech, to communicate what they saw, heard, felt, or thought to others. But speech limits the range of communication to the distance a voice can carry, and limits the audience to those present when the speech is uttered. The invention of writing, which converted spoken language into visual symbols, extended the range of communication across space and time.

Exam Probability: **High**

17. *Answer choices:*

(see index for correct answer)

- a. deep-level diversity
- b. surface-level diversity
- c. Code
- d. hierarchical

Guidance: level 1

:: Google services ::

__________ is a word processor included as part of a free, web-based software office suite offered by Google within its Google Drive service. This service also includes Google Sheets and Google Slides, a spreadsheet and presentation program respectively. __________ is available as a web application, mobile app for Android, iOS, Windows, BlackBerry, and as a desktop application on Google`s ChromeOS. The app is compatible with Microsoft Office file formats.The application allows users to create and edit files online while collaborating with other users in real-time. Edits are tracked by user with a revision history presenting changes. An editor`s position is highlighted with an editor-specific color and cursor. A permissions system regulates what users can do. Updates have introduced features using machine learning, including "Explore", offering search results based on the contents of a document, and "Action items", allowing users to assign tasks to other users.

Exam Probability: **Medium**

18. *Answer choices:*

(see index for correct answer)

- a. Google Docs
- b. Google Mobile Services
- c. Google Blog Search
- d. Google Web History

Guidance: level 1

:: Management ::

__________ is the kind of knowledge that is difficult to transfer to another person by means of writing it down or verbalizing it. For example, that London is in the United Kingdom is a piece of explicit knowledge that can be written down, transmitted, and understood by a recipient. However, the ability to speak a language, ride a bicycle, knead dough, play a musical instrument, or design and use complex equipment requires all sorts of knowledge that is not always known explicitly, even by expert practitioners, and which is difficult or impossible to explicitly transfer to other people.

Exam Probability: **Low**

19. *Answer choices:*

(see index for correct answer)

- a. Resource breakdown structure
- b. Supplier performance management
- c. Office management
- d. Overtime rate

Guidance: level 1

:: ::

Collaborative software or _________ is application software designed to help people involved in a common task to achieve their goals. One of the earliest definitions of collaborative software is "intentional group processes plus software to support them".

Exam Probability: **High**

20. *Answer choices:*

(see index for correct answer)

- a. Groupware
- b. surface-level diversity
- c. personal values
- d. functional perspective

Guidance: level 1

:: ::

Within the Internet, _________ s are formed by the rules and procedures of the _________ System . Any name registered in the DNS is a _________ . _________ s are used in various networking contexts and for application-specific naming and addressing purposes. In general, a _________ represents an Internet Protocol resource, such as a personal computer used to access the Internet, a server computer hosting a web site, or the web site itself or any other service communicated via the Internet. In 2017, 330.6 million _________ s had been registered.

Exam Probability: **High**

21. *Answer choices:*

(see index for correct answer)

- a. similarity-attraction theory
- b. open system
- c. surface-level diversity
- d. Domain name

Guidance: level 1

:: ::

_______ rate is the ratio of users who click on a specific link to the number of total users who view a page, email, or advertisement. It is commonly used to measure the success of an online advertising campaign for a particular website as well as the effectiveness of email campaigns.

Exam Probability: **Low**

22. *Answer choices:*

(see index for correct answer)

- a. Click-through
- b. empathy
- c. personal values
- d. hierarchical

Guidance: level 1

:: Database theory ::

A _______ is a digital database based on the relational model of data, as proposed by E. F. Codd in 1970.A software system used to maintain _______ s is a _______ management system . Virtually all _______ systems use SQL for querying and maintaining the database.

Exam Probability: **Medium**

23. *Answer choices:*

(see index for correct answer)

- a. Relational database
- b. Data cube
- c. Single Table Inheritance
- d. Transitive dependency

Guidance: level 1

:: ::

Sustainability is the process of people maintaining change in a balanced environment, in which the exploitation of resources, the direction of investments, the orientation of technological development and institutional change are all in harmony and enhance both current and future potential to meet human needs and aspirations. For many in the field, sustainability is defined through the following interconnected domains or pillars: environment, economic and social, which according to Fritjof Capra is based on the principles of Systems Thinking. Sub-domains of _________ development have been considered also: cultural, technological and political. While _________ development may be the organizing principle for sustainability for some, for others, the two terms are paradoxical . _________ development is the development that meets the needs of the present without compromising the ability of future generations to meet their own needs. Brundtland Report for the World Commission on Environment and Development introduced the term of _________ development.

Exam Probability: **High**

24. *Answer choices:*

(see index for correct answer)

- a. deep-level diversity
- b. Sustainable
- c. hierarchical
- d. personal values

Guidance: level 1

:: Information systems ::

_________s are information systems that are developed in response to corporate business initiative. They are intended to give competitive advantage to the organization. They may deliver a product or service that is at a lower cost, that is differentiated, that focuses on a particular market segment, or is innovative.

Exam Probability: **High**

25. *Answer choices:*

(see index for correct answer)

- a. Disparate system
- b. Joint application design
- c. Data flow diagram
- d. Strategic information system

Guidance: level 1

:: Information technology organisations ::

The Internet Corporation for Assigned Names and Numbers is a nonprofit organization responsible for coordinating the maintenance and procedures of several databases related to the namespaces and numerical spaces of the Internet, ensuring the network`s stable and secure operation. _________ performs the actual technical maintenance work of the Central Internet Address pools and DNS root zone registries pursuant to the Internet Assigned Numbers Authority function contract. The contract regarding the IANA stewardship functions between _________ and the National Telecommunications and Information Administration of the United States Department of Commerce ended on October 1, 2016, formally transitioning the functions to the global multistakeholder community.

Exam Probability: **Low**

26. *Answer choices:*

(see index for correct answer)

- a. Information Technology Association of America
- b. WOUGNET
- c. Information Technology Association of Canada
- d. ICANN

Guidance: level 1

:: Data modeling languages ::

An entity–relationship model describes interrelated things of interest in a specific domain of knowledge. A basic ER model is composed of entity types and specifies relationships that can exist between entities .

Exam Probability: **High**

27. *Answer choices:*

(see index for correct answer)

- a. Entity-relationship
- b. IDEF4
- c. CODASYL
- d. Regular Language description for XML

Guidance: level 1

:: Digital rights management ::

_________ tools or technological protection measures are a set of access control technologies for restricting the use of proprietary hardware and copyrighted works. DRM technologies try to control the use, modification, and distribution of copyrighted works , as well as systems within devices that enforce these policies.

Exam Probability: **Medium**

28. *Answer choices:*

(see index for correct answer)

- a. InterTrust Technologies
- b. Seed
- c. Digital rights management
- d. Broadcast encryption

Guidance: level 1

:: Management ::

Porter`s Five Forces Framework is a tool for analyzing competition of a business. It draws from industrial organization economics to derive five forces that determine the competitive intensity and, therefore, the attractiveness of an industry in terms of its profitability. An "unattractive" industry is one in which the effect of these five forces reduces overall profitability. The most unattractive industry would be one approaching "pure competition", in which available profits for all firms are driven to normal profit levels. The five-forces perspective is associated with its originator, Michael E. Porter of Harvard University. This framework was first published in Harvard Business Review in 1979.

Exam Probability: **Medium**

29. *Answer choices:*

(see index for correct answer)

- a. Organizational space
- b. Management buyout
- c. Managerial hubris
- d. Porter five forces analysis

Guidance: level 1

:: Intelligence (information gathering) ::

__________ comprises the strategies and technologies used by enterprises for the data analysis of business information. BI technologies provide historical, current and predictive views of business operations. Common functions of __________ technologies include reporting, online analytical processing, analytics, data mining, process mining, complex event processing, business performance management, benchmarking, text mining, predictive analytics and prescriptive analytics. BI technologies can handle large amounts of structured and sometimes unstructured data to help identify, develop and otherwise create new strategic business opportunities. They aim to allow for the easy interpretation of these big data. Identifying new opportunities and implementing an effective strategy based on insights can provide businesses with a competitive market advantage and long-term stability.

Exam Probability: **Medium**

30. *Answer choices:*

(see index for correct answer)

- a. Intelligence analysis management
- b. Stovepiping
- c. Measurement and signature intelligence
- d. Business intelligence

Guidance: level 1

:: Content management systems ::

__________ is the textual, visual, or aural content that is encountered as part of the user experience on websites. It may include—among other things—text, images, sounds, videos, and animations.

Exam Probability: **Medium**

31. *Answer choices:*

(see index for correct answer)

- a. Backbase
- b. Mixedink
- c. Edicy
- d. KnowledgeTree

Guidance: level 1

:: Information science ::

In discourse-based grammatical theory, _________ is any tracking of referential information by speakers. Information may be new, just introduced into the conversation; given, already active in the speakers` consciousness; or old, no longer active. The various types of activation, and how these are defined, are model-dependent.

Exam Probability: **Medium**

32. *Answer choices:*

(see index for correct answer)

- a. Computational informatics
- b. Recording format
- c. Information flow
- d. Library Literature and Information Science

Guidance: level 1

:: ::

A _________ is a system designed to capture, store, manipulate, analyze, manage, and present spatial or geographic data. GIS applications are tools that allow users to create interactive queries , analyze spatial information, edit data in maps, and present the results of all these operations. GIS sometimes refers to geographic information science , the science underlying geographic concepts, applications, and systems.

Exam Probability: **Medium**

33. *Answer choices:*

(see index for correct answer)

- a. Geographic information system

- b. similarity-attraction theory
- c. Sarbanes-Oxley act of 2002
- d. information systems assessment

Guidance: level 1

:: Teams ::

A _________ usually refers to a group of individuals who work together from different geographic locations and rely on communication technology such as email, FAX, and video or voice conferencing services in order to collaborate. The term can also refer to groups or teams that work together asynchronously or across organizational levels. Powell, Piccoli and Ives define _________ s as "groups of geographically, organizationally and/or time dispersed workers brought together by information and telecommunication technologies to accomplish one or more organizational tasks." According to Ale Ebrahim et. al. , _________ s can also be defined as "small temporary groups of geographically, organizationally and/or time dispersed knowledge workers who coordinate their work predominantly with electronic information and communication technologies in order to accomplish one or more organization tasks."

Exam Probability: **High**

34. *Answer choices:*

(see index for correct answer)

- a. Team-building
- b. Virtual team

Guidance: level 1

:: Computer file formats ::

_________ is a communication protocol for peer-to-peer file sharing which is used to distribute data and electronic files over the Internet.

Exam Probability: **High**

35. *Answer choices:*

(see index for correct answer)

- a. Position-independent code
- b. Open Financial Exchange

- c. BitTorrent
- d. VMessage

Guidance: level 1

:: ::

The __________ , commonly known as the Web, is an information system where documents and other web resources are identified by Uniform Resource Locators , which may be interlinked by hypertext, and are accessible over the Internet. The resources of the WWW may be accessed by users by a software application called a web browser.

Exam Probability: **Medium**

36. *Answer choices:*

(see index for correct answer)

- a. empathy
- b. imperative
- c. cultural
- d. open system

Guidance: level 1

:: Data transmission ::

In telecommunication a __________ is the means of connecting one location to another for the purpose of transmitting and receiving digital information. It can also refer to a set of electronics assemblies, consisting of a transmitter and a receiver and the interconnecting data telecommunication circuit. These are governed by a link protocol enabling digital data to be transferred from a data source to a data sink.

Exam Probability: **High**

37. *Answer choices:*

(see index for correct answer)

- a. NAK
- b. Syncword
- c. IOPS
- d. Data link

Guidance: level 1

:: Data collection ::

__________ is information that either does not have a pre-defined data model or is not organized in a pre-defined manner. Unstructured information is typically text-heavy, but may contain data such as dates, numbers, and facts as well. This results in irregularities and ambiguities that make it difficult to understand using traditional programs as compared to data stored in fielded form in databases or annotated in documents.

Exam Probability: **Medium**

38. *Answer choices:*

(see index for correct answer)

- a. SensoMotoric Instruments
- b. General Social Survey
- c. Datalogix
- d. Multi-channel analytics

Guidance: level 1

:: Industrial design ::

Across the many fields concerned with __________, including information science, computer science, human-computer interaction, communication, and industrial design, there is little agreement over the meaning of the term " __________ ", although all are related to interaction with computers and other machines with a user interface.

Exam Probability: **High**

39. *Answer choices:*

(see index for correct answer)

- a. Design 1st
- b. Interactivity
- c. field study
- d. Japanese design law

Guidance: level 1

:: Computer networking ::

_________ is a method of grouping data that is transmitted over a digital network into packets. Packets are made of a header and a payload. Data in the header are used by networking hardware to direct the packet to its destination where the payload is extracted and used by application software. _________ is the primary basis for data communications in computer networks worldwide.

Exam Probability: **Medium**

40. *Answer choices:*

(see index for correct answer)

- a. IGMP snooping
- b. Cisco Certified Entry Networking Technician
- c. Packet switching
- d. Link level

Guidance: level 1

:: ::

A _________ is an abstract model that organizes elements of data and standardizes how they relate to one another and to properties of the real world entities. For instance, a _________ may specify that the data element representing a car be composed of a number of other elements which, in turn, represent the color and size of the car and define its owner.

Exam Probability: **Medium**

41. *Answer choices:*

(see index for correct answer)

- a. Data model
- b. open system
- c. deep-level diversity
- d. interpersonal communication

Guidance: level 1

:: Data management ::

Data aggregation is the compiling of information from databases with intent to prepare combined datasets for data processing.

Exam Probability: **High**

42. *Answer choices:*
(see index for correct answer)

- a. WCF Data Services
- b. PL/Perl
- c. Data aggregator
- d. Data proliferation

Guidance: level 1

:: Strategic management ::

In marketing strategy, first-mover advantage is the advantage gained by the initial significant occupant of a market segment. First-mover advantage may be gained by technological leadership, or early purchase of resources.

Exam Probability: **Medium**

43. *Answer choices:*
(see index for correct answer)

- a. Strategic fit
- b. Complexity management
- c. First mover advantage
- d. E-learning Maturity Model

Guidance: level 1

:: Systems theory ::

A _________ is a group of interacting or interrelated entities that form a unified whole. A _________ is delineated by its spatial and temporal boundaries, surrounded and influenced by its environment, described by its structure and purpose and expressed in its functioning.

Exam Probability: **Medium**

44. *Answer choices:*
(see index for correct answer)

- a. decentralized system
- b. System
- c. subsystem
- d. steady state

Guidance: level 1

:: Monopoly (economics) ::

A __________ exists when a specific person or enterprise is the only supplier of a particular commodity. This contrasts with a monopsony which relates to a single entity`s control of a market to purchase a good or service, and with oligopoly which consists of a few sellers dominating a market. Monopolies are thus characterized by a lack of economic competition to produce the good or service, a lack of viable substitute goods, and the possibility of a high __________ price well above the seller`s marginal cost that leads to a high __________ profit. The verb monopolise or monopolize refers to the process by which a company gains the ability to raise prices or exclude competitors. In economics, a __________ is a single seller. In law, a __________ is a business entity that has significant market power, that is, the power to charge overly high prices. Although monopolies may be big businesses, size is not a characteristic of a __________ . A small business may still have the power to raise prices in a small industry .

Exam Probability: **High**

45. *Answer choices:*

(see index for correct answer)

- a. Chamberlinian monopolistic competition
- b. Motion Picture Patents Company
- c. Copyright law of the European Union
- d. Monopoly

Guidance: level 1

:: Data management ::

__________ is a data management concept concerning the capability that enables an organization to ensure that high data quality exists throughout the complete lifecycle of the data. The key focus areas of __________ include availability, usability, consistency, data integrity and data security and includes establishing processes to ensure effective data management throughout the enterprise such as accountability for the adverse effects of poor data quality and ensuring that the data which an enterprise has can be used by the entire organization.

Exam Probability: **High**

46. *Answer choices:*

(see index for correct answer)

- a. Data governance
- b. Copyright
- c. Data field
- d. Cloud Data Management Interface

Guidance: level 1

:: Information technology management ::

In information technology to _________ means to move from one place to another, information to detailed data by focusing in on something. In a GUI-environment, "drilling-down" may involve clicking on some representation in order to reveal more detail.

Exam Probability: **High**

47. *Answer choices:*

(see index for correct answer)

- a. Mobile business development
- b. OMII-UK
- c. Capability Maturity Model
- d. Drill down

Guidance: level 1

:: Business process ::

A _________ or business method is a collection of related, structured activities or tasks by people or equipment which in a specific sequence produce a service or product for a particular customer or customers. _________ es occur at all organizational levels and may or may not be visible to the customers. A _________ may often be visualized as a flowchart of a sequence of activities with interleaving decision points or as a process matrix of a sequence of activities with relevance rules based on data in the process. The benefits of using _________ es include improved customer satisfaction and improved agility for reacting to rapid market change. Process-oriented organizations break down the barriers of structural departments and try to avoid functional silos.

Exam Probability: **Low**

48. *Answer choices:*

(see index for correct answer)

- a. Business process
- b. Social BPM
- c. Bonita BPM
- d. Process mining

Guidance: level 1

:: Information systems ::

A _________ manages the creation and modification of digital content. It typically supports multiple users in a collaborative environment.

Exam Probability: **Low**

49. *Answer choices:*

(see index for correct answer)

- a. Laws of information systems
- b. Content management system
- c. Sticky information
- d. Association for Information Systems

Guidance: level 1

:: Big data ::

__________ is the discovery, interpretation, and communication of meaningful patterns in data; and the process of applying those patterns towards effective decision making. In other words, __________ can be understood as the connective tissue between data and effective decision making, within an organization. Especially valuable in areas rich with recorded information, __________ relies on the simultaneous application of statistics, computer programming and operations research to quantify performance.

Exam Probability: **Low**

50. *Answer choices:*

(see index for correct answer)

- a. Talend
- b. Flytxt
- c. MonetDB
- d. Social IT

Guidance: level 1

:: Google services ::

A blog is a discussion or informational website published on the World Wide Web consisting of discrete, often informal diary-style text entries . Posts are typically displayed in reverse chronological order, so that the most recent post appears first, at the top of the web page. Until 2009, blogs were usually the work of a single individual, occasionally of a small group, and often covered a single subject or topic. In the 2010s, "multi-author blogs" emerged, featuring the writing of multiple authors and sometimes professionally edited. MABs from newspapers, other media outlets, universities, think tanks, advocacy groups, and similar institutions account for an increasing quantity of blog traffic. The rise of Twitter and other "microblogging" systems helps integrate MABs and single-author blogs into the news media. Blog can also be used as a verb, meaning to maintain or add content to a blog.

Exam Probability: **Medium**

51. *Answer choices:*

(see index for correct answer)

- a. Google Apps Marketplace
- b. Blogger
- c. Google Patents

- d. Gizmo5

Guidance: level 1

:: Marketing ::

__________ , in marketing, manufacturing, call centres and management, is the use of flexible computer-aided manufacturing systems to produce custom output. Such systems combine the low unit costs of mass production processes with the flexibility of individual customization.

Exam Probability: **High**

52. *Answer choices:*

(see index for correct answer)

- a. societal marketing
- b. Mass affluent
- c. Pricing objectives
- d. Product naming convention

Guidance: level 1

:: Data management ::

__________ is "data [information] that provides information about other data". Many distinct types of __________ exist, among these descriptive __________ , structural __________ , administrative __________ , reference __________ and statistical __________ .

Exam Probability: **Low**

53. *Answer choices:*

(see index for correct answer)

- a. Record linkage
- b. Metadata
- c. Dynamic knowledge repository
- d. Open Compute Project

Guidance: level 1

:: Marketing ::

__________ is a business model in which consumers create value and businesses consume that value. For example, when a consumer writes reviews or when a consumer gives a useful idea for new product development then that consumer is creating value for the business if the business adopts the input. In the C2B model, a reverse auction or demand collection model, enables buyers to name or demand their own price, which is often binding, for a specific good or service. Inside of a consumer to business market the roles involved in the transaction must be established and the consumer must offer something of value to the business.

Exam Probability: **Low**

54. *Answer choices:*

(see index for correct answer)

- a. Mass market
- b. LGBT marketing
- c. societal marketing
- d. Book of business

Guidance: level 1

:: Data management ::

" __________ " is a field that treats ways to analyze, systematically extract information from, or otherwise deal with data sets that are too large or complex to be dealt with by traditional data-processing application software. Data with many cases offer greater statistical power, while data with higher complexity may lead to a higher false discovery rate. __________ challenges include capturing data, data storage, data analysis, search, sharing, transfer, visualization, querying, updating, information privacy and data source. __________ was originally associated with three key concepts: volume, variety, and velocity. Other concepts later attributed with __________ are veracity and value.

Exam Probability: **Low**

55. *Answer choices:*

(see index for correct answer)

- a. Data classification
- b. Big data
- c. Concurrency control

- d. datum

Guidance: level 1

:: Data management ::

An _________ is a term used in data warehousing to refer to a system that is used to process the day-to-day transactions of an organization. These systems are designed in a manner that processing of day-to-day transactions is performed efficiently and the integrity of the transactional data is preserved.

Exam Probability: **High**

56. *Answer choices:*

(see index for correct answer)

- a. Content migration
- b. Operational system
- c. Operational historian
- d. Data management plan

Guidance: level 1

:: ::

A _________ is a computer network that interconnects computers within a limited area such as a residence, school, laboratory, university campus or office building. By contrast, a wide area network not only covers a larger geographic distance, but also generally involves leased telecommunication circuits.

Exam Probability: **Medium**

57. *Answer choices:*

(see index for correct answer)

- a. Character
- b. hierarchical
- c. hierarchical perspective
- d. deep-level diversity

Guidance: level 1

:: E-commerce ::

__________ is a type of fraud that occurs on the Internet in pay-per-click online advertising. In this type of advertising, the owners of websites that post the ads are paid an amount of money determined by how many visitors to the sites click on the ads. Fraud occurs when a person, automated script or computer program imitates a legitimate user of a web browser, clicking on such an ad without having an actual interest in the target of the ad's link. __________ is the subject of some controversy and increasing litigation due to the advertising networks being a key beneficiary of the fraud.

Exam Probability: **Medium**

58. *Answer choices:*

(see index for correct answer)

- a. Click fraud
- b. APazari
- c. Yemeksepeti
- d. Public exchange

Guidance: level 1

:: Ergonomics ::

__________ is the design of products, devices, services, or environments for people with disabilities. The concept of accessible design and practice of accessible development ensures both "direct access" and "indirect access" meaning compatibility with a person's assistive technology .

Exam Probability: **Low**

59. *Answer choices:*

(see index for correct answer)

- a. Anthropometry
- b. Full-spectrum light
- c. Ergonomic glove
- d. Light ergonomics

Guidance: level 1

Marketing

Marketing is the study and management of exchange relationships. Marketing is the business process of creating relationships with and satisfying customers. With its focus on the customer, marketing is one of the premier components of business management.

Marketing is defined by the American Marketing Association as "the activity, set of institutions, and processes for creating, communicating, delivering, and exchanging offerings that have value for customers, clients, partners, and society at large."

:: ::

_________ characterises the behaviour of a system or model whose components interact in multiple ways and follow local rules, meaning there is no reasonable higher instruction to define the various possible interactions.

Exam Probability: **High**

1. *Answer choices:*

(see index for correct answer)

- a. Complexity
- b. hierarchical
- c. deep-level diversity
- d. levels of analysis

Guidance: level 1

:: Business ::

The seller, or the provider of the goods or services, completes a sale in response to an acquisition, appropriation, requisition or a direct interaction with the buyer at the point of sale. There is a passing of title of the item, and the settlement of a price, in which agreement is reached on a price for which transfer of ownership of the item will occur. The seller, not the purchaser typically executes the sale and it may be completed prior to the obligation of payment. In the case of indirect interaction, a person who sells goods or service on behalf of the owner is known as a salesman or saleswoman or salesperson, but this often refers to someone _________ goods in a store/shop, in which case other terms are also common, including salesclerk, shop assistant, and retail clerk.

Exam Probability: **High**

2. *Answer choices:*

(see index for correct answer)

- a. Business development
- b. Policy capturing
- c. Selling
- d. Ian McLeod

Guidance: level 1

:: Marketing ::

_________ is a marketing practice of individuals or organizations . It allows them to sell products or services to other companies or organizations that resell them, use them in their products or services or use them to support their works.

Exam Probability: **Medium**

3. *Answer choices:*

(see index for correct answer)

- a. Price umbrella
- b. Business marketing
- c. Decoy effect
- d. Nano-campaigning

Guidance: level 1

:: Advertising techniques ::

In promotion and of advertising, a _________ or show consists of a person`s written or spoken statement extolling the virtue of a product. The term " _________ " most commonly applies to the sales-pitches attributed to ordinary citizens, whereas the word "endorsement" usually applies to pitches by celebrities. _________ s can be part of communal marketing. Sometimes, the cartoon character can be a _________ in a commercial.

Exam Probability: **Medium**

4. *Answer choices:*

(see index for correct answer)

- a. Hard sell
- b. Debranding
- c. Incomplete comparison
- d. Transpromotional

Guidance: level 1

:: ::

In communications and information processing, _________ is a system of rules to convert information—such as a letter, word, sound, image, or gesture—into another form or representation, sometimes shortened or secret, for communication through a communication channel or storage in a storage medium. An early example is the invention of language, which enabled a person, through speech, to communicate what they saw, heard, felt, or thought to others. But speech limits the range of communication to the distance a voice can carry, and limits the audience to those present when the speech is uttered. The invention of writing, which converted spoken language into visual symbols, extended the range of communication across space and time.

Exam Probability: **Medium**

5. *Answer choices:*

(see index for correct answer)

- a. information systems assessment
- b. functional perspective
- c. Code
- d. process perspective

Guidance: level 1

:: Data ::

Data has two ways of being created or generated. The first is what is called `captured data`, and is found through purposeful investigation or analysis. The second is called `exhaust data`, and is gathered usually by machines or terminals as a secondary function. For example, cash registers, smartphones, and speedometers serve a main function but may collect data as a secondary task. Exhaustive data is usually too large or of little use to process and becomes `transient` or thrown away.

Exam Probability: **Medium**

6. *Answer choices:*

(see index for correct answer)

- a. MVP tree
- b. Primary data
- c. Data acquisition
- d. DataSplice

Guidance: level 1

:: Behaviorism ::

In behavioral psychology, _________ is a consequence applied that will strengthen an organism`s future behavior whenever that behavior is preceded by a specific antecedent stimulus. This strengthening effect may be measured as a higher frequency of behavior , longer duration , greater magnitude , or shorter latency . There are two types of _________ , known as positive _________ and negative _________ ; positive is where by a reward is offered on expression of the wanted behaviour and negative is taking away an undesirable element in the persons environment whenever the desired behaviour is achieved.

Exam Probability: **Low**

7. *Answer choices:*

(see index for correct answer)

- a. social facilitation
- b. contingency management
- c. chaining
- d. Reinforcement

Guidance: level 1

:: Data management ::

In computing, a _________ , also known as an enterprise _________ , is a system used for reporting and data analysis, and is considered a core component of business intelligence. DWs are central repositories of integrated data from one or more disparate sources. They store current and historical data in one single place that are used for creating analytical reports for workers throughout the enterprise.

Exam Probability: **Low**

8. *Answer choices:*

(see index for correct answer)

- a. Enterprise data management
- b. Data management plan
- c. Data warehouse
- d. Government Performance Management

Guidance: level 1

:: Stock market ::

_________ is freedom from, or resilience against, potential harm caused by others. Beneficiaries of _________ may be of persons and social groups, objects and institutions, ecosystems or any other entity or phenomenon vulnerable to unwanted change by its environment.

Exam Probability: **High**

9. *Answer choices:*

(see index for correct answer)

- a. CEE Stock Exchange Group
- b. Slippage
- c. Security
- d. Trader

Guidance: level 1

:: ::

A __________ is a professional who provides expert advice in a particular area such as security , management, education, accountancy, law, human resources, marketing , finance, engineering, science or any of many other specialized fields.

Exam Probability: **High**

10. *Answer choices:*

(see index for correct answer)

- a. hierarchical
- b. Consultant
- c. imperative
- d. corporate values

Guidance: level 1

:: Auctioneering ::

An __________ is a process of buying and selling goods or services by offering them up for bid, taking bids, and then selling the item to the highest bidder. The open ascending price __________ is arguably the most common form of __________ in use today. Participants bid openly against one another, with each subsequent bid required to be higher than the previous bid. An __________ eer may announce prices, bidders may call out their bids themselves , or bids may be submitted electronically with the highest current bid publicly displayed. In a Dutch __________ , the __________ eer begins with a high asking price for some quantity of like items; the price is lowered until a participant is willing to accept the __________ eer`s price for some quantity of the goods in the lot or until the seller`s reserve price is met. While __________ s are most associated in the public imagination with the sale of antiques, paintings, rare collectibles and expensive wines, __________ s are also used for commodities, livestock, radio spectrum and used cars. In economic theory, an __________ may refer to any mechanism or set of trading rules for exchange.

Exam Probability: **Low**

11. *Answer choices:*

(see index for correct answer)

- a. Pie supper
- b. Unique bid auction
- c. Auction

- d. Virginity auction

Guidance: level 1

:: Marketing ::

_________ is research conducted for a problem that has not been studied more clearly, intended to establish priorities, develop operational definitions and improve the final research design. _________ helps determine the best research design, data-collection method and selection of subjects. It should draw definitive conclusions only with extreme caution. Given its fundamental nature, _________ often relies on techniques such as.

Exam Probability: **High**

12. *Answer choices:*

(see index for correct answer)

- a. Customer newsletter service
- b. Exploratory research
- c. Franchise disclosure document
- d. Experiential marketing

Guidance: level 1

:: Evaluation methods ::

In natural and social sciences, and sometimes in other fields, _________ is the systematic empirical investigation of observable phenomena via statistical, mathematical, or computational techniques. The objective of _________ is to develop and employ mathematical models, theories, and hypotheses pertaining to phenomena. The process of measurement is central to _________ because it provides the fundamental connection between empirical observation and mathematical expression of quantitative relationships.

Exam Probability: **Low**

13. *Answer choices:*

(see index for correct answer)

- a. Self-assessment
- b. Quantitative research
- c. Event correlation
- d. Advanced Concept Technology Demonstration

Guidance: level 1

:: Monopoly (economics) ::

The _________ of 1890 was a United States antitrust law that regulates competition among enterprises, which was passed by Congress under the presidency of Benjamin Harrison.

Exam Probability: **Medium**

14. *Answer choices:*

(see index for correct answer)

- a. Intellectual property
- b. Privatization
- c. Private finance initiative
- d. Sherman Antitrust Act

Guidance: level 1

:: Data analysis ::

_________ is a process of inspecting, cleansing, transforming, and modeling data with the goal of discovering useful information, informing conclusions, and supporting decision-making. _________ has multiple facets and approaches, encompassing diverse techniques under a variety of names, and is used in different business, science, and social science domains. In today`s business world, _________ plays a role in making decisions more scientific and helping businesses operate more effectively.

Exam Probability: **Low**

15. *Answer choices:*

(see index for correct answer)

- a. Aggregative Contingent Estimation
- b. Data analysis
- c. Multiscale geometric analysis
- d. FSA-Red Algorithm

Guidance: level 1

:: Logistics ::

__________ is generally the detailed organization and implementation of a complex operation. In a general business sense, __________ is the management of the flow of things between the point of origin and the point of consumption in order to meet requirements of customers or corporations. The resources managed in __________ may include tangible goods such as materials, equipment, and supplies, as well as food and other consumable items. The __________ of physical items usually involves the integration of information flow, materials handling, production, packaging, inventory, transportation, warehousing, and often security.

Exam Probability: **Low**

16. *Answer choices:*

(see index for correct answer)

- a. Logistics
- b. Distribution resource planning
- c. DASH7
- d. Freightos

Guidance: level 1

:: Reputation management ::

A __________ is an astronomical object consisting of a luminous spheroid of plasma held together by its own gravity. The nearest __________ to Earth is the Sun. Many other __________ s are visible to the naked eye from Earth during the night, appearing as a multitude of fixed luminous points in the sky due to their immense distance from Earth. Historically, the most prominent __________ s were grouped into constellations and asterisms, the brightest of which gained proper names. Astronomers have assembled __________ catalogues that identify the known __________ s and provide standardized stellar designations. However, most of the estimated 300 sextillion __________ s in the Universe are invisible to the naked eye from Earth, including all __________ s outside our galaxy, the Milky Way.

Exam Probability: **Low**

17. *Answer choices:*

(see index for correct answer)

- a. ClaimID
- b. Moderation system

- c. TrustRank
- d. Whuffie

Guidance: level 1

:: Business law ::

A _________ is an arrangement where parties, known as partners, agree to cooperate to advance their mutual interests. The partners in a _________ may be individuals, businesses, interest-based organizations, schools, governments or combinations. Organizations may partner to increase the likelihood of each achieving their mission and to amplify their reach. A _________ may result in issuing and holding equity or may be only governed by a contract.

Exam Probability: **Medium**

18. *Answer choices:*

(see index for correct answer)

- a. Partnership
- b. Output contract
- c. Lessor
- d. Participation

Guidance: level 1

:: Credit cards ::

The _________ Company, also known as Amex, is an American multinational financial services corporation headquartered in Three World Financial Center in New York City. The company was founded in 1850 and is one of the 30 components of the Dow Jones Industrial Average. The company is best known for its charge card, credit card, and traveler's cheque businesses.

Exam Probability: **High**

19. *Answer choices:*

(see index for correct answer)

- a. The Everything Card
- b. InteliSpend Prepaid Solutions
- c. Accolades Card
- d. Credit CARD Act

Guidance: level 1

:: ::

An __________ is a systematic and independent examination of books, accounts, statutory records, documents and vouchers of an organization to ascertain how far the financial statements as well as non-financial disclosures present a true and fair view of the concern. It also attempts to ensure that the books of accounts are properly maintained by the concern as required by law. __________ ing has become such a ubiquitous phenomenon in the corporate and the public sector that academics started identifying an " __________ Society". The __________ or perceives and recognises the propositions before them for examination, obtains evidence, evaluates the same and formulates an opinion on the basis of his judgement which is communicated through their __________ ing report.

Exam Probability: **High**

20. *Answer choices:*

(see index for correct answer)

- a. functional perspective
- b. deep-level diversity
- c. similarity-attraction theory
- d. Audit

Guidance: level 1

:: ::

Distribution is one of the four elements of the marketing mix. Distribution is the process of making a product or service available for the consumer or business user who needs it. This can be done directly by the producer or service provider, or using indirect channels with distributors or intermediaries. The other three elements of the marketing mix are product, pricing, and promotion.

Exam Probability: **Low**

21. *Answer choices:*

(see index for correct answer)

- a. Distribution channel
- b. levels of analysis
- c. hierarchical perspective

- d. empathy

Guidance: level 1

:: Management ::

A __________ is a comprehensive document or blueprint that outlines the advertising and marketing efforts for the coming year. It describes business activities involved in accomplishing specific marketing objectives within a set time frame. A __________ also includes a description of the current marketing position of a business, a discussion of the target market and a description of the marketing mix that a business will use to achieve their marketing goals. A __________ has a formal structure, but can be used as a formal or informal document which makes it very flexible. It contains some historical data, future predictions, and methods or strategies to achieve the marketing objectives. __________s start with the identification of customer needs through a market research and how the business can satisfy these needs while generating an acceptable return. This includes processes such as market situation analysis, action programs, budgets, sales forecasts, strategies and projected financial statements. A __________ can also be described as a technique that helps a business to decide on the best use of its resources to achieve corporate objectives. It can also contain a full analysis of the strengths and weaknesses of a company, its organization and its products.

Exam Probability: **Low**

22. *Answer choices:*

(see index for correct answer)

- a. Narcissistic leadership
- b. Mushroom management
- c. Marketing plan
- d. Maryland StateStat

Guidance: level 1

:: ::

_________ is the provision of service to customers before, during and after a purchase. The perception of success of such interactions is dependent on employees "who can adjust themselves to the personality of the guest". _________ concerns the priority an organization assigns to _________ relative to components such as product innovation and pricing. In this sense, an organization that values good _________ may spend more money in training employees than the average organization or may proactively interview customers for feedback.

Exam Probability: **Medium**

23. *Answer choices:*

(see index for correct answer)

- a. imperative
- b. hierarchical perspective
- c. Customer service
- d. process perspective

Guidance: level 1

:: Monopoly (economics) ::

A _________ is a form of intellectual property that gives its owner the legal right to exclude others from making, using, selling, and importing an invention for a limited period of years, in exchange for publishing an enabling public disclosure of the invention. In most countries _________ rights fall under civil law and the _________ holder needs to sue someone infringing the _________ in order to enforce his or her rights. In some industries _________ s are an essential form of competitive advantage; in others they are irrelevant.

Exam Probability: **Low**

24. *Answer choices:*

(see index for correct answer)

- a. Patent
- b. Trust
- c. Building block model
- d. Government-granted monopoly

Guidance: level 1

:: Evaluation methods ::

__________ is a scientific method of observation to gather non-numerical data. This type of research "refers to the meanings, concepts definitions, characteristics, metaphors, symbols, and description of things" and not to their "counts or measures." This research answers why and how a certain phenomenon may occur rather than how often. __________ approaches are employed across many academic disciplines, focusing particularly on the human elements of the social and natural sciences; in less academic contexts, areas of application include qualitative market research, business, service demonstrations by non-profits, and journalism.

Exam Probability: **High**

25. *Answer choices:*

(see index for correct answer)

- a. Moral statistics
- b. Qualitative research
- c. Proof of concept
- d. Poll average

Guidance: level 1

:: Marketing ::

A __________ is the people, organizations, and activities necessary to transfer the ownership of goods from the point of production to the point of consumption. It is the way products get to the end-user, the consumer; and is also known as a distribution channel. A __________ is a useful tool for management, and is crucial to creating an effective and well-planned marketing strategy.

Exam Probability: **Low**

26. *Answer choices:*

(see index for correct answer)

- a. Marketing channel
- b. Engagement marketing
- c. Mass-market theory
- d. Affective design

Guidance: level 1

:: Library science ::

_________ refers to data which is collected by someone who is someone other than the user. Common sources of _________ for social science include censuses, information collected by government departments, organizational records and data that was originally collected for other research purposes. Primary data, by contrast, are collected by the investigator conducting the research.

Exam Probability: **High**

27. *Answer choices:*

(see index for correct answer)

- a. Source literature
- b. OpenURL
- c. Beta Phi Mu Award
- d. Secondary data

Guidance: level 1

:: Market research ::

_________ is the action of defining, gathering, analyzing, and distributing intelligence about products, customers, competitors, and any aspect of the environment needed to support executives and managers in strategic decision making for an organization.

Exam Probability: **Medium**

28. *Answer choices:*

(see index for correct answer)

- a. Competitive intelligence
- b. Qualtrics
- c. Computer-assisted web interviewing
- d. Omnibus

Guidance: level 1

:: Organizational structure ::

An __________ defines how activities such as task allocation, coordination, and supervision are directed toward the achievement of organizational aims.

Exam Probability: **Medium**

29. *Answer choices:*

(see index for correct answer)

- a. Organization of the New York City Police Department
- b. Unorganisation
- c. The Starfish and the Spider
- d. Automated Bureaucracy

Guidance: level 1

:: Marketing ::

A __________ is an overall experience of a customer that distinguishes an organization or product from its rivals in the eyes of the customer. __________ s are used in business, marketing, and advertising. Name __________ s are sometimes distinguished from generic or store __________ s.

Exam Probability: **Medium**

30. *Answer choices:*

(see index for correct answer)

- a. Brand
- b. Neuromarketing
- c. Bluetooth advertising
- d. Customer acquisition cost

Guidance: level 1

:: Consumer behaviour ::

__________ is an activity in which a customer browses the available goods or services presented by one or more retailers with the potential intent to purchase a suitable selection of them. A typology of shopper types has been developed by scholars which identifies one group of shoppers as recreational shoppers, that is, those who enjoy __________ and view it as a leisure activity.

Exam Probability: **Medium**

31. *Answer choices:*

(see index for correct answer)

- a. Shopping
- b. Consumer confidence index
- c. Marketing buzz
- d. Post-consumerism

Guidance: level 1

:: ::

A _________ or sample _________ is a single measure of some attribute of a sample . It is calculated by applying a function to the values of the items of the sample, which are known together as a set of data.

Exam Probability: **High**

32. *Answer choices:*

(see index for correct answer)

- a. functional perspective
- b. co-culture
- c. corporate values
- d. Statistic

Guidance: level 1

:: ::

_________ is a term frequently used in marketing. It is a measure of how products and services supplied by a company meet or surpass customer expectation. _________ is defined as "the number of customers, or percentage of total customers, whose reported experience with a firm, its products, or its services exceeds specified satisfaction goals."

Exam Probability: **High**

33. *Answer choices:*

(see index for correct answer)

- a. Customer satisfaction
- b. corporate values
- c. functional perspective

- d. cultural

Guidance: level 1

:: Commerce ::

A _________ is a company or individual that purchases goods or services with the intention of selling them rather than consuming or using them. This is usually done for profit . One example can be found in the industry of telecommunications, where companies buy excess amounts of transmission capacity or call time from other carriers and resell it to smaller carriers.

Exam Probability: **Medium**

34. *Answer choices:*

(see index for correct answer)

- a. Coincidence of wants
- b. Contingent payment sales
- c. Church sale
- d. Reseller

Guidance: level 1

:: ::

In _________ relations and communication science, _________ s are groups of individual people, and the _________ is the totality of such groupings. This is a different concept to the sociological concept of the Öffentlichkeit or _________ sphere. The concept of a _________ has also been defined in political science, psychology, marketing, and advertising. In _________ relations and communication science, it is one of the more ambiguous concepts in the field. Although it has definitions in the theory of the field that have been formulated from the early 20th century onwards, it has suffered in more recent years from being blurred, as a result of conflation of the idea of a _________ with the notions of audience, market segment, community, constituency, and stakeholder.

Exam Probability: **High**

35. *Answer choices:*

(see index for correct answer)

- a. Public
- b. Character
- c. interpersonal communication
- d. similarity-attraction theory

Guidance: level 1

:: Generally Accepted Accounting Principles ::

In accounting, _________ is the income that a business have from its normal business activities, usually from the sale of goods and services to customers. _________ is also referred to as sales or turnover.Some companies receive _________ from interest, royalties, or other fees. _________ may refer to business income in general, or it may refer to the amount, in a monetary unit, earned during a period of time, as in "Last year, Company X had _________ of $42 million". Profits or net income generally imply total _________ minus total expenses in a given period. In accounting, in the balance statement it is a subsection of the Equity section and _________ increases equity, it is often referred to as the "top line" due to its position on the income statement at the very top. This is to be contrasted with the "bottom line" which denotes net income .

Exam Probability: **High**

36. *Answer choices:*

(see index for correct answer)

- a. Gross profit
- b. Standard Business Reporting
- c. French generally accepted accounting principles
- d. Cash method of accounting

Guidance: level 1

:: Basic financial concepts ::

__________ is a sustained increase in the general price level of goods and services in an economy over a period of time.When the general price level rises, each unit of currency buys fewer goods and services; consequently, __________ reflects a reduction in the purchasing power per unit of money a loss of real value in the medium of exchange and unit of account within the economy. The measure of __________ is the __________ rate, the annualized percentage change in a general price index, usually the consumer price index, over time. The opposite of __________ is deflation.

Exam Probability: **Low**

37. *Answer choices:*

(see index for correct answer)

- a. Present value of benefits
- b. Leverage cycle
- c. Deflation
- d. Present value of costs

Guidance: level 1

:: Marketing ::

__________ is multi-channel online marketing technique focused at reaching a specific audience on their smartphones, tablets, or any other related devices through websites, E-mail, SMS and MMS, social media, or mobile applications. __________ can provide customers with time and location sensitive, personalized information that promotes goods, services and ideas. In a more theoretical manner, academic Andreas Kaplan defines __________ as "any marketing activity conducted through a ubiquitous network to which consumers are constantly connected using a personal mobile device".

Exam Probability: **Medium**

38. *Answer choices:*

(see index for correct answer)

- a. Corporate anniversary
- b. Field research
- c. Postmodern branding
- d. Multichannel marketing

Guidance: level 1

:: Sales ::

_________ is a business discipline which is focused on the practical application of sales techniques and the management of a firm`s sales operations. It is an important business function as net sales through the sale of products and services and resulting profit drive most commercial business. These are also typically the goals and performance indicators of _________ .

Exam Probability: **High**

39. *Answer choices:*

(see index for correct answer)

- a. System sales
- b. Sales decision process
- c. Souvenir
- d. Sales management

Guidance: level 1

:: ::

Market segmentation is the activity of dividing a broad consumer or business market, normally consisting of existing and potential customers, into sub-groups of consumers based on some type of shared characteristics. In dividing or segmenting markets, researchers typically look for common characteristics such as shared needs, common interests, similar lifestyles or even similar demographic profiles. The overall aim of segmentation is to identify high yield segments – that is, those segments that are likely to be the most profitable or that have growth potential – so that these can be selected for special attention .

Exam Probability: **High**

40. *Answer choices:*

(see index for correct answer)

- a. functional perspective
- b. Market segments
- c. process perspective
- d. cultural

Guidance: level 1

:: ::

In financial markets, a share is a unit used as mutual funds, limited partnerships, and real estate investment trusts. The owner of _________ in the corporation/company is a shareholder of the corporation. A share is an indivisible unit of capital, expressing the ownership relationship between the company and the shareholder. The denominated value of a share is its face value, and the total of the face value of issued _________ represent the capital of a company, which may not reflect the market value of those _________ .

Exam Probability: **Low**

41. *Answer choices:*

(see index for correct answer)

- a. Character
- b. empathy
- c. Shares
- d. personal values

Guidance: level 1

:: ::

_________ is a concept of English common law and is a necessity for simple contracts but not for special contracts . The concept has been adopted by other common law jurisdictions, including the US.

Exam Probability: **High**

42. *Answer choices:*

(see index for correct answer)

- a. Consideration
- b. hierarchical perspective
- c. information systems assessment
- d. levels of analysis

Guidance: level 1

:: ::

__________ refers to a diverse array of media technologies that reach a large audience via mass communication. The technologies through which this communication takes place include a variety of outlets.

Exam Probability: **High**

43. *Answer choices:*

(see index for correct answer)

- a. corporate values
- b. co-culture
- c. surface-level diversity
- d. deep-level diversity

Guidance: level 1

:: ::

__________, or auditory perception, is the ability to perceive sounds by detecting vibrations, changes in the pressure of the surrounding medium through time, through an organ such as the ear. The academic field concerned with __________ is auditory science.

Exam Probability: **High**

44. *Answer choices:*

(see index for correct answer)

- a. levels of analysis
- b. personal values
- c. Hearing
- d. deep-level diversity

Guidance: level 1

:: Brokered programming ::

An _________ is a form of television commercial, which generally includes a toll-free telephone number or website. Most often used as a form of direct response television , long-form _________ s are typically 28:30 or 58:30 minutes in length. _________ s are also known as paid programming . This phenomenon started in the United States, where _________ s were typically shown overnight , outside peak prime time hours for commercial broadcasters. Some television stations chose to air _________ s as an alternative to the former practice of signing off. Some channels air _________ s 24 hours. Some stations also choose to air _________ s during the daytime hours mostly on weekends to fill in for unscheduled network or syndicated programming. By 2009, most _________ spending in the U.S. occurred during the early morning, daytime and evening hours, or in the afternoon. Stations in most countries around the world have instituted similar media structures. The _________ industry is worth over $200 billion.

Exam Probability: **Low**

45. *Answer choices:*

(see index for correct answer)

- a. Leased access
- b. Brokered programming
- c. One Magnificent Morning
- d. Infomercial

Guidance: level 1

:: Electronic feedback ::

_________ occurs when outputs of a system are routed back as inputs as part of a chain of cause-and-effect that forms a circuit or loop. The system can then be said to feed back into itself. The notion of cause-and-effect has to be handled carefully when applied to _________ systems.

Exam Probability: **Medium**

46. *Answer choices:*

(see index for correct answer)

- a. Feedback
- b. Positive feedback

Guidance: level 1

:: ::

__________ is an abstract concept of management of complex systems according to a set of rules and trends. In systems theory, these types of rules exist in various fields of biology and society, but the term has slightly different meanings according to context. For example.

Exam Probability: **Medium**

47. *Answer choices:*

(see index for correct answer)

- a. hierarchical perspective
- b. functional perspective
- c. co-culture
- d. Regulation

Guidance: level 1

:: Marketing ::

__________ is based on a marketing concept which can be adopted by an organization as a strategy for business expansion. Where implemented, a franchisor licenses its know-how, procedures, intellectual property, use of its business model, brand, and rights to sell its branded products and services to a franchisee. In return the franchisee pays certain fees and agrees to comply with certain obligations, typically set out in a Franchise Agreement.

Exam Probability: **Low**

48. *Answer choices:*

(see index for correct answer)

- a. Immersion marketing
- b. Franchising
- c. Paddock girl
- d. Intent scale translation

Guidance: level 1

:: ::

_________ or accountancy is the measurement, processing, and communication of financial information about economic entities such as businesses and corporations. The modern field was established by the Italian mathematician Luca Pacioli in 1494. _________ , which has been called the "language of business", measures the results of an organization`s economic activities and conveys this information to a variety of users, including investors, creditors, management, and regulators. Practitioners of _________ are known as accountants. The terms " _________ " and "financial reporting" are often used as synonyms.

Exam Probability: **Medium**

49. *Answer choices:*
(see index for correct answer)

- a. deep-level diversity
- b. imperative
- c. open system
- d. Accounting

Guidance: level 1

:: Legal terms ::

A _________ is a person who is called upon to issue a response to a communication made by another. The term is used in legal contexts, in survey methodology, and in psychological conditioning.

Exam Probability: **Low**

50. *Answer choices:*
(see index for correct answer)

- a. Legal recourse
- b. Black letter law
- c. Adjudication
- d. Respondent

Guidance: level 1

:: Survey methodology ::

An _________ is a conversation where questions are asked and answers are given. In common parlance, the word " _________ " refers to a one-on-one conversation between an _________ er and an _________ ee. The _________ er asks questions to which the _________ ee responds, usually so information may be transferred from _________ ee to _________ er . Sometimes, information can be transferred in both directions. It is a communication, unlike a speech, which produces a one-way flow of information.

Exam Probability: **High**

51. *Answer choices:*

(see index for correct answer)

- a. Interview
- b. Sampling
- c. Swiss Centre of Expertise in the Social Sciences
- d. Self-report

Guidance: level 1

:: Marketing ::

_________ is a market strategy in which a firm decides to ignore market segment differences and appeal the whole market with one offer or one strategy, which supports the idea of broadcasting a message that will reach the largest number of people possible. Traditionally _________ has focused on radio, television and newspapers as the media used to reach this broad audience. By reaching the largest audience possible, exposure to the product is maximized, and in theory this would directly correlate with a larger number of sales or buys into the product.

Exam Probability: **High**

52. *Answer choices:*

(see index for correct answer)

- a. Decoy effect
- b. Customer newsletter service
- c. Mass marketing
- d. Price point

Guidance: level 1

:: ::

_________ is the means to see, hear, or become aware of something or someone through our fundamental senses. The term _________ derives from the Latin word perceptio, and is the organization, identification, and interpretation of sensory information in order to represent and understand the presented information, or the environment.

Exam Probability: **Medium**

53. *Answer choices:*

(see index for correct answer)

- a. Perception
- b. Character
- c. similarity-attraction theory
- d. functional perspective

Guidance: level 1

:: Television terminology ::

A _________ organization , also known as a non-business entity, not-for-profit organization, or _________ institution, is dedicated to furthering a particular social cause or advocating for a shared point of view. In economic terms, it is an organization that uses its surplus of the revenues to further achieve its ultimate objective, rather than distributing its income to the organization`s shareholders, leaders, or members. _________ s are tax exempt or charitable, meaning they do not pay income tax on the money that they receive for their organization. They can operate in religious, scientific, research, or educational settings.

Exam Probability: **High**

54. *Answer choices:*

(see index for correct answer)

- a. multiplexing
- b. distance learning
- c. Satellite television
- d. not-for-profit

Guidance: level 1

:: Marketing ::

_________ uses different marketing channels and tools in combination: Marketing communication channels focus on any way a business communicates a message to its desired market, or the market in general. A marketing communication tool can be anything from: advertising, personal selling, direct marketing, sponsorship, communication, and promotion to public relations.

Exam Probability: **Low**

55. *Answer choices:*

(see index for correct answer)

- a. Cult brand
- b. Digital native
- c. Cumulative prospect theory
- d. Performance-based advertising

Guidance: level 1

:: Human resource management ::

_________ encompasses values and behaviors that contribute to the unique social and psychological environment of a business. The _________ influences the way people interact, the context within which knowledge is created, the resistance they will have towards certain changes, and ultimately the way they share knowledge. _________ represents the collective values, beliefs and principles of organizational members and is a product of factors such as history, product, market, technology, strategy, type of employees, management style, and national culture; culture includes the organization`s vision, values, norms, systems, symbols, language, assumptions, environment, location, beliefs and habits.

Exam Probability: **Medium**

56. *Answer choices:*

(see index for correct answer)

- a. Induction programme
- b. Chartered Institute of Personnel and Development
- c. T-shaped skills
- d. Organizational culture

Guidance: level 1

:: ::

A __________ is an organized collection of data, generally stored and accessed electronically from a computer system. Where __________ s are more complex they are often developed using formal design and modeling techniques.

Exam Probability: **Low**

57. *Answer choices:*

(see index for correct answer)

- a. corporate values
- b. co-culture
- c. surface-level diversity
- d. empathy

Guidance: level 1

:: Marketing techniques ::

__________ is the activity of dividing a broad consumer or business market, normally consisting of existing and potential customers, into sub-groups of consumers based on some type of shared characteristics. In dividing or segmenting markets, researchers typically look for common characteristics such as shared needs, common interests, similar lifestyles or even similar demographic profiles. The overall aim of segmentation is to identify high yield segments – that is, those segments that are likely to be the most profitable or that have growth potential – so that these can be selected for special attention .

Exam Probability: **Medium**

58. *Answer choices:*

(see index for correct answer)

- a. Market segmentation
- b. Co-promotion
- c. Blackout dates
- d. Product life cycle

Guidance: level 1

:: ::

__________ LLC is an American multinational technology company that specializes in Internet-related services and products, which include online advertising technologies, search engine, cloud computing, software, and hardware. It is considered one of the Big Four technology companies, alongside Amazon, Apple and Facebook.

Exam Probability: **Medium**

59. *Answer choices:*

(see index for correct answer)

- a. cultural
- b. Sarbanes-Oxley act of 2002
- c. Google
- d. open system

Guidance: level 1

Manufacturing

Manufacturing is the production of merchandise for use or sale using labor and machines, tools, chemical and biological processing, or formulation. The term may refer to a range of human activity, from handicraft to high tech, but is most commonly applied to industrial design , in which raw materials are transformed into finished goods on a large scale. Such finished goods may be sold to other manufacturers for the production of other, more complex products, such as aircraft, household appliances, furniture, sports equipment or automobiles, or sold to wholesalers, who in turn sell them to retailers, who then sell them to end users and consumers.

:: Production economics ::

_________ is the creation of a whole that is greater than the simple sum of its parts. The term _________ comes from the Attic Greek word sea synergia from synergos, , meaning "working together".

Exam Probability: **Low**

1. *Answer choices:*

(see index for correct answer)

- a. Factor price
- b. Returns to scale
- c. Synergy
- d. Ramp up

Guidance: level 1

:: Project management ::

_________ is a process of setting goals, planning and/or controlling the organizing and leading the execution of any type of activity, such as.

Exam Probability: **High**

2. *Answer choices:*

(see index for correct answer)

- a. Stages of project finance
- b. Concept note
- c. Theory Z of Ouchi
- d. Management process

Guidance: level 1

:: Knowledge representation ::

__________ s are causal diagrams created by Kaoru Ishikawa that show the causes of a specific event.

Exam Probability: **High**

3. *Answer choices:*

(see index for correct answer)

- a. Knowledge integration
- b. Defeasible reasoning
- c. Linguistic value
- d. Dublin Core

Guidance: level 1

:: Business process ::

A committee is a body of one or more persons that is subordinate to a deliberative assembly. Usually, the assembly sends matters into a committee as a way to explore them more fully than would be possible if the assembly itself were considering them. Committees may have different functions and their type of work differ depending on the type of the organization and its needs.

Exam Probability: **High**

4. *Answer choices:*

(see index for correct answer)

- a. Business process outsourcing to India
- b. Business Process Modeling Language
- c. Tenant screening
- d. ProcessEdge

Guidance: level 1

:: Industrial engineering ::

The __________ is the design of any task that aims to describe or explain the variation of information under conditions that are hypothesized to reflect the variation. The term is generally associated with experiments in which the design introduces conditions that directly affect the variation, but may also refer to the design of quasi-experiments, in which natural conditions that influence the variation are selected for observation.

Exam Probability: **Low**

5. *Answer choices:*

(see index for correct answer)

- a. Standard time
- b. Indian Institution of Industrial Engineering
- c. Design of experiments
- d. Harold and Inge Marcus Department of Industrial and Manufacturing Engineering

Guidance: level 1

:: Gas technologies ::

A __________ is a rotary mechanical device that extracts energy from a fluid flow and converts it into useful work. The work produced by a __________ can be used for generating electrical power when combined with a generator. A __________ is a turbomachine with at least one moving part called a rotor assembly, which is a shaft or drum with blades attached. Moving fluid acts on the blades so that they move and impart rotational energy to the rotor. Early __________ examples are windmills and waterwheels.

Exam Probability: **High**

6. *Answer choices:*

(see index for correct answer)

- a. Turbine
- b. Vacuum cleaner
- c. Molecular sieve
- d. HEPA

Guidance: level 1

:: Lean manufacturing ::

__________ is a Japanese term that means "mistake-proofing" or "inadvertent error prevention". A __________ is any mechanism in any process that helps an equipment operator avoid mistakes . Its purpose is to eliminate product defects by preventing, correcting, or drawing attention to human errors as they occur. The concept was formalised, and the term adopted, by Shigeo Shingo as part of the Toyota Production System. It was originally described as baka-yoke, but as this means "fool-proofing" the name was changed to the milder __________ .

Exam Probability: **High**

7. *Answer choices:*

(see index for correct answer)

- a. Oobeya
- b. Mura
- c. Poka-yoke
- d. Supply chain responsiveness matrix

Guidance: level 1

:: Product development ::

In business and engineering, __________ covers the complete process of bringing a new product to market. A central aspect of NPD is product design, along with various business considerations. __________ is described broadly as the transformation of a market opportunity into a product available for sale. The product can be tangible or intangible , though sometimes services and other processes are distinguished from "products." NPD requires an understanding of customer needs and wants, the competitive environment, and the nature of the market.Cost, time and quality are the main variables that drive customer needs. Aiming at these three variables, innovative companies develop continuous practices and strategies to better satisfy customer requirements and to increase their own market share by a regular development of new products. There are many uncertainties and challenges which companies must face throughout the process. The use of best practices and the elimination of barriers to communication are the main concerns for the management of the NPD .

Exam Probability: **High**

8. *Answer choices:*
(see index for correct answer)

- a. New product development
- b. Walter Heidenfels
- c. Product line extension
- d. EXtreme Manufacturing

Guidance: level 1

:: Risk analysis ::

Supply-chain risk management is "the implementation of strategies to manage both everyday and exceptional risks along the supply chain based on continuous risk assessment with the objective of reducing vulnerability and ensuring continuity".

Exam Probability: **Medium**

9. *Answer choices:*
(see index for correct answer)

- a. Precautionary principle
- b. Fault tree analysis
- c. Wilderness Risk Management Conference
- d. Supply chain risk management

Guidance: level 1

:: Monopoly (economics) ::

__________ are "efficiencies formed by variety, not volume" . For example, a gas station that sells gasoline can sell soda, milk, baked goods, etc through their customer service representatives and thus achieve gasoline companies __________ .

Exam Probability: **Medium**

10. *Answer choices:*
(see index for correct answer)

- a. Economies of scope
- b. Third-party access
- c. Legal monopoly
- d. Revenue-cap regulation

Guidance: level 1

:: ::

In production, research, retail, and accounting, a __________ is the value of money that has been used up to produce something or deliver a service, and hence is not available for use anymore. In business, the __________ may be one of acquisition, in which case the amount of money expended to acquire it is counted as __________. In this case, money is the input that is gone in order to acquire the thing. This acquisition __________ may be the sum of the __________ of production as incurred by the original producer, and further __________s of transaction as incurred by the acquirer over and above the price paid to the producer. Usually, the price also includes a mark-up for profit over the __________ of production.

Exam Probability: **Medium**

11. *Answer choices:*

(see index for correct answer)

- a. Character
- b. imperative
- c. Cost
- d. interpersonal communication

Guidance: level 1

:: Software testing ::

__________ 1 was the first artificial Earth satellite. The Soviet Union launched it into an elliptical low Earth orbit on 4 October 1957, orbiting for three weeks before its batteries died, then silently for two more months before falling back into the atmosphere. It was a 58 cm diameter polished metal sphere, with four external radio antennas to broadcast radio pulses. Its radio signal was easily detectable even by radio amateurs, and the 65° inclination and duration of its orbit made its flight path cover virtually the entire inhabited Earth. This surprise success precipitated the American __________ crisis and triggered the Space Race, a part of the Cold War. The launch was the beginning of a new era of political, military, technological, and scientific developments.

Exam Probability: **Low**

12. *Answer choices:*

(see index for correct answer)

- a. Sputnik
- b. Test data generation
- c. Agile testing
- d. Augmented reality-based testing

Guidance: level 1

:: Production and manufacturing ::

_________ is a systematic method to improve the "value" of goods or products and services by using an examination of function. Value, as defined, is the ratio of function to cost. Value can therefore be manipulated by either improving the function or reducing the cost. It is a primary tenet of _________ that basic functions be preserved and not be reduced as a consequence of pursuing value improvements.

Exam Probability: **Low**

13. *Answer choices:*

(see index for correct answer)

- a. Value engineering
- b. Managed services
- c. Variable rate feeder
- d. Zero Defects

Guidance: level 1

:: Information technology management ::

_________ is the discipline of engineering concerned with the principles and practice of product and service quality assurance and control. In the software development, it is the management, development, operation and maintenance of IT systems and enterprise architectures with a high quality standard.

Exam Probability: **High**

14. *Answer choices:*

(see index for correct answer)

- a. Incident management
- b. Quality Engineering
- c. Business transformation
- d. ISO/IEC 19770

Guidance: level 1

:: Distribution, retailing, and wholesaling ::

_________ measures the performance of a system. Certain goals are defined and the _________ gives the percentage to which those goals should be achieved. Fill rate is different from _________ .

Exam Probability: **Medium**

15. *Answer choices:*
(see index for correct answer)

- a. Service level
- b. Independent Publishers Group
- c. Fast Fiction
- d. Direct market

Guidance: level 1

:: ::

_________ refers to a business or organization attempting to acquire goods or services to accomplish its goals. Although there are several organizations that attempt to set standards in the _________ process, processes can vary greatly between organizations. Typically the word " _________ " is not used interchangeably with the word "procurement", since procurement typically includes expediting, supplier quality, and transportation and logistics in addition to _________ .

Exam Probability: **High**

16. *Answer choices:*
(see index for correct answer)

- a. cultural
- b. deep-level diversity
- c. Purchasing
- d. process perspective

Guidance: level 1

:: Semiconductor companies ::

__________ Corporation is a Japanese multinational conglomerate corporation headquartered in Konan, Minato, Tokyo. Its diversified business includes consumer and professional electronics, gaming, entertainment and financial services. The company owns the largest music entertainment business in the world, the largest video game console business and one of the largest video game publishing businesses, and is one of the leading manufacturers of electronic products for the consumer and professional markets, and a leading player in the film and television entertainment industry. __________ was ranked 97th on the 2018 Fortune Global 500 list.

Exam Probability: **Low**

17. *Answer choices:*

(see index for correct answer)

- a. Conemtech
- b. CML Microcircuits
- c. Sony
- d. Entropic Communications

Guidance: level 1

:: ::

__________ is the production of products for use or sale using labour and machines, tools, chemical and biological processing, or formulation. The term may refer to a range of human activity, from handicraft to high tech, but is most commonly applied to industrial design, in which raw materials are transformed into finished goods on a large scale. Such finished goods may be sold to other manufacturers for the production of other, more complex products, such as aircraft, household appliances, furniture, sports equipment or automobiles, or sold to wholesalers, who in turn sell them to retailers, who then sell them to end users and consumers.

Exam Probability: **High**

18. *Answer choices:*

(see index for correct answer)

- a. Character
- b. co-culture
- c. open system
- d. Manufacturing

Guidance: level 1

:: Promotion and marketing communications ::

The _________ of American Manufacturers, now ThomasNet, is an online platform for supplier discovery and product sourcing in the US and Canada. It was once known as the "big green books" and "Thomas Registry", and was a multi-volume directory of industrial product information covering 650,000 distributors, manufacturers and service companies within 67,000-plus industrial categories that is now published on ThomasNet.

Exam Probability: **High**

19. *Answer choices:*

(see index for correct answer)

- a. Propaganda
- b. Worthy Book
- c. Social network advertising
- d. E-Marketing Collateral

Guidance: level 1

:: Project management ::

_________ is the right to exercise power, which can be formalized by a state and exercised by way of judges, appointed executives of government, or the ecclesiastical or priestly appointed representatives of a God or other deities.

Exam Probability: **Low**

20. *Answer choices:*

(see index for correct answer)

- a. ISO 31000
- b. Dependency
- c. Authority
- d. The International Association of Project and Program Management

Guidance: level 1

:: Product management ::

__________ s, also known as Shewhart charts or process-behavior charts, are a statistical process control tool used to determine if a manufacturing or business process is in a state of control.

Exam Probability: **Medium**

21. *Answer choices:*

(see index for correct answer)

- a. Pareto chart
- b. Obsolescence
- c. Product information
- d. Product manager

Guidance: level 1

:: Commercial item transport and distribution ::

In commerce, supply-chain management , the management of the flow of goods and services, involves the movement and storage of raw materials, of work-in-process inventory, and of finished goods from point of origin to point of consumption. Interconnected or interlinked networks, channels and node businesses combine in the provision of products and services required by end customers in a supply chain. Supply-chain management has been defined as the "design, planning, execution, control, and monitoring of supply-chain activities with the objective of creating net value, building a competitive infrastructure, leveraging worldwide logistics, synchronizing supply with demand and measuring performance globally."SCM practice draws heavily from the areas of industrial engineering, systems engineering, operations management, logistics, procurement, information technology, and marketing and strives for an integrated approach. Marketing channels play an important role in supply-chain management. Current research in supply-chain management is concerned with topics related to sustainability and risk management, among others. Some suggest that the "people dimension" of SCM, ethical issues, internal integration, transparency/visibility, and human capital/talent management are topics that have, so far, been underrepresented on the research agenda.

Exam Probability: **Low**

22. *Answer choices:*
(see index for correct answer)

- a. Supply chain management
- b. Lowboy
- c. Gas carrier
- d. Shuttle tanker

Guidance: level 1

:: Costs ::

In process improvement efforts, _________ or cost of quality is a means to quantify the total cost of quality-related efforts and deficiencies. It was first described by Armand V. Feigenbaum in a 1956 Harvard Business Review article.

Exam Probability: **Low**

23. *Answer choices:*
(see index for correct answer)

- a. Joint cost
- b. Social cost
- c. Average variable cost
- d. Direct materials cost

Guidance: level 1

:: Outsourcing ::

_________ is the practice of sourcing from the global market for goods and services across geopolitical boundaries. _________ often aims to exploit global efficiencies in the delivery of a product or service. These efficiencies include low cost skilled labor, low cost raw material and other economic factors like tax breaks and low trade tariffs. A large number of Information Technology projects and Services, including IS Applications and Mobile Apps and database services are outsourced globally to countries like Pakistan and India for more economical pricing.

Exam Probability: **Medium**

24. *Answer choices:*

(see index for correct answer)

- a. Sourcing agent
- b. Application Management Services Framework
- c. IGATE
- d. Global sourcing

Guidance: level 1

:: Metalworking ::

A _________ is a round object with various uses. It is used in _________ games, where the play of the game follows the state of the _________ as it is hit, kicked or thrown by players. _________ s can also be used for simpler activities, such as catch or juggling. _________ s made from hard-wearing materials are used in engineering applications to provide very low friction bearings, known as _________ bearings. Black-powder weapons use stone and metal _________ s as projectiles.

Exam Probability: **Low**

25. *Answer choices:*

(see index for correct answer)

- a. Centerless grinding
- b. Damascus steel
- c. Hot working
- d. Soldering

Guidance: level 1

:: Supply chain management terms ::

In business and finance, _________ is a system of organizations, people, activities, information, and resources involved inmoving a product or service from supplier to customer. _________ activities involve the transformation of natural resources, raw materials, and components into a finished product that is delivered to the end customer. In sophisticated _________ systems, used products may re-enter the _________ at any point where residual value is recyclable. _________ s link value chains.

Exam Probability: **High**

26. *Answer choices:*

(see index for correct answer)

- a. Supply chain
- b. Supply-chain management
- c. Consumables
- d. Overstock

Guidance: level 1

:: Production economics ::

_________ is the joint use of a resource or space. It is also the process of dividing and distributing. In its narrow sense, it refers to joint or alternating use of inherently finite goods, such as a common pasture or a shared residence. Still more loosely, " _________ " can actually mean giving something as an outright gift: for example, to "share" one`s food really means to give some of it as a gift. _________ is a basic component of human interaction, and is responsible for strengthening social ties and ensuring a person's well-being.

Exam Probability: **High**

27. *Answer choices:*

(see index for correct answer)

- a. Diminishing returns
- b. Sharing
- c. Post-Fordism
- d. Marginal cost

Guidance: level 1

:: Outsourcing ::

A _________ is a document that solicits proposal, often made through a bidding process, by an agency or company interested in procurement of a commodity, service, or valuable asset, to potential suppliers to submit business proposals. It is submitted early in the procurement cycle, either at the preliminary study, or procurement stage.

Exam Probability: **High**

28. *Answer choices:*

(see index for correct answer)

- a. IGATE
- b. Service review
- c. Service level objective
- d. Government of Nova Scotia

Guidance: level 1

:: Production and manufacturing ::

__________ was a management-led program to eliminate defects in industrial production that enjoyed brief popularity in American industry from 1964 to the early 1970s. Quality expert Philip Crosby later incorporated it into his "Absolutes of Quality Management" and it enjoyed a renaissance in the American automobile industry—as a performance goal more than as a program—in the 1990s. Although applicable to any type of enterprise, it has been primarily adopted within supply chains wherever large volumes of components are being purchased .

Exam Probability: **Low**

29. *Answer choices:*

(see index for correct answer)

- a. Zero Defects
- b. Back-story
- c. product lifecycle
- d. Division of labour

Guidance: level 1

:: Costs ::

In microeconomic theory, the __________ , or alternative cost, of making a particular choice is the value of the most valuable choice out of those that were not taken. In other words, opportunity that will require sacrifices.

Exam Probability: **High**

30. *Answer choices:*

(see index for correct answer)

- a. Total cost
- b. Quality costs
- c. Incremental cost-effectiveness ratio
- d. Opportunity cost

Guidance: level 1

:: Project management ::

A _________ is a professional in the field of project management. _________ s have the responsibility of the planning, procurement and execution of a project, in any undertaking that has a defined scope, defined start and a defined finish; regardless of industry. _________ s are first point of contact for any issues or discrepancies arising from within the heads of various departments in an organization before the problem escalates to higher authorities. Project management is the responsibility of a _________ . This individual seldom participates directly in the activities that produce the end result, but rather strives to maintain the progress, mutual interaction and tasks of various parties in such a way that reduces the risk of overall failure, maximizes benefits, and minimizes costs.

Exam Probability: **High**

31. *Answer choices:*

(see index for correct answer)

- a. Operational bill
- b. Gantt chart
- c. Project manager
- d. Financial plan

Guidance: level 1

:: Production economics ::

In economics and related disciplines, a _________ is a cost in making any economic trade when participating in a market.

Exam Probability: **Medium**

32. *Answer choices:*

(see index for correct answer)

- a. Transaction cost
- b. Productive capacity
- c. Capitalist mode of production
- d. Marginal product of labor

Guidance: level 1

:: Waste ::

_________ are unwanted or unusable materials. _________ is any substance which is discarded after primary use, or is worthless, defective and of no use. A by-product by contrast is a joint product of relatively minor economic value. A _________ product may become a by-product, joint product or resource through an invention that raises a _________ product`s value above zero.

Exam Probability: **High**

33. *Answer choices:*

(see index for correct answer)

- a. Bulky waste
- b. Uncontrolled waste
- c. Waste
- d. Trash Inc: The Secret Life of Garbage

Guidance: level 1

:: Management ::

_________, also known as natural process limits, are horizontal lines drawn on a statistical process control chart, usually at a distance of ±3 standard deviations of the plotted statistic from the statistic`s mean.

Exam Probability: **High**

34. *Answer choices:*

(see index for correct answer)

- a. Concept of operations
- b. Certified management consultant
- c. Performance management
- d. Action item

Guidance: level 1

:: Information technology management ::

__________ is a collective term for all approaches to prepare , support and help individuals, teams, and organizations in making organizational change. The most common change drivers include: technological evolution, process reviews, crisis, and consumer habit changes; pressure from new business entrants, acquisitions, mergers, and organizational restructuring. It includes methods that redirect or redefine the use of resources, business process, budget allocations, or other modes of operation that significantly change a company or organization. Organizational __________ considers the full organization and what needs to change, while __________ may be used solely to refer to how people and teams are affected by such organizational transition. It deals with many different disciplines, from behavioral and social sciences to information technology and business solutions.

Exam Probability: **Low**

35. *Answer choices:*

(see index for correct answer)

- a. Cumulus
- b. Infrastructure optimization
- c. Business transformation
- d. Change management

Guidance: level 1

:: Inventory ::

The __________ is the level of inventory which triggers an action to replenish that particular inventory stock. It is a minimum amount of an item which a firm holds in stock, such that, when stock falls to this amount, the item must be reordered. It is normally calculated as the forecast usage during the replenishment lead time plus safety stock. In the EOQ model, it was assumed that there is no time lag between ordering and procuring of materials. Therefore the __________ for replenishing the stocks occurs at that level when the inventory level drops to zero and because instant delivery by suppliers, the stock level bounce back.

Exam Probability: **Medium**

36. *Answer choices:*

(see index for correct answer)

- a. Reorder point
- b. Inventory bounce
- c. Buffer stock
- d. Order picking

Guidance: level 1

:: Production and manufacturing ::

A BOM can define products as they are designed , as they are ordered , as they are built , or as they are maintained . The different types of BOMs depend on the business need and use for which they are intended. In process industries, the BOM is also known as the formula, recipe, or ingredients list. The phrase "bill of material" is frequently used by engineers as an adjective to refer not to the literal bill, but to the current production configuration of a product, to distinguish it from modified or improved versions under study or in test.

Exam Probability: **Medium**

37. *Answer choices:*
(see index for correct answer)

- a. Simatic S5 PLC
- b. Predetermined motion time system
- c. Bill of materials
- d. Alarm fatigue

Guidance: level 1

:: Decision theory ::

__________ is a method developed in Japan beginning in 1966 to help transform the voice of the customer into engineering characteristics for a product. Yoji Akao, the original developer, described QFD as a "method to transform qualitative user demands into quantitative parameters, to deploy the functions forming quality, and to deploy methods for achieving the design quality into subsystems and component parts, and ultimately to specific elements of the manufacturing process." The author combined his work in quality assurance and quality control points with function deployment used in value engineering.

Exam Probability: **High**

38. *Answer choices:*
(see index for correct answer)

- a. Statistical murder
- b. Decision tree
- c. Ellsberg paradox
- d. Social and Decision Sciences

Guidance: level 1

:: Management ::

__________ is the identification, evaluation, and prioritization of risks followed by coordinated and economical application of resources to minimize, monitor, and control the probability or impact of unfortunate events or to maximize the realization of opportunities.

Exam Probability: **Medium**

39. *Answer choices:*
(see index for correct answer)

- a. Business plan
- b. Fleet management
- c. Risk management
- d. Managing stage boundaries

Guidance: level 1

:: Project management ::

__________ is a work methodology emphasizing the parallelisation of tasks , which is sometimes called simultaneous engineering or integrated product development using an integrated product team approach. It refers to an approach used in product development in which functions of design engineering, manufacturing engineering, and other functions are integrated to reduce the time required to bring a new product to market.

Exam Probability: **Medium**

40. *Answer choices:*
(see index for correct answer)

- a. Project charter
- b. Concurrent engineering

- c. Pre-construction services
- d. Project initiation document

Guidance: level 1

:: Information technology management ::

The term _________ is used to refer to periods when a system is unavailable. _________ or outage duration refers to a period of time that a system fails to provide or perform its primary function. Reliability, availability, recovery, and unavailability are related concepts.The unavailability is the proportion of a time-span that a system is unavailable or offline.This is usually a result of the system failing to function because of an unplanned event, or because of routine maintenance .

Exam Probability: **High**

41. *Answer choices:*

(see index for correct answer)

- a. Library Review
- b. Downtime
- c. One-to-one marketing
- d. Operational-level agreement

Guidance: level 1

:: Quality control tools ::

A _________ is a type of diagram that represents an algorithm, workflow or process. _________ can also be defined as a diagramatic representation of an algorithm .

Exam Probability: **High**

42. *Answer choices:*

(see index for correct answer)

- a. X-bar chart
- b. Western Electric rules
- c. Flowchart
- d. Run chart

Guidance: level 1

:: Retailing ::

_________ is the process of selling consumer goods or services to customers through multiple channels of distribution to earn a profit. _________ ers satisfy demand identified through a supply chain. The term " _________ er" is typically applied where a service provider fills the small orders of a large number of individuals, who are end-users, rather than large orders of a small number of wholesale, corporate or government clientele. Shopping generally refers to the act of buying products. Sometimes this is done to obtain final goods, including necessities such as food and clothing; sometimes it takes place as a recreational activity. Recreational shopping often involves window shopping and browsing: it does not always result in a purchase.

Exam Probability: **High**

43. *Answer choices:*

(see index for correct answer)

- a. Planogram
- b. Pop-up retail
- c. Chocolaterie
- d. Retail

Guidance: level 1

:: Quality awards ::

The _________ recognizes U.S. organizations in the business, health care, education, and nonprofit sectors for performance excellence. The Baldrige Award is the only formal recognition of the performance excellence of both public and private U.S. organizations given by the President of the United States. It is administered by the Baldrige Performance Excellence Program, which is based at and managed by the National Institute of Standards and Technology , an agency of the U.S. Department of Commerce.

Exam Probability: **Low**

44. *Answer choices:*

(see index for correct answer)

- a. Malcolm Baldrige National Quality Award
- b. European Quality Award
- c. Rajiv Gandhi National Quality Award
- d. Philippine Quality Award

Guidance: level 1

:: Project management ::

_________ is a marketing activity that does an aggregate plan for the production process, in advance of 6 to 18 months, to give an idea to management as to what quantity of materials and other resources are to be procured and when, so that the total cost of operations of the organization is kept to the minimum over that period.

Exam Probability: **Low**

45. *Answer choices:*

(see index for correct answer)

- a. Risk management plan
- b. Aggregate planning
- c. The Practice Standard for Scheduling
- d. Schedule

Guidance: level 1

:: ::

A _________ or till is a mechanical or electronic device for registering and calculating transactions at a point of sale. It is usually attached to a drawer for storing cash and other valuables. A modern _________ is usually attached to a printer that can print out receipts for record-keeping purposes.

Exam Probability: **High**

46. *Answer choices:*

(see index for correct answer)

- a. surface-level diversity
- b. Cash register
- c. information systems assessment
- d. similarity-attraction theory

Guidance: level 1

:: ::

Catalysis is the process of increasing the rate of a chemical reaction by adding a substance known as a _________ , which is not consumed in the catalyzed reaction and can continue to act repeatedly. Because of this, only very small amounts of _________ are required to alter the reaction rate in principle.

Exam Probability: **High**

47. *Answer choices:*

(see index for correct answer)

- a. Character
- b. personal values
- c. information systems assessment
- d. co-culture

Guidance: level 1

:: Industrial processes ::

A _________ is a device used for high-temperature heating. The name derives from Latin word fornax, which means oven. The heat energy to fuel a _________ may be supplied directly by fuel combustion, by electricity such as the electric arc _________ , or through induction heating in induction _________ s.

Exam Probability: **Low**

48. *Answer choices:*

(see index for correct answer)

- a. Furnace
- b. Olefin metathesis
- c. Conveyor belt furnace
- d. Dry-ice blasting

Guidance: level 1

:: Management ::

_________ is a formal technique useful where many possible courses of action are competing for attention. In essence, the problem-solver estimates the benefit delivered by each action, then selects a number of the most effective actions that deliver a total benefit reasonably close to the maximal possible one.

Exam Probability: **Medium**

49. *Answer choices:*

(see index for correct answer)

- a. Provectus IT Inc
- b. Information excellence
- c. Pareto analysis
- d. Business rule

Guidance: level 1

:: Packaging ::

In work place, _________ or job _________ means good ranking with the hypothesized conception of requirements of a role. There are two types of job _________ s: contextual and task. Task _________ is related to cognitive ability while contextual _________ is dependent upon personality. Task _________ are behavioral roles that are recognized in job descriptions and by remuneration systems, they are directly related to organizational _________ , whereas, contextual _________ are value based and additional behavioral roles that are not recognized in job descriptions and covered by compensation; they are extra roles that are indirectly related to organizational _________ . Citizenship _________ like contextual _________ means a set of individual activity/contribution that supports the organizational culture.

Exam Probability: **High**

50. *Answer choices:*

(see index for correct answer)

- a. Obi
- b. Performance
- c. Food labeling regulations
- d. ISPM 15

Guidance: level 1

:: Management ::

In organizational studies, _________ is the efficient and effective development of an organization`s resources when they are needed. Such resources may include financial resources, inventory, human skills, production resources, or information technology and natural resources.

Exam Probability: **Medium**

51. *Answer choices:*

(see index for correct answer)

- a. Management by exception
- b. Management buyout
- c. Marketing science
- d. Virtual customer environment

Guidance: level 1

:: Quality management ::

In quality management system, a _________ is a document developed by management to express the directive of the top management with respect to quality. _________ management is a strategic item.

Exam Probability: **Low**

52. *Answer choices:*

(see index for correct answer)

- a. Common Assessment Framework
- b. Product quality risk in supply chain
- c. Quality policy
- d. QC Reporting

Guidance: level 1

:: Management ::

__________ is a method of quality control which employs statistical methods to monitor and control a process. This helps to ensure that the process operates efficiently, producing more specification-conforming products with less waste . SPC can be applied to any process where the "conforming product" output can be measured. Key tools used in SPC include run charts, control charts, a focus on continuous improvement, and the design of experiments. An example of a process where SPC is applied is manufacturing lines.

Exam Probability: **High**

53. *Answer choices:*
(see index for correct answer)

- a. Information excellence
- b. Staff management
- c. Twelve leverage points
- d. Statistical process control

Guidance: level 1

:: Production and manufacturing ::

__________ consists of organization-wide efforts to "install and make permanent climate where employees continuously improve their ability to provide on demand products and services that customers will find of particular value." "Total" emphasizes that departments in addition to production are obligated to improve their operations; "management" emphasizes that executives are obligated to actively manage quality through funding, training, staffing, and goal setting. While there is no widely agreed-upon approach, TQM efforts typically draw heavily on the previously developed tools and techniques of quality control. TQM enjoyed widespread attention during the late 1980s and early 1990s before being overshadowed by ISO 9000, Lean manufacturing, and Six Sigma.

Exam Probability: **Low**

54. *Answer choices:*
(see index for correct answer)

- a. Nesting
- b. Industrial engineering
- c. Total quality management
- d. product lifecycle

Guidance: level 1

:: Production and manufacturing ::

__________ is the production under license of technology developed elsewhere. It is an especially prominent commercial practice in developing nations, which often approach __________ as a starting point for indigenous industrial development.

Exam Probability: **High**

55. *Answer choices:*

(see index for correct answer)

- a. Fieldbus Foundation
- b. Memo motion
- c. Nesting
- d. Licensed production

Guidance: level 1

:: Industrial engineering ::

__________ , in its contemporary conceptualisation, is a comparison of perceived expectations of a service with perceived performance , giving rise to the equation SQ=P-E. This conceptualistion of __________ has its origins in the expectancy-disconfirmation paradigm.

Exam Probability: **Low**

56. *Answer choices:*

(see index for correct answer)

- a. PFD allowance
- b. Therblig
- c. Service quality
- d. Operations and technology management

Guidance: level 1

:: Time management ::

__________ is the process of planning and exercising conscious control of time spent on specific activities, especially to increase effectiveness, efficiency, and productivity. It involves a juggling act of various demands upon a person relating to work, social life, family, hobbies, personal interests and commitments with the finiteness of time. Using time effectively gives the person "choice" on spending/managing activities at their own time and expediency.

Exam Probability: **Low**

57. *Answer choices:*
(see index for correct answer)

- a. Sufficient unto the day is the evil thereof
- b. Time Trek
- c. waiting room
- d. Getting Things Done

Guidance: level 1

:: Management accounting ::

" __________ s are the structural determinants of the cost of an activity, reflecting any linkages or interrelationships that affect it". Therefore we could assume that the __________ s determine the cost behavior within the activities, reflecting the links that these have with other activities and relationships that affect them.

Exam Probability: **High**

58. *Answer choices:*
(see index for correct answer)

- a. Certified Management Accountant
- b. Accounting management
- c. Cost driver
- d. Managerial risk accounting

Guidance: level 1

:: Business planning ::

__________ is an organization`s process of defining its strategy, or direction, and making decisions on allocating its resources to pursue this strategy. It may also extend to control mechanisms for guiding the implementation of the strategy. __________ became prominent in corporations during the 1960s and remains an important aspect of strategic management. It is executed by strategic planners or strategists, who involve many parties and research sources in their analysis of the organization and its relationship to the environment in which it competes.

Exam Probability: **High**

59. *Answer choices:*

(see index for correct answer)

- a. Gap analysis
- b. Customer Demand Planning
- c. Business war games
- d. Joint decision trap

Guidance: level 1

Commerce

Commerce relates to "the exchange of goods and services, especially on a large scale." It includes legal, economic, political, social, cultural and technological systems that operate in any country or internationally.

:: Project management ::

Contemporary business and science treat as a _________ any undertaking, carried out individually or collaboratively and possibly involving research or design, that is carefully planned to achieve a particular aim.

Exam Probability: **Medium**

1. *Answer choices:*

(see index for correct answer)

- a. Level of Effort
- b. Expected commercial value
- c. Resource leveling
- d. Punch list

Guidance: level 1

:: Statutory law ::

_________ or statute law is written law set down by a body of legislature or by a singular legislator . This is as opposed to oral or customary law; or regulatory law promulgated by the executive or common law of the judiciary. Statutes may originate with national, state legislatures or local municipalities.

Exam Probability: **Medium**

2. *Answer choices:*

(see index for correct answer)

- a. statute law
- b. Statutory law
- c. incorporation by reference
- d. Statute of repose

Guidance: level 1

:: Project management ::

In political science, an _________ is a means by which a petition signed by a certain minimum number of registered voters can force a government to choose to either enact a law or hold a public vote in parliament in what is called indirect _________ , or under direct _________ , the proposition is immediately put to a plebiscite or referendum, in what is called a Popular initiated Referendum or citizen-initiated referendum).

Exam Probability: **High**

3. *Answer choices:*

(see index for correct answer)

- a. Association for Project Management
- b. Initiative
- c. Executive sponsor
- d. The Goal

Guidance: level 1

:: ::

A _________ is a graphic mark, emblem, or symbol used to aid and promote public identification and recognition. It may be of an abstract or figurative design or include the text of the name it represents as in a wordmark.

Exam Probability: **Medium**

4. *Answer choices:*

(see index for correct answer)

- a. similarity-attraction theory
- b. Logo
- c. process perspective
- d. open system

Guidance: level 1

:: Auctioneering ::

_________ are electronic auctions, which can be used by sellers to sell their items to many potential buyers. Sellers and buyers can be individuals, organizations etc.

Exam Probability: **High**

5. *Answer choices:*

(see index for correct answer)

- a. English auction
- b. Forward auction
- c. Vehicle impoundment
- d. Public auction

Guidance: level 1

:: Behavior modification ::

In psychotherapy and mental health, _________ has a positive sense of empowering individuals, or a negative sense of encouraging dysfunctional behavior.

Exam Probability: **Medium**

6. *Answer choices:*

(see index for correct answer)

- a. Thought stopping
- b. Enabling

Guidance: level 1

:: ::

In legal terminology, a _________ is any formal legal document that sets out the facts and legal reasons that the filing party or parties believes are sufficient to support a claim against the party or parties against whom the claim is brought that entitles the plaintiff to a remedy . For example, the Federal Rules of Civil Procedure that govern civil litigation in United States courts provide that a civil action is commenced with the filing or service of a pleading called a _________ . Civil court rules in states that have incorporated the Federal Rules of Civil Procedure use the same term for the same pleading.

Exam Probability: **Medium**

7. *Answer choices:*

(see index for correct answer)

- a. co-culture
- b. Complaint
- c. imperative
- d. personal values

Guidance: level 1

:: Business models ::

A _________ is "an autonomous association of persons united voluntarily to meet their common economic, social, and cultural needs and aspirations through a jointly-owned and democratically-controlled enterprise". _________ s may include.

Exam Probability: **High**

8. *Answer choices:*

(see index for correct answer)

- a. Product-service system
- b. Inclusive business model
- c. Technology push
- d. Sailing Ship Effect

Guidance: level 1

:: ::

__________ s and acquisitions are transactions in which the ownership of companies, other business organizations, or their operating units are transferred or consolidated with other entities. As an aspect of strategic management, M&A can allow enterprises to grow or downsize, and change the nature of their business or competitive position.

Exam Probability: **Medium**

9. *Answer choices:*

(see index for correct answer)

- a. interpersonal communication
- b. empathy
- c. Merger
- d. similarity-attraction theory

Guidance: level 1

:: Marketing ::

__________ or stock control can be broadly defined as "the activity of checking a shop's stock." However, a more focused definition takes into account the more science-based, methodical practice of not only verifying a business' inventory but also focusing on the many related facets of inventory management "within an organisation to meet the demand placed upon that business economically." Other facets of __________ include supply chain management, production control, financial flexibility, and customer satisfaction. At the root of __________, however, is the __________ problem, which involves determining when to order, how much to order, and the logistics of those decisions.

Exam Probability: **Medium**

10. *Answer choices:*

(see index for correct answer)

- a. Product proliferation
- b. Inventory control
- c. Predatory pricing
- d. Bayesian inference in marketing

Guidance: level 1

:: Securities (finance) ::

A __________ is a container that is traditionally constructed from stiff fibers, and can be made from a range of materials, including wood splints, runners, and cane. While most __________ s are made from plant materials, other materials such as horsehair, baleen, or metal wire can be used. __________ s are generally woven by hand. Some __________ s are fitted with a lid, while others are left open on top.

Exam Probability: **Low**

11. *Answer choices:*

(see index for correct answer)

- a. Exempt market securities
- b. UNIDROIT
- c. Basket
- d. Place of the Relevant Intermediary Approach

Guidance: level 1

:: ::

In marketing jargon, product lining is offering several related products for sale individually. Unlike product bundling, where several products are combined into one group, which is then offered for sale as a units, product lining involves offering the products for sale separately. A line can comprise related products of various sizes, types, colors, qualities, or prices. Line depth refers to the number of subcategories a category has. Line consistency refers to how closely related the products that make up the line are. Line vulnerability refers to the percentage of sales or profits that are derived from only a few products in the line.

Exam Probability: **Medium**

12. *Answer choices:*

(see index for correct answer)

- a. Sarbanes-Oxley act of 2002
- b. co-culture
- c. Product line
- d. corporate values

Guidance: level 1

:: ::

A ________ or GM is an executive who has overall responsibility for managing both the revenue and cost elements of a company`s income statement, known as profit & loss responsibility. A ________ usually oversees most or all of the firm`s marketing and sales functions as well as the day-to-day operations of the business. Frequently, the ________ is responsible for effective planning, delegating, coordinating, staffing, organizing, and decision making to attain desirable profit making results for an organization .

Exam Probability: **Medium**

13. *Answer choices:*

(see index for correct answer)

- a. information systems assessment
- b. hierarchical perspective
- c. deep-level diversity
- d. General manager

Guidance: level 1

:: ::

________ is an emotion involving pleasure, , or anxiety in considering or awaiting an expected event.

Exam Probability: **Low**

14. *Answer choices:*

(see index for correct answer)

- a. functional perspective
- b. Anticipation
- c. levels of analysis
- d. personal values

Guidance: level 1

:: ::

_________ , in general use, is a devotion and faithfulness to a nation, cause, philosophy, country, group, or person. Philosophers disagree on what can be an object of _________ , as some argue that _________ is strictly interpersonal and only another human being can be the object of _________ . The definition of _________ in law and political science is the fidelity of an individual to a nation, either one`s nation of birth, or one`s declared home nation by oath .

Exam Probability: **High**

15. *Answer choices:*

(see index for correct answer)

- a. Sarbanes-Oxley act of 2002
- b. Loyalty
- c. corporate values
- d. hierarchical perspective

Guidance: level 1

:: ::

In a supply chain, a _________ , or a seller, is an enterprise that contributes goods or services. Generally, a supply chain _________ manufactures inventory/stock items and sells them to the next link in the chain. Today, these terms refer to a supplier of any good or service.

Exam Probability: **Low**

16. *Answer choices:*

(see index for correct answer)

- a. personal values
- b. empathy
- c. co-culture
- d. hierarchical

Guidance: level 1

:: ::

A _________ is a sworn body of people convened to render an impartial verdict officially submitted to them by a court, or to set a penalty or judgment. Modern juries tend to be found in courts to ascertain the guilt or lack thereof in a crime. In Anglophone jurisdictions, the verdict may be guilty or not guilty . The old institution of grand juries still exists in some places, particularly the United States, to investigate whether enough evidence of a crime exists to bring someone to trial.

Exam Probability: **High**

17. *Answer choices:*

(see index for correct answer)

- a. hierarchical perspective
- b. imperative
- c. Jury
- d. process perspective

Guidance: level 1

:: Costs ::

In economics, _________ is the total economic cost of production and is made up of variable cost, which varies according to the quantity of a good produced and includes inputs such as labour and raw materials, plus fixed cost, which is independent of the quantity of a good produced and includes inputs that cannot be varied in the short term: fixed costs such as buildings and machinery, including sunk costs if any. Since cost is measured per unit of time, it is a flow variable.

Exam Probability: **Low**

18. *Answer choices:*

(see index for correct answer)

- a. Quality costs
- b. Incremental cost-effectiveness ratio
- c. Cost competitiveness of fuel sources
- d. Average variable cost

Guidance: level 1

:: ::

In financial markets, a share is a unit used as mutual funds, limited partnerships, and real estate investment trusts. The owner of _________ in the corporation/company is a shareholder of the corporation. A share is an indivisible unit of capital, expressing the ownership relationship between the company and the shareholder. The denominated value of a share is its face value, and the total of the face value of issued _________ represent the capital of a company, which may not reflect the market value of those _________ .

Exam Probability: **Low**

19. *Answer choices:*

(see index for correct answer)

- a. empathy
- b. imperative
- c. cultural
- d. Shares

Guidance: level 1

:: Dot-com bubble ::

_________ was an online grocery business that filed bankruptcy in 2001 after 3 years of operation and was later folded into Amazon.com. It was headquartered in Foster City, California, United States. It delivered products to customers' homes within a 30-minute window of their choosing. At its peak, it offered service in ten US markets: the San Francisco Bay Area; Dallas; Sacramento; San Diego; Los Angeles; Orange County, California; Chicago; Seattle; Portland, Oregon; and Atlanta, Georgia. The company had hoped to expand to 26 cities by 2001.

Exam Probability: **Low**

20. *Answer choices:*

(see index for correct answer)

- a. Dot-com company
- b. Pay to surf
- c. Webvan
- d. Paid to surf

Guidance: level 1

:: ::

__________ or accountancy is the measurement, processing, and communication of financial information about economic entities such as businesses and corporations. The modern field was established by the Italian mathematician Luca Pacioli in 1494. __________ , which has been called the "language of business", measures the results of an organization`s economic activities and conveys this information to a variety of users, including investors, creditors, management, and regulators. Practitioners of __________ are known as accountants. The terms " __________ " and "financial reporting" are often used as synonyms.

Exam Probability: **Medium**

21. *Answer choices:*

(see index for correct answer)

- a. hierarchical
- b. surface-level diversity
- c. hierarchical perspective
- d. empathy

Guidance: level 1

:: Export and import control ::

" __________ " means the Government Service which is responsible for the administration of __________ law and the collection of duties and taxes and which also has the responsibility for the application of other laws and regulations relating to the importation, exportation, movement or storage of goods.

Exam Probability: **Low**

22. *Answer choices:*

(see index for correct answer)

- a. Export parity price
- b. Customs Modernization Act
- c. Customs
- d. Plant Protection and Quarantine

Guidance: level 1

:: Credit cards ::

The _________ Company, also known as Amex, is an American multinational financial services corporation headquartered in Three World Financial Center in New York City. The company was founded in 1850 and is one of the 30 components of the Dow Jones Industrial Average. The company is best known for its charge card, credit card, and traveler's cheque businesses.

Exam Probability: **Low**

23. *Answer choices:*

(see index for correct answer)

- a. Universal Air Travel Plan
- b. American Express
- c. Visa Black Card
- d. Medi Script

Guidance: level 1

:: ::

The _________ of 1990 is a civil rights law that prohibits discrimination based on disability. It affords similar protections against discrimination to Americans with disabilities as the Civil Rights Act of 1964, which made discrimination based on race, religion, sex, national origin, and other characteristics illegal. In addition, unlike the Civil Rights Act, the ADA also requires covered employers to provide reasonable accommodations to employees with disabilities, and imposes accessibility requirements on public accommodations.

Exam Probability: **Medium**

24. *Answer choices:*

(see index for correct answer)

- a. Americans with Disabilities Act
- b. corporate values
- c. co-culture
- d. levels of analysis

Guidance: level 1

:: ::

_________ Corporation is an American multinational technology company with headquarters in Redmond, Washington. It develops, manufactures, licenses, supports and sells computer software, consumer electronics, personal computers, and related services. Its best known software products are the _________ Windows line of operating systems, the _________ Office suite, and the Internet Explorer and Edge Web browsers. Its flagship hardware products are the Xbox video game consoles and the _________ Surface lineup of touchscreen personal computers. As of 2016, it is the world`s largest software maker by revenue, and one of the world`s most valuable companies. The word " _________ " is a portmanteau of "microcomputer" and "software". _________ is ranked No. 30 in the 2018 Fortune 500 rankings of the largest United States corporations by total revenue.

Exam Probability: **Medium**

25. *Answer choices:*

(see index for correct answer)

- a. surface-level diversity
- b. levels of analysis
- c. Character
- d. Microsoft

Guidance: level 1

:: Marketing ::

_________ is the percentage of a market accounted for by a specific entity. In a survey of nearly 200 senior marketing managers, 67% responded that they found the revenue- "dollar _________ " metric very useful, while 61% found "unit _________ " very useful.

Exam Probability: **Low**

26. *Answer choices:*

(see index for correct answer)

- a. Franchise disclosure document
- b. Cultural consumer
- c. Price on application
- d. Market share

Guidance: level 1

:: Credit cards ::

A _________ is a payment card issued to users to enable the cardholder to pay a merchant for goods and services based on the cardholder`s promise to the card issuer to pay them for the amounts plus the other agreed charges. The card issuer creates a revolving account and grants a line of credit to the cardholder, from which the cardholder can borrow money for payment to a merchant or as a cash advance.

Exam Probability: **Low**

27. *Answer choices:*

(see index for correct answer)

- a. Fuel card
- b. MPP Global Solutions
- c. Wirecard
- d. Credit card

Guidance: level 1

:: Organizational structure ::

An _________ defines how activities such as task allocation, coordination, and supervision are directed toward the achievement of organizational aims.

Exam Probability: **High**

28. *Answer choices:*

(see index for correct answer)

- a. Organization of the New York City Police Department
- b. Organizational structure
- c. The Starfish and the Spider
- d. Blessed Unrest

Guidance: level 1

:: ::

In law, a _________ is a coming together of parties to a dispute, to present information in a tribunal, a formal setting with the authority to adjudicate claims or disputes. One form of tribunal is a court. The tribunal, which may occur before a judge, jury, or other designated trier of fact, aims to achieve a resolution to their dispute.

Exam Probability: **Medium**

29. *Answer choices:*

(see index for correct answer)

- a. empathy
- b. Trial
- c. similarity-attraction theory
- d. hierarchical

Guidance: level 1

:: ::

_________ is an American restaurant chain and international franchise which was founded in 1958 by Dan and Frank Carney. The company is known for its Italian-American cuisine menu, including pizza and pasta, as well as side dishes and desserts. _________ has 18,431 restaurants worldwide as of December 31, 2018, making it the world`s largest pizza chain in terms of locations. It is a subsidiary of Yum! Brands, Inc., one of the world`s largest restaurant companies.

Exam Probability: **Low**

30. *Answer choices:*

(see index for correct answer)

- a. imperative
- b. surface-level diversity
- c. process perspective
- d. corporate values

Guidance: level 1

:: Marketing ::

__________ or stock is the goods and materials that a business holds for the ultimate goal of resale .

Exam Probability: **High**

31. *Answer choices:*

(see index for correct answer)

- a. Inventory
- b. Boston matrix
- c. Target market
- d. Licensing International Expo

Guidance: level 1

:: Banking ::

A __________ is a financial institution that accepts deposits from the public and creates credit. Lending activities can be performed either directly or indirectly through capital markets. Due to their importance in the financial stability of a country, __________ s are highly regulated in most countries. Most nations have institutionalized a system known as fractional reserve __________ ing under which __________ s hold liquid assets equal to only a portion of their current liabilities. In addition to other regulations intended to ensure liquidity, __________ s are generally subject to minimum capital requirements based on an international set of capital standards, known as the Basel Accords.

Exam Probability: **Low**

32. *Answer choices:*

(see index for correct answer)

- a. Master transaction agreement
- b. U-turn
- c. Personal account
- d. Market discipline

Guidance: level 1

:: ::

A _________ is a structured form of play, usually undertaken for enjoyment and sometimes used as an educational tool. _________ s are distinct from work, which is usually carried out for remuneration, and from art, which is more often an expression of aesthetic or ideological elements. However, the distinction is not clear-cut, and many _________ s are also considered to be work or art .

Exam Probability: **Low**

33. *Answer choices:*

(see index for correct answer)

- a. Character
- b. Game
- c. corporate values
- d. open system

Guidance: level 1

:: Payment systems ::

A _________ is any system used to settle financial transactions through the transfer of monetary value. This includes the institutions, instruments, people, rules, procedures, standards, and technologies that make it exchange possible. A common type of _________ is called an operational network that links bank accounts and provides for monetary exchange using bank deposits. Some _________ s also include credit mechanisms, which are essentially a different aspect of payment.

Exam Probability: **Medium**

34. *Answer choices:*

(see index for correct answer)

- a. Ebillz
- b. GrIDsure
- c. Payment processor
- d. Payment system

Guidance: level 1

:: E-commerce ::

Customer to customer markets provide an innovative way to allow customers to interact with each other. Traditional markets require business to customer relationships, in which a customer goes to the business in order to purchase a product or service. In customer to customer markets, the business facilitates an environment where customers can sell goods or services to each other. Other types of markets include business to business and business to customer .

Exam Probability: **Low**

35. *Answer choices:*

(see index for correct answer)

- a. Silent commerce
- b. Consumer-to-consumer
- c. Boston Computer Exchange
- d. APazari

Guidance: level 1

:: Business terms ::

_________ ning is an organization`s process of defining its strategy, or direction, and making decisions on allocating its resources to pursue this strategy. It may also extend to control mechanisms for guiding the implementation of the strategy. _________ ning became prominent in corporations during the 1960s and remains an important aspect of strategic management. It is executed by _________ ners or strategists, who involve many parties and research sources in their analysis of the organization and its relationship to the environment in which it competes.

Exam Probability: **Low**

36. *Answer choices:*

(see index for correct answer)

- a. back office
- b. year-to-date
- c. operating cost
- d. Strategic plan

Guidance: level 1

:: Minimum wage ::

A _________ is the lowest remuneration that employers can legally pay their workers—the price floor below which workers may not sell their labor. Most countries had introduced _________ legislation by the end of the 20th century.

Exam Probability: **Medium**

37. *Answer choices:*

(see index for correct answer)

- a. Minimum wage in Taiwan
- b. Working poor
- c. Guaranteed minimum income
- d. National Anti-Sweating League

Guidance: level 1

:: ::

A _________ , or also known as foreman, overseer, facilitator, monitor, area coordinator, or sometimes gaffer, is the job title of a low level management position that is primarily based on authority over a worker or charge of a workplace. A _________ can also be one of the most senior in the staff at the place of work, such as a Professor who oversees a PhD dissertation. Supervision, on the other hand, can be performed by people without this formal title, for example by parents. The term _________ itself can be used to refer to any personnel who have this task as part of their job description.

Exam Probability: **Low**

38. *Answer choices:*

(see index for correct answer)

- a. information systems assessment
- b. interpersonal communication
- c. surface-level diversity
- d. Supervisor

Guidance: level 1

:: International trade ::

_________ involves the transfer of goods or services from one person or entity to another, often in exchange for money. A system or network that allows _________ is called a market.

Exam Probability: **Low**

39. *Answer choices:*

(see index for correct answer)

- a. Agreement on Government Procurement
- b. Trade creation
- c. Hilton Quota
- d. Trade

Guidance: level 1

:: Market structure and pricing ::

_________ has historically emerged in two separate types of discussions in economics, that of Adam Smith on the one hand, and that of Karl Marx on the other hand. Adam Smith in his writing on economics stressed the importance of laissez-faire principles outlining the operation of the market in the absence of dominant political mechanisms of control, while Karl Marx discussed the working of the market in the presence of a controlled economy sometimes referred to as a command economy in the literature. Both types of _________ have been in historical evidence throughout the twentieth century and twenty-first century.

Exam Probability: **Medium**

40. *Answer choices:*

(see index for correct answer)

- a. Market structure
- b. Open source
- c. industry concentration
- d. Open-source economics

Guidance: level 1

:: Production economics ::

In economics long run is a theoretical concept where all markets are in equilibrium, and all prices and quantities have fully adjusted and are in equilibrium. The long run contrasts with the _________ where there are some constraints and markets are not fully in equilibrium.

Exam Probability: **Low**

41. *Answer choices:*
(see index for correct answer)

- a. Specialization
- b. Diminishing returns
- c. Value and Capital
- d. Short run

Guidance: level 1

:: Marketing ::

_________ comes from the Latin neg and otsia referring to businessmen who, unlike the patricians, had no leisure time in their industriousness; it held the meaning of business until the 17th century when it took on the diplomatic connotation as a dialogue between two or more people or parties intended to reach a beneficial outcome over one or more issues where a conflict exists with respect to at least one of these issues. Thus, _________ is a process of combining divergent positions into a joint agreement under a decision rule of unanimity.

Exam Probability: **Low**

42. *Answer choices:*
(see index for correct answer)

- a. Davie-Brown Index
- b. Gimmick
- c. Marketing channel
- d. elaboration likelihood model

Guidance: level 1

:: Management accounting ::

_________ s are costs that change as the quantity of the good or service that a business produces changes. _________ s are the sum of marginal costs over all units produced. They can also be considered normal costs. Fixed costs and _________ s make up the two components of total cost. Direct costs are costs that can easily be associated with a particular cost object. However, not all _________ s are direct costs. For example, variable manufacturing overhead costs are _________ s that are indirect costs, not direct costs. _________ s are sometimes called unit-level costs as they vary with the number of units produced.

Exam Probability: **High**

43. *Answer choices:*

(see index for correct answer)

- a. Cash and cash equivalents
- b. Direct material price variance
- c. Chartered Cost Accountant
- d. Variable cost

Guidance: level 1

:: ::

_________ are electronic transfer of money from one bank account to another, either within a single financial institution or across multiple institutions, via computer-based systems, without the direct intervention of bank staff.

Exam Probability: **High**

44. *Answer choices:*

(see index for correct answer)

- a. deep-level diversity
- b. surface-level diversity
- c. Electronic funds transfer
- d. imperative

Guidance: level 1

:: ::

An __________ is a systematic and independent examination of books, accounts, statutory records, documents and vouchers of an organization to ascertain how far the financial statements as well as non-financial disclosures present a true and fair view of the concern. It also attempts to ensure that the books of accounts are properly maintained by the concern as required by law. __________ ing has become such a ubiquitous phenomenon in the corporate and the public sector that academics started identifying an " __________ Society". The __________ or perceives and recognises the propositions before them for examination, obtains evidence, evaluates the same and formulates an opinion on the basis of his judgement which is communicated through their __________ ing report.

Exam Probability: **Medium**

45. *Answer choices:*

(see index for correct answer)

- a. open system
- b. Sarbanes-Oxley act of 2002
- c. similarity-attraction theory
- d. Audit

Guidance: level 1

:: Commercial item transport and distribution ::

In a contract of carriage, the __________ is the entity who is financially responsible for the receipt of a shipment. Generally, but not always, the __________ is the same as the receiver.

Exam Probability: **Medium**

46. *Answer choices:*

(see index for correct answer)

- a. Oversize load
- b. EPCglobal Network
- c. Euro container
- d. Lowboy

Guidance: level 1

:: ::

_________ is "property consisting of land and the buildings on it, along with its natural resources such as crops, minerals or water; immovable property of this nature; an interest vested in this an item of real property, buildings or housing in general. Also: the business of _________ ; the profession of buying, selling, or renting land, buildings, or housing." It is a legal term used in jurisdictions whose legal system is derived from English common law, such as India, England, Wales, Northern Ireland, United States, Canada, Pakistan, Australia, and New Zealand.

Exam Probability: **High**

47. *Answer choices:*

(see index for correct answer)

- a. Character
- b. interpersonal communication
- c. corporate values
- d. surface-level diversity

Guidance: level 1

:: Stock market ::

The _________ of a corporation is all of the shares into which ownership of the corporation is divided. In American English, the shares are commonly known as " _________ s". A single share of the _________ represents fractional ownership of the corporation in proportion to the total number of shares. This typically entitles the _________ holder to that fraction of the company`s earnings, proceeds from liquidation of assets , or voting power, often dividing these up in proportion to the amount of money each _________ holder has invested. Not all _________ is necessarily equal, as certain classes of _________ may be issued for example without voting rights, with enhanced voting rights, or with a certain priority to receive profits or liquidation proceeds before or after other classes of shareholders.

Exam Probability: **High**

48. *Answer choices:*

(see index for correct answer)

- a. Stock
- b. Matchbook FX
- c. Bellwether

- d. Automated trading system

Guidance: level 1

:: Supply chain management ::

__________ is a variable pricing strategy, based on understanding, anticipating and influencing consumer behavior in order to maximize revenue or profits from a fixed, time-limited resource . As a specific, inventory-focused branch of revenue management, __________ involves strategic control of inventory to sell the right product to the right customer at the right time for the right price. This process can result in price discrimination, in which customers consuming identical goods or services are charged different prices. __________ is a large revenue generator for several major industries; Robert Crandall, former Chairman and CEO of American Airlines, gave __________ its name and has called it "the single most important technical development in transportation management since we entered deregulation."

Exam Probability: **Medium**

49. *Answer choices:*

(see index for correct answer)

- a. Cross-border leasing
- b. Supply chain cyber security
- c. Certified Supply Chain Professional
- d. Yield management

Guidance: level 1

:: Auctioneering ::

A __________ is a type of sealed-bid auction. Bidders submit written bids without knowing the bid of the other people in the auction. The highest bidder wins but the price paid is the second-highest bid. This type of auction is strategically similar to an English auction and gives bidders an incentive to bid their true value. The auction was first described academically by Columbia University professor William Vickrey in 1961 though it had been used by stamp collectors since 1893. In 1797 Johann Wolfgang von Goethe sold a manuscript using a sealed-bid, second-price auction.

Exam Probability: **Low**

50. *Answer choices:*

(see index for correct answer)

- a. Name Your Own Price
- b. Bid shading
- c. Calcutta auction
- d. Vickrey auction

Guidance: level 1

:: ::

In economics _________ is a theoretical concept where all markets are in equilibrium, and all prices and quantities have fully adjusted and are in equilibrium. The _________ contrasts with the short run where there are some constraints and markets are not fully in equilibrium.

Exam Probability: **Medium**

51. *Answer choices:*

(see index for correct answer)

- a. hierarchical perspective
- b. Long run
- c. functional perspective
- d. Character

Guidance: level 1

:: Business law ::

A _________ is a business entity created by two or more parties, generally characterized by shared ownership, shared returns and risks, and shared governance. Companies typically pursue _________ s for one of four reasons: to access a new market, particularly emerging markets; to gain scale efficiencies by combining assets and operations; to share risk for major investments or projects; or to access skills and capabilities.

Exam Probability: **Low**

52. *Answer choices:*

(see index for correct answer)

- a. Joint venture
- b. Arbitration clause

- c. WIPO Copyright Treaty
- d. TRIPS Agreement

Guidance: level 1

:: Evaluation ::

__________ is a way of preventing mistakes and defects in manufactured products and avoiding problems when delivering products or services to customers; which ISO 9000 defines as "part of quality management focused on providing confidence that quality requirements will be fulfilled". This defect prevention in __________ differs subtly from defect detection and rejection in quality control and has been referred to as a shift left since it focuses on quality earlier in the process .

Exam Probability: **Medium**

53. *Answer choices:*

(see index for correct answer)

- a. XTS-400
- b. Continuous assessment
- c. Technology assessment
- d. Quality assurance

Guidance: level 1

:: Strategic alliances ::

A __________ is an agreement between two or more parties to pursue a set of agreed upon objectives needed while remaining independent organizations. A __________ will usually fall short of a legal partnership entity, agency, or corporate affiliate relationship. Typically, two companies form a __________ when each possesses one or more business assets or have expertise that will help the other by enhancing their businesses. __________ s can develop in outsourcing relationships where the parties desire to achieve long-term win-win benefits and innovation based on mutually desired outcomes.

Exam Probability: **High**

54. *Answer choices:*

(see index for correct answer)

- a. International joint venture

- b. Defensive termination
- c. Cross-licensing
- d. Bridge Alliance

Guidance: level 1

:: Insolvency ::

_________ is the process in accounting by which a company is brought to an end in the United Kingdom, Republic of Ireland and United States. The assets and property of the company are redistributed. _________ is also sometimes referred to as winding-up or dissolution, although dissolution technically refers to the last stage of _________ . The process of _________ also arises when customs, an authority or agency in a country responsible for collecting and safeguarding customs duties, determines the final computation or ascertainment of the duties or drawback accruing on an entry.

Exam Probability: **Low**

55. *Answer choices:*

(see index for correct answer)

- a. Financial distress
- b. Insolvency law of Russia
- c. Liquidator
- d. Debt consolidation

Guidance: level 1

:: Production economics ::

In economics, _________ is the change in the total cost that arises when the quantity produced is incremented by one unit; that is, it is the cost of producing one more unit of a good. Intuitively, _________ at each level of production includes the cost of any additional inputs required to produce the next unit. At each level of production and time period being considered, _________ s include all costs that vary with the level of production, whereas other costs that do not vary with production are fixed and thus have no _________ . For example, the _________ of producing an automobile will generally include the costs of labor and parts needed for the additional automobile but not the fixed costs of the factory that have already been incurred. In practice, marginal analysis is segregated into short and long-run cases, so that, over the long run, all costs become marginal. Where there are economies of scale, prices set at _________ will fail to cover total costs, thus requiring a subsidy. _________ pricing is not a matter of merely lowering the general level of prices with the aid of a subsidy; with or without subsidy it calls for a drastic restructuring of pricing practices, with opportunities for very substantial improvements in efficiency at critical points.

Exam Probability: **High**

56. *Answer choices:*

(see index for correct answer)

- a. Learning-by-doing
- b. Marginal cost
- c. Productive capacity
- d. Marginal rate of technical substitution

Guidance: level 1

:: Business law ::

A _________ is a group of people who jointly supervise the activities of an organization, which can be either a for-profit business, nonprofit organization, or a government agency. Such a board`s powers, duties, and responsibilities are determined by government regulations and the organization`s own constitution and bylaws. These authorities may specify the number of members of the board, how they are to be chosen, and how often they are to meet.

Exam Probability: **High**

57. *Answer choices:*

(see index for correct answer)

- a. Industrial relations
- b. Enhanced use lease
- c. Board of directors
- d. Forged endorsement

Guidance: level 1

:: Business terms ::

The __________ or reception is an area where visitors arrive and first encounter a staff at a place of business. __________ staff will deal with whatever question the visitor has and put them in contact with a relevant person at the company. Broadly speaking, the __________ includes roles that affect the revenues of the business. The term __________ is in contrast to the term back office which refers to a company's operations, personnel, accounting, payroll and financial departments which do not interact directly with customers.

Exam Probability: **Medium**

58. *Answer choices:*

(see index for correct answer)

- a. Front office
- b. customer base
- c. operating cost
- d. churn rate

Guidance: level 1

:: ::

In Western musical notation, the staff or stave is a set of five horizontal lines and four spaces that each represent a different musical pitch or in the case of a percussion staff, different percussion instruments. Appropriate music symbols, depending on the intended effect, are placed on the staff according to their corresponding pitch or function. Musical notes are placed by pitch, percussion notes are placed by instrument, and rests and other symbols are placed by convention.

Exam Probability: **Low**

59. *Answer choices:*

(see index for correct answer)

- a. Staff position
- b. imperative
- c. functional perspective
- d. corporate values

Guidance: level 1

Business ethics

Business ethics (also known as corporate ethics) is a form of applied ethics or professional ethics, that examines ethical principles and moral or ethical problems that can arise in a business environment. It applies to all aspects of business conduct and is relevant to the conduct of individuals and entire organizations. These ethics originate from individuals, organizational statements or from the legal system. These norms, values, ethical, and unethical practices are what is used to guide business. They help those businesses maintain a better connection with their stakeholders.

:: Workplace ::

In business management, _________ is a management style whereby a manager closely observes and/or controls the work of his/her subordinates or employees.

Exam Probability: **Low**

1. *Answer choices:*

(see index for correct answer)

- a. Micromanagement
- b. Staff turnover
- c. Workplace conflict
- d. Workplace relationships

Guidance: level 1

:: ::

__________ is the means to see, hear, or become aware of something or someone through our fundamental senses. The term __________ derives from the Latin word perceptio, and is the organization, identification, and interpretation of sensory information in order to represent and understand the presented information, or the environment.

Exam Probability: **Medium**

2. *Answer choices:*

(see index for correct answer)

- a. levels of analysis
- b. Sarbanes-Oxley act of 2002
- c. Perception
- d. hierarchical

Guidance: level 1

:: ::

__________ is a non-governmental environmental organization with offices in over 39 countries and an international coordinating body in Amsterdam, the Netherlands. __________ was founded in 1971 by Irving Stowe, and Dorothy Stowe, Canadian and US ex-pat environmental activists. __________ states its goal is to "ensure the ability of the Earth to nurture life in all its diversity" and focuses its campaigning on worldwide issues such as climate change, deforestation, overfishing, commercial whaling, genetic engineering, and anti-nuclear issues. It uses direct action, lobbying, research, and ecotage to achieve its goals. The global organization does not accept funding from governments, corporations, or political parties, relying on three million individual supporters and foundation grants. __________ has a general consultative status with the United Nations Economic and Social Council and is a founding member of the INGO Accountability Charter, an international non-governmental organization that intends to foster accountability and transparency of non-governmental organizations.

Exam Probability: **Low**

3. *Answer choices:*

(see index for correct answer)

- a. empathy
- b. Greenpeace

- c. open system
- d. hierarchical

Guidance: level 1

:: ::

In regulatory jurisdictions that provide for it , _________ is a group of laws and organizations designed to ensure the rights of consumers as well as fair trade, competition and accurate information in the marketplace. The laws are designed to prevent the businesses that engage in fraud or specified unfair practices from gaining an advantage over competitors. They may also provides additional protection for those most vulnerable in society. _________ laws are a form of government regulation that aim to protect the rights of consumers. For example, a government may require businesses to disclose detailed information about products—particularly in areas where safety or public health is an issue, such as food.

Exam Probability: **Low**

4. *Answer choices:*

(see index for correct answer)

- a. cultural
- b. Consumer Protection
- c. surface-level diversity
- d. levels of analysis

Guidance: level 1

:: Corporate scandals ::

The _________ was a privately held international group of financial services companies controlled by Allen Stanford, until it was seized by United States authorities in early 2009. Headquartered in the Galleria Tower II in Uptown Houston, Texas, it had 50 offices in several countries, mainly in the Americas, included the Stanford International Bank, and said it managed US$8.5 billion of assets for more than 30,000 clients in 136 countries on six continents. On February 17, 2009, U.S. Federal agents placed the company into receivership due to charges of fraud. Ten days later, the U.S. Securities and Exchange Commission amended its complaint to accuse Stanford of turning the company into a "massive Ponzi scheme".

Exam Probability: **Low**

5. *Answer choices:*

(see index for correct answer)

- a. Milberg
- b. PurchasePro
- c. Saradha Group financial scandal
- d. Lerner Newspapers

Guidance: level 1

:: Utilitarianism ::

__________ is a family of consequentialist ethical theories that promotes actions that maximize happiness and well-being for the majority of a population. Although different varieties of __________ admit different characterizations, the basic idea behind all of them is to in some sense maximize utility, which is often defined in terms of well-being or related concepts. For instance, Jeremy Bentham, the founder of __________, described utility as

Exam Probability: **Low**

6. *Answer choices:*

(see index for correct answer)

- a. Utilitarianism
- b. Preference utilitarianism
- c. Informed judge
- d. Felicific calculus

Guidance: level 1

:: Human resource management ::

_________ encompasses values and behaviors that contribute to the unique social and psychological environment of a business. The _________ influences the way people interact, the context within which knowledge is created, the resistance they will have towards certain changes, and ultimately the way they share knowledge. _________ represents the collective values, beliefs and principles of organizational members and is a product of factors such as history, product, market, technology, strategy, type of employees, management style, and national culture; culture includes the organization`s vision, values, norms, systems, symbols, language, assumptions, environment, location, beliefs and habits.

Exam Probability: **High**

7. *Answer choices:*

(see index for correct answer)

- a. Competency-based recruitment
- b. Organizational culture
- c. T-shaped skills
- d. Job enrichment

Guidance: level 1

:: ::

A _________ is an astronomical body orbiting a star or stellar remnant that is massive enough to be rounded by its own gravity, is not massive enough to cause thermonuclear fusion, and has cleared its neighbouring region of _________ esimals.

Exam Probability: **Low**

8. *Answer choices:*

(see index for correct answer)

- a. Planet
- b. corporate values
- c. cultural
- d. personal values

Guidance: level 1

:: Separation of investment and commercial banking ::

The _________ refers to § 619 of the Dodd–Frank Wall Street Reform and Consumer Protection Act . The rule was originally proposed by American economist and former United States Federal Reserve Chairman Paul Volcker to restrict United States banks from making certain kinds of speculative investments that do not benefit their customers. Volcker argued that such speculative activity played a key role in the financial crisis of 2007–2008. The rule is often referred to as a ban on proprietary trading by commercial banks, whereby deposits are used to trade on the bank`s own accounts, although a number of exceptions to this ban were included in the Dodd-Frank law.

Exam Probability: **Low**

9. *Answer choices:*

(see index for correct answer)

- a. Merchant bank
- b. Bank holding company
- c. Volcker Rule
- d. Commercial bank

Guidance: level 1

:: ::

_________ or accountancy is the measurement, processing, and communication of financial information about economic entities such as businesses and corporations. The modern field was established by the Italian mathematician Luca Pacioli in 1494. _________ , which has been called the "language of business", measures the results of an organization`s economic activities and conveys this information to a variety of users, including investors, creditors, management, and regulators. Practitioners of _________ are known as accountants. The terms " _________ " and "financial reporting" are often used as synonyms.

Exam Probability: **Medium**

10. *Answer choices:*

(see index for correct answer)

- a. co-culture
- b. open system
- c. Accounting
- d. interpersonal communication

Guidance: level 1

:: Occupational safety and health ::

_________ is a chemical element with symbol Pb and atomic number 82. It is a heavy metal that is denser than most common materials. _________ is soft and malleable, and also has a relatively low melting point. When freshly cut, _________ is silvery with a hint of blue; it tarnishes to a dull gray color when exposed to air. _________ has the highest atomic number of any stable element and three of its isotopes are endpoints of major nuclear decay chains of heavier elements.

Exam Probability: **High**

11. *Answer choices:*

(see index for correct answer)

- a. Asbestos-related diseases
- b. Manganese
- c. Defensible space
- d. Lead

Guidance: level 1

:: Television terminology ::

A _________ organization , also known as a non-business entity, not-for-profit organization, or _________ institution, is dedicated to furthering a particular social cause or advocating for a shared point of view. In economic terms, it is an organization that uses its surplus of the revenues to further achieve its ultimate objective, rather than distributing its income to the organization`s shareholders, leaders, or members. _________ s are tax exempt or charitable, meaning they do not pay income tax on the money that they receive for their organization. They can operate in religious, scientific, research, or educational settings.

Exam Probability: **Medium**

12. *Answer choices:*

(see index for correct answer)

- a. Satellite television
- b. not-for-profit

- c. Nonprofit
- d. distance learning

Guidance: level 1

:: Hazard analysis ::

Broadly speaking, a _________ is the combined effort of 1. identifying and analyzing potential events that may negatively impact individuals, assets, and/or the environment ; and 2. making judgments "on the tolerability of the risk on the basis of a risk analysis" while considering influencing factors . Put in simpler terms, a _________ analyzes what can go wrong, how likely it is to happen, what the potential consequences are, and how tolerable the identified risk is. As part of this process, the resulting determination of risk may be expressed in a quantitative or qualitative fashion. The _________ is an inherent part of an overall risk management strategy, which attempts to, after a _________ , "introduce control measures to eliminate or reduce" any potential risk-related consequences.

Exam Probability: **Low**

13. *Answer choices:*

(see index for correct answer)

- a. Risk assessment
- b. Swiss cheese model
- c. Hazard identification

Guidance: level 1

:: Decentralization ::

_________ or sub _________ mainly refers to the unrestricted growth in many urban areas of housing, commercial development, and roads over large expanses of land, with little concern for urban planning. In addition to describing a particular form of urbanization, the term also relates to the social and environmental consequences associated with this development. In Continental Europe the term "peri-urbanisation" is often used to denote similar dynamics and phenomena, although the term _________ is currently being used by the European Environment Agency. There is widespread disagreement about what constitutes sprawl and how to quantify it. For example, some commentators measure sprawl only with the average number of residential units per acre in a given area. But others associate it with decentralization , discontinuity , segregation of uses, and so forth.

Exam Probability: **High**

14. *Answer choices:*

(see index for correct answer)

- a. Federated state
- b. Fiscal federalism
- c. Political innovation
- d. Middlebury Institute

Guidance: level 1

:: Market-based policy instruments ::

Cause marketing is defined as a type of corporate social responsibility, in which a company's promotional campaign has the dual purpose of increasing profitability while bettering society.

Exam Probability: **Medium**

15. *Answer choices:*

(see index for correct answer)

- a. Energy Tax Act
- b. Feebate
- c. Regional Clean Air Incentives Market
- d. Tree credits

Guidance: level 1

:: ::

The American Recovery and Reinvestment Act of 2009 , nicknamed the _________ , was a stimulus package enacted by the 111th U.S. Congress and signed into law by President Barack Obama in February 2009. Developed in response to the Great Recession, the ARRA`s primary objective was to save existing jobs and create new ones as soon as possible. Other objectives were to provide temporary relief programs for those most affected by the recession and invest in infrastructure, education, health, and renewable energy.

Exam Probability: **Medium**

16. *Answer choices:*

(see index for correct answer)

- a. similarity-attraction theory
- b. Recovery Act
- c. surface-level diversity
- d. functional perspective

Guidance: level 1

:: ::

_________ is the study and management of exchange relationships. _________ is the business process of creating relationships with and satisfying customers. With its focus on the customer, _________ is one of the premier components of business management.

Exam Probability: **Low**

17. *Answer choices:*

(see index for correct answer)

- a. deep-level diversity
- b. Marketing
- c. similarity-attraction theory
- d. co-culture

Guidance: level 1

:: Electronic feedback ::

__________ occurs when outputs of a system are routed back as inputs as part of a chain of cause-and-effect that forms a circuit or loop. The system can then be said to feed back into itself. The notion of cause-and-effect has to be handled carefully when applied to __________ systems.

Exam Probability: **High**

18. *Answer choices:*
(see index for correct answer)

- a. Feedback
- b. feedback loop

Guidance: level 1

:: Organizational structure ::

An __________ defines how activities such as task allocation, coordination, and supervision are directed toward the achievement of organizational aims.

Exam Probability: **Medium**

19. *Answer choices:*
(see index for correct answer)

- a. The Starfish and the Spider
- b. Blessed Unrest
- c. Organization of the New York City Police Department
- d. Organizational structure

Guidance: level 1

:: Renewable energy ::

A __________ is a fuel that is produced through contemporary biological processes, such as agriculture and anaerobic digestion, rather than a fuel produced by geological processes such as those involved in the formation of fossil fuels, such as coal and petroleum, from prehistoric biological matter. If the source biomatter can regrow quickly, the resulting fuel is said to be a form of renewable energy.

Exam Probability: **High**

20. *Answer choices:*

(see index for correct answer)

- a. Waste heat recovery unit
- b. GREEN Cell Shipping
- c. Agency for Renewable Resources
- d. Biofuel

Guidance: level 1

:: ::

Bernard Lawrence _________ is an American former market maker, investment advisor, financier, fraudster, and convicted felon, who is currently serving a federal prison sentence for offenses related to a massive Ponzi scheme. He is the former non-executive chairman of the NASDAQ stock market, the confessed operator of the largest Ponzi scheme in world history, and the largest financial fraud in U.S. history. Prosecutors estimated the fraud to be worth $64.8 billion based on the amounts in the accounts of _________ `s 4,800 clients as of November 30, 2008.

Exam Probability: **Medium**

21. *Answer choices:*

(see index for correct answer)

- a. open system
- b. Madoff
- c. imperative
- d. process perspective

Guidance: level 1

:: ::

An _________ is the release of a liquid petroleum hydrocarbon into the environment, especially the marine ecosystem, due to human activity, and is a form of pollution. The term is usually given to marine _________ s, where oil is released into the ocean or coastal waters, but spills may also occur on land. _________ s may be due to releases of crude oil from tankers, offshore platforms, drilling rigs and wells, as well as spills of refined petroleum products and their by-products, heavier fuels used by large ships such as bunker fuel, or the spill of any oily refuse or waste oil.

Exam Probability: **High**

22. *Answer choices:*

(see index for correct answer)

- a. information systems assessment
- b. interpersonal communication
- c. corporate values
- d. Oil spill

Guidance: level 1

:: ::

The _________ is an 1848 political pamphlet by the German philosophers Karl Marx and Friedrich Engels. Commissioned by the Communist League and originally published in London just as the Revolutions of 1848 began to erupt, the Manifesto was later recognised as one of the world`s most influential political documents. It presents an analytical approach to the class struggle and the conflicts of capitalism and the capitalist mode of production, rather than a prediction of communism`s potential future forms.

Exam Probability: **Medium**

23. *Answer choices:*

(see index for correct answer)

- a. levels of analysis
- b. open system
- c. surface-level diversity
- d. Communist Manifesto

Guidance: level 1

:: ::

A _________ is a form of business network, for example, a local organization of businesses whose goal is to further the interests of businesses. Business owners in towns and cities form these local societies to advocate on behalf of the business community. Local businesses are members, and they elect a board of directors or executive council to set policy for the chamber. The board or council then hires a President, CEO or Executive Director, plus staffing appropriate to size, to run the organization.

Exam Probability: **Low**

24. *Answer choices:*

(see index for correct answer)

- a. empathy
- b. process perspective
- c. corporate values
- d. cultural

Guidance: level 1

:: Business ethics ::

_______ is a type of international private business self-regulation. While once it was possible to describe CSR as an internal organisational policy or a corporate ethic strategy, that time has passed as various international laws have been developed and various organisations have used their authority to push it beyond individual or even industry-wide initiatives. While it has been considered a form of corporate self-regulation for some time, over the last decade or so it has moved considerably from voluntary decisions at the level of individual organisations, to mandatory schemes at regional, national and even transnational levels.

Exam Probability: **Medium**

25. *Answer choices:*

(see index for correct answer)

- a. Burson-Marsteller
- b. Hostile work environment
- c. Foreign official
- d. Corporate social responsibility

Guidance: level 1

:: Progressive Era in the United States ::

The Clayton Antitrust Act of 1914 , was a part of United States antitrust law with the goal of adding further substance to the U.S. antitrust law regime; the _________ sought to prevent anticompetitive practices in their incipiency. That regime started with the Sherman Antitrust Act of 1890, the first Federal law outlawing practices considered harmful to consumers . The _________ specified particular prohibited conduct, the three-level enforcement scheme, the exemptions, and the remedial measures.

Exam Probability: **High**

26. *Answer choices:*

(see index for correct answer)

- a. Clayton Act
- b. Clayton Antitrust Act
- c. pragmatism

Guidance: level 1

:: Management ::

_________ or executive pay is composed of the financial compensation and other non-financial awards received by an executive from their firm for their service to the organization. It is typically a mixture of salary, bonuses, shares of or call options on the company stock, benefits, and perquisites, ideally configured to take into account government regulations, tax law, the desires of the organization and the executive, and rewards for performance.

Exam Probability: **Low**

27. *Answer choices:*

(see index for correct answer)

- a. Executive compensation
- b. Dominant design
- c. Project management simulation
- d. Meeting

Guidance: level 1

:: Business ::

__________ , or built-in obsolescence, in industrial design and economics is a policy of planning or designing a product with an artificially limited useful life, so that it becomes obsolete after a certain period of time. The rationale behind this strategy is to generate long-term sales volume by reducing the time between repeat purchases .

Exam Probability: **Medium**

28. *Answer choices:*
(see index for correct answer)

- a. Planned obsolescence
- b. Ian McLeod
- c. Disappointment
- d. Absentee business owner

Guidance: level 1

:: ::

The __________ is an agency of the United States Department of Labor. Congress established the agency under the Occupational Safety and Health Act , which President Richard M. Nixon signed into law on December 29, 1970. OSHA`s mission is to "assure safe and healthy working conditions for working men and women by setting and enforcing standards and by providing training, outreach, education and assistance". The agency is also charged with enforcing a variety of whistleblower statutes and regulations. OSHA is currently headed by Acting Assistant Secretary of Labor Loren Sweatt. OSHA`s workplace safety inspections have been shown to reduce injury rates and injury costs without adverse effects to employment, sales, credit ratings, or firm survival.

Exam Probability: **Low**

29. *Answer choices:*
(see index for correct answer)

- a. hierarchical perspective
- b. surface-level diversity
- c. interpersonal communication
- d. similarity-attraction theory

Guidance: level 1

:: ::

_________ is the collection of mechanisms, processes and relations by which corporations are controlled and operated. Governance structures and principles identify the distribution of rights and responsibilities among different participants in the corporation and include the rules and procedures for making decisions in corporate affairs. _________ is necessary because of the possibility of conflicts of interests between stakeholders, primarily between shareholders and upper management or among shareholders.

Exam Probability: **High**

30. *Answer choices:*

(see index for correct answer)

- a. cultural
- b. Corporate governance
- c. levels of analysis
- d. Character

Guidance: level 1

:: United Kingdom labour law ::

The _________ was a series of programs, public work projects, financial reforms, and regulations enacted by President Franklin D. Roosevelt in the United States between 1933 and 1936. It responded to needs for relief, reform, and recovery from the Great Depression. Major federal programs included the Civilian Conservation Corps , the Civil Works Administration , the Farm Security Administration , the National Industrial Recovery Act of 1933 and the Social Security Administration . They provided support for farmers, the unemployed, youth and the elderly. The _________ included new constraints and safeguards on the banking industry and efforts to re-inflate the economy after prices had fallen sharply. _________ programs included both laws passed by Congress as well as presidential executive orders during the first term of the presidency of Franklin D. Roosevelt.

Exam Probability: **High**

31. *Answer choices:*

(see index for correct answer)

- a. Information and Consultation of Employees Regulations 2004
- b. Employment Act 2008

- c. Truck Acts
- d. Eleventh and Final Report of the Royal Commissioners appointed to Inquire into the Organization and Rules of Trades Unions and Other Associations

Guidance: level 1

:: Confidence tricks ::

A _________ is a business model that recruits members via a promise of payments or services for enrolling others into the scheme, rather than supplying investments or sale of products. As recruiting multiplies, recruiting becomes quickly impossible, and most members are unable to profit; as such, _________ s are unsustainable and often illegal.

Exam Probability: **High**

32. *Answer choices:*

(see index for correct answer)

- a. BioPerformance
- b. Sucker list
- c. Shell game
- d. First International Bank of Grenada

Guidance: level 1

:: Business ethics ::

_________ is a type of harassment technique that relates to a sexual nature and the unwelcome or inappropriate promise of rewards in exchange for sexual favors. _________ includes a range of actions from mild transgressions to sexual abuse or assault. Harassment can occur in many different social settings such as the workplace, the home, school, churches, etc. Harassers or victims may be of any gender.

Exam Probability: **High**

33. *Answer choices:*

(see index for correct answer)

- a. Nishkam Karma
- b. International Association for Business and Society
- c. Ethical corporate social responsibility
- d. Sexual harassment

Guidance: level 1

:: ::

A __________ is a proceeding by a party or parties against another in the civil court of law.The archaic term "suit in law" is found in only a small number of laws still in effect today.The term " __________ " is used in reference to a civil action brought in a court of law in which a plaintiff, a party who claims to have incurred loss as a result of a defendant's actions, demands a legal or equitable remedy. The defendant is required to respond to the plaintiff's complaint. If the plaintiff is successful, judgment is in the plaintiff's favor, and a variety of court orders may be issued to enforce a right, award damages, or impose a temporary or permanent injunction to prevent an act or compel an act. A declaratory judgment may be issued to prevent future legal disputes.

Exam Probability: **High**

34. *Answer choices:*

(see index for correct answer)

- a. deep-level diversity
- b. Lawsuit
- c. corporate values
- d. hierarchical

Guidance: level 1

:: Employment compensation ::

A __________ is the minimum income necessary for a worker to meet their basic needs. Needs are defined to include food, housing, and other essential needs such as clothing. The goal of a __________ is to allow a worker to afford a basic but decent standard of living. Due to the flexible nature of the term "needs", there is not one universally accepted measure of what a __________ is and as such it varies by location and household type.

Exam Probability: **Medium**

35. *Answer choices:*

(see index for correct answer)

- a. Living wage

- b. Basic Income Earth Network
- c. Annual enrollment
- d. General Schedule

Guidance: level 1

:: Timber industry ::

The _________ is an international non-profit, multi-stakeholder organization established in 1993 to promote responsible management of the world's forests. The FSC does this by setting standards on forest products, along with certifying and labeling them as eco-friendly.

Exam Probability: **Medium**

36. *Answer choices:*

(see index for correct answer)

- a. Brettstapel
- b. Ottawa River timber trade
- c. Timber recycling
- d. Forest Stewardship Council

Guidance: level 1

:: Coal ::

_________ is a combustible black or brownish-black sedimentary rock, formed as rock strata called _________ seams. _________ is mostly carbon with variable amounts of other elements; chiefly hydrogen, sulfur, oxygen, and nitrogen. _________ is formed if dead plant matter decays into peat and over millions of years the heat and pressure of deep burial converts the peat into _________ . Vast deposits of _________ originates in former wetlands—called _________ forests—that covered much of the Earth's tropical land areas during the late Carboniferous and Permian times.

Exam Probability: **Low**

37. *Answer choices:*

(see index for correct answer)

- a. Lignite
- b. Coal
- c. Ethanol from coal
- d. Leonardite

Guidance: level 1

:: Offshoring ::

A _________ is the temporary suspension or permanent termination of employment of an employee or, more commonly, a group of employees for business reasons, such as personnel management or downsizing an organization. Originally, _________ referred exclusively to a temporary interruption in work, or employment but this has evolved to a permanent elimination of a position in both British and US English, requiring the addition of "temporary" to specify the original meaning of the word. A _________ is not to be confused with wrongful termination. Laid off workers or displaced workers are workers who have lost or left their jobs because their employer has closed or moved, there was insufficient work for them to do, or their position or shift was abolished . Downsizing in a company is defined to involve the reduction of employees in a workforce. Downsizing in companies became a popular practice in the 1980s and early 1990s as it was seen as a way to deliver better shareholder value as it helps to reduce the costs of employers . Indeed, recent research on downsizing in the U.S., UK, and Japan suggests that downsizing is being regarded by management as one of the preferred routes to help declining organizations, cutting unnecessary costs, and improve organizational performance. Usually a _________ occurs as a cost cutting measure.

Exam Probability: **High**

38. *Answer choices:*

(see index for correct answer)

- a. Antex
- b. Avasant
- c. Offshore outsourcing
- d. American Jobs

Guidance: level 1

:: ::

__________ in the United States is a federal and state program that helps with medical costs for some people with limited income and resources. __________ also offers benefits not normally covered by Medicare, including nursing home care and personal care services. The Health Insurance Association of America describes __________ as "a government insurance program for persons of all ages whose income and resources are insufficient to pay for health care." __________ is the largest source of funding for medical and health-related services for people with low income in the United States, providing free health insurance to 74 million low-income and disabled people as of 2017. It is a means-tested program that is jointly funded by the state and federal governments and managed by the states, with each state currently having broad leeway to determine who is eligible for its implementation of the program. States are not required to participate in the program, although all have since 1982. __________ recipients must be U.S. citizens or qualified non-citizens, and may include low-income adults, their children, and people with certain disabilities. Poverty alone does not necessarily qualify someone for __________ .

Exam Probability: **Low**

39. *Answer choices:*

(see index for correct answer)

- a. functional perspective
- b. interpersonal communication
- c. Sarbanes-Oxley act of 2002
- d. Medicaid

Guidance: level 1

:: ::

The _________ of 1973 serves as the enacting legislation to carry out the provisions outlined in The Convention on International Trade in Endangered Species of Wild Fauna and Flora . Designed to protect critically imperiled species from extinction as a "consequence of economic growth and development untempered by adequate concern and conservation", the ESA was signed into law by President Richard Nixon on December 28, 1973. The law requires federal agencies to consult with the Fish and Wildlife Service &/or the NOAA Fisheries Service to ensure their actions are not likely to jeopardize the continued existence of any listed species or result in the destruction or adverse modification of designated critical habitat of such species. The U.S. Supreme Court found that "the plain intent of Congress in enacting" the ESA "was to halt and reverse the trend toward species extinction, whatever the cost." The Act is administered by two federal agencies, the United States Fish and Wildlife Service and the National Marine Fisheries Service .

Exam Probability: **Medium**

40. *Answer choices:*

(see index for correct answer)

- a. Endangered Species Act
- b. levels of analysis
- c. cultural
- d. information systems assessment

Guidance: level 1

:: Leadership ::

_________ is leadership that is directed by respect for ethical beliefs and values and for the dignity and rights of others. It is thus related to concepts such as trust, honesty, consideration, charisma, and fairness.

Exam Probability: **Low**

41. *Answer choices:*

(see index for correct answer)

- a. Evolutionary leadership theory
- b. Sex differences in leadership
- c. Transformational leadership
- d. Ethical leadership

Guidance: level 1

:: ::

_________ is "property consisting of land and the buildings on it, along with its natural resources such as crops, minerals or water; immovable property of this nature; an interest vested in this an item of real property, buildings or housing in general. Also: the business of _________ ; the profession of buying, selling, or renting land, buildings, or housing." It is a legal term used in jurisdictions whose legal system is derived from English common law, such as India, England, Wales, Northern Ireland, United States, Canada, Pakistan, Australia, and New Zealand.

Exam Probability: **Low**

42. *Answer choices:*
(see index for correct answer)

- a. Sarbanes-Oxley act of 2002
- b. process perspective
- c. Real estate
- d. corporate values

Guidance: level 1

:: Real estate ::

_________ s serve several societal needs – primarily as shelter from weather, security, living space, privacy, to store belongings, and to comfortably live and work. A _________ as a shelter represents a physical division of the human habitat and the outside .

Exam Probability: **Low**

43. *Answer choices:*
(see index for correct answer)

- a. 3D floor plan
- b. Rent control
- c. Building
- d. Property cycle

Guidance: level 1

:: Patent law ::

A __________ is generally any statement intended to specify or delimit the scope of rights and obligations that may be exercised and enforced by parties in a legally recognized relationship. In contrast to other terms for legally operative language, the term __________ usually implies situations that involve some level of uncertainty, waiver, or risk.

Exam Probability: **Low**

44. *Answer choices:*

(see index for correct answer)

- a. SCRIPDB
- b. Opposition proceeding
- c. Patent Busting Project
- d. Disclaimer

Guidance: level 1

:: Majority–minority relations ::

It was established as axiomatic in anthropological research by Franz Boas in the first few decades of the 20th century and later popularized by his students. Boas first articulated the idea in 1887: "civilization is not something absolute, but ... is relative, and ... our ideas and conceptions are true only so far as our civilization goes". However, Boas did not coin the term.

Exam Probability: **Medium**

45. *Answer choices:*

(see index for correct answer)

- a. positive discrimination
- b. Cultural relativism
- c. Affirmative action

Guidance: level 1

:: United States federal labor legislation ::

The __________ of 1988 is a United States federal law that generally prevents employers from using polygraph tests, either for pre-employment screening or during the course of employment, with certain exemptions.

Exam Probability: **High**

46. *Answer choices:*

(see index for correct answer)

- a. Age Discrimination in Employment Act
- b. Employee Polygraph Protection Act
- c. Title 29 of the United States Code
- d. Alien Contract Labor Law

Guidance: level 1

:: Industrial ecology ::

__________ is a strategy for reducing the amount of waste created and released into the environment, particularly by industrial facilities, agriculture, or consumers. Many large corporations view P2 as a method of improving the efficiency and profitability of production processes by technology advancements. Legislative bodies have enacted P2 measures, such as the __________ Act of 1990 and the Clean Air Act Amendments of 1990 by the United States Congress.

Exam Probability: **High**

47. *Answer choices:*

(see index for correct answer)

- a. Eco-costs value ratio
- b. Material flow management
- c. Design for the Environment
- d. Pollution Prevention

Guidance: level 1

:: Corporate scandals ::

Exxon Mobil Corporation, doing business as _________ , is an American multinational oil and gas corporation headquartered in Irving, Texas. It is the largest direct descendant of John D. Rockefeller`s Standard Oil Company, and was formed on November 30, 1999 by the merger of Exxon and Mobil . _________ `s primary brands are Exxon, Mobil, Esso, and _________ Chemical.

Exam Probability: **Low**

48. *Answer choices:*

(see index for correct answer)

- a. Service Corporation of America
- b. ExxonMobil
- c. Aluminium price-fixing conspiracy
- d. Trustor affair

Guidance: level 1

:: ::

Sustainability is the process of people maintaining change in a balanced environment, in which the exploitation of resources, the direction of investments, the orientation of technological development and institutional change are all in harmony and enhance both current and future potential to meet human needs and aspirations. For many in the field, sustainability is defined through the following interconnected domains or pillars: environment, economic and social, which according to Fritjof Capra is based on the principles of Systems Thinking. Sub-domains of _________ development have been considered also: cultural, technological and political. While _________ development may be the organizing principle for sustainability for some, for others, the two terms are paradoxical . _________ development is the development that meets the needs of the present without compromising the ability of future generations to meet their own needs. Brundtland Report for the World Commission on Environment and Development introduced the term of _________ development.

Exam Probability: **Medium**

49. *Answer choices:*

(see index for correct answer)

- a. Sustainable
- b. Character
- c. information systems assessment

- d. hierarchical

Guidance: level 1

:: Business law ::

A _________ is an arrangement where parties, known as partners, agree to cooperate to advance their mutual interests. The partners in a _________ may be individuals, businesses, interest-based organizations, schools, governments or combinations. Organizations may partner to increase the likelihood of each achieving their mission and to amplify their reach. A _________ may result in issuing and holding equity or may be only governed by a contract.

Exam Probability: **Medium**

50. *Answer choices:*

(see index for correct answer)

- a. Partnership
- b. Advertising regulation
- c. Bulk sale
- d. Unfair Commercial Practices Directive

Guidance: level 1

:: ::

_________ was a philosopher during the Classical period in Ancient Greece, the founder of the Lyceum and the Peripatetic school of philosophy and Aristotelian tradition. Along with his teacher Plato, he is considered the "Father of Western Philosophy". His writings cover many subjects – including physics, biology, zoology, metaphysics, logic, ethics, aesthetics, poetry, theatre, music, rhetoric, psychology, linguistics, economics, politics and government. _________ provided a complex synthesis of the various philosophies existing prior to him, and it was above all from his teachings that the West inherited its intellectual lexicon, as well as problems and methods of inquiry. As a result, his philosophy has exerted a unique influence on almost every form of knowledge in the West and it continues to be a subject of contemporary philosophical discussion.

Exam Probability: **Low**

51. *Answer choices:*

(see index for correct answer)

- a. similarity-attraction theory
- b. hierarchical perspective
- c. Sarbanes-Oxley act of 2002
- d. Aristotle

Guidance: level 1

:: Ethically disputed business practices ::

__________ is the trading of a public company's stock or other securities by individuals with access to nonpublic information about the company. In various countries, some kinds of trading based on insider information is illegal. This is because it is seen as unfair to other investors who do not have access to the information, as the investor with insider information could potentially make larger profits than a typical investor could make. The rules governing __________ are complex and vary significantly from country to country. The extent of enforcement also varies from one country to another. The definition of insider in one jurisdiction can be broad, and may cover not only insiders themselves but also any persons related to them, such as brokers, associates and even family members. A person who becomes aware of non-public information and trades on that basis may be guilty of a crime.

Exam Probability: **Medium**

52. *Answer choices:*

(see index for correct answer)

- a. Reassignment centers
- b. Boiler room
- c. Sugging
- d. Suicide bidding

Guidance: level 1

:: Trade unions ::

A _________ was a group formed of private citizens to administer law and order where they considered governmental structures to be inadequate. The term is commonly associated with the frontier areas of the American West in the mid-19th century, where groups attacked cattle rustlers and gangs, and people at gold mining claims. As non-state organizations no functioning checks existed to protect against excessive force or safeguard due process from the committees. In the years prior to the Civil War, some committees worked to free slaves and transport them to freedom.

Exam Probability: **Medium**

53. *Answer choices:*

(see index for correct answer)

- a. Vigilance committee
- b. Union wage premium
- c. National trade union center
- d. Directly Affiliated Local Union

Guidance: level 1

:: ::

_________ is the practice of deliberately managing the spread of information between an individual or an organization and the public. _________ may include an organization or individual gaining exposure to their audiences using topics of public interest and news items that do not require direct payment. This differentiates it from advertising as a form of marketing communications. _________ is the idea of creating coverage for clients for free, rather than marketing or advertising. But now, advertising is also a part of greater PR Activities.An example of good _________ would be generating an article featuring a client, rather than paying for the client to be advertised next to the article. The aim of _________ is to inform the public, prospective customers, investors, partners, employees, and other stakeholders and ultimately persuade them to maintain a positive or favorable view about the organization, its leadership, products, or political decisions. _________ professionals typically work for PR and marketing firms, businesses and companies, government, and public officials as PIOs and nongovernmental organizations, and nonprofit organizations. Jobs central to _________ include account coordinator, account executive, account supervisor, and media relations manager.

Exam Probability: **High**

54. *Answer choices:*

(see index for correct answer)

- a. hierarchical
- b. Character
- c. surface-level diversity
- d. process perspective

Guidance: level 1

:: Agricultural labor ::

The _________ of America, or more commonly just _________ , is a labor union for farmworkers in the United States. It originated from the merger of two workers' rights organizations, the Agricultural Workers Organizing Committee led by organizer Larry Itliong, and the National Farm Workers Association led by César Chávez and Dolores Huerta. They became allied and transformed from workers' rights organizations into a union as a result of a series of strikes in 1965, when the mostly Filipino farmworkers of the AWOC in Delano, California initiated a grape strike, and the NFWA went on strike in support. As a result of the commonality in goals and methods, the NFWA and the AWOC formed the _________ Organizing Committee on August 22, 1966.This organization was accepted into the AFL-CIO in 1972 and changed its name to the _________ Union.

Exam Probability: **Medium**

55. *Answer choices:*

(see index for correct answer)

- a. Collective farming
- b. Salad Bowl strike
- c. United Farm Workers
- d. Moshav

Guidance: level 1

:: Marketing ::

_________ is the marketing of products that are presumed to be environmentally safe. It incorporates a broad range of activities, including product modification, changes to the production process, sustainable packaging, as well as modifying advertising. Yet defining _________ is not a simple task where several meanings intersect and contradict each other; an example of this will be the existence of varying social, environmental and retail definitions attached to this term. Other similar terms used are environmental marketing and ecological marketing.

Exam Probability: **Low**

56. *Answer choices:*

(see index for correct answer)

- a. Configurator
- b. Marchitecture

- c. Green marketing
- d. Masstige

Guidance: level 1

:: Pyramid and Ponzi schemes ::

__________ was an Italian swindler and con artist in the U.S. and Canada. His aliases include Charles Ponci, Carlo, and Charles P. Bianchi. Born and raised in Italy, he became known in the early 1920s as a swindler in North America for his money-making scheme. He promised clients a 50% profit within 45 days or 100% profit within 90 days, by buying discounted postal reply coupons in other countries and redeeming them at face value in the United States as a form of arbitrage. In reality, Ponzi was paying earlier investors using the investments of later investors. While this type of fraudulent investment scheme was not originally invented by Ponzi, it became so identified with him that it now is referred to as a "Ponzi scheme". His scheme ran for over a year before it collapsed, costing his "investors" $20 million.

Exam Probability: **High**

57. *Answer choices:*

(see index for correct answer)

- a. Bayou Hedge Fund Group
- b. Joseph S. Forte
- c. Charles Ponzi
- d. Equinox

Guidance: level 1

:: Corporations law ::

A normal _________ consists of various departments that contribute to the company`s overall mission and goals. Common departments include Marketing, [Finance, [[Operations managementOperations, Human Resource, and IT. These five divisions represent the major departments within a publicly traded company, though there are often smaller departments within autonomous firms. There is typically a CEO, and Board of Directors composed of the directors of each department. There are also company presidents, vice presidents, and CFOs.There is a great diversity in corporate forms as enterprises may range from single company to multi-corporate conglomerate. The four main _________ s are Functional, Divisional, Geographic, and the Matrix.Realistically, most corporations tend to have a "hybrid" structure, which is a combination of different models with one dominant strategy.

Exam Probability: **Low**

58. *Answer choices:*

(see index for correct answer)

- a. Creature of statute
- b. South African company law
- c. Corporate lawyer
- d. United Kingdom company law

Guidance: level 1

:: ::

The _________ is an institution of the European Union, responsible for proposing legislation, implementing decisions, upholding the EU treaties and managing the day-to-day business of the EU. Commissioners swear an oath at the European Court of Justice in Luxembourg City, pledging to respect the treaties and to be completely independent in carrying out their duties during their mandate. Unlike in the Council of the European Union, where members are directly and indirectly elected, and the European Parliament, where members are directly elected, the Commissioners are proposed by the Council of the European Union, on the basis of suggestions made by the national governments, and then appointed by the European Council after the approval of the European Parliament.

Exam Probability: **High**

59. *Answer choices:*

(see index for correct answer)

- a. corporate values
- b. European Commission
- c. functional perspective
- d. surface-level diversity

Guidance: level 1

Accounting

Accounting or accountancy is the measurement, processing, and communication of financial information about economic entities such as businesses and corporations. The modern field was established by the Italian mathematician Luca Pacioli in 1494. Accounting, which has been called the "language of business", measures the results of an organization's economic activities and conveys this information to a variety of users, including investors, creditors, management, and regulators.

:: Legal terms ::

_________ is a state of prolonged public dispute or debate, usually concerning a matter of conflicting opinion or point of view. The word was coined from the Latin controversia, as a composite of controversus – "turned in an opposite direction," from contra – "against" – and vertere – to turn, or versus , hence, "to turn against."

Exam Probability: **Low**

1. *Answer choices:*

(see index for correct answer)

- a. Adjustment
- b. All rights reserved
- c. Medical advice
- d. Plurality opinion

Guidance: level 1

:: Tax reform ::

_________ is the process of changing the way taxes are collected or managed by the government and is usually undertaken to improve tax administration or to provide economic or social benefits. _________ can include reducing the level of taxation of all people by the government, making the tax system more progressive or less progressive, or simplifying the tax system and making the system more understandable or more accountable.

Exam Probability: **Medium**

2. *Answer choices:*

(see index for correct answer)

- a. Enterprise Value Tax
- b. Tax reform
- c. Single tax
- d. John Sherwin Crosby

Guidance: level 1

:: Management ::

Business _________ is a discipline in operations management in which people use various methods to discover, model, analyze, measure, improve, optimize, and automate business processes. BPM focuses on improving corporate performance by managing business processes. Any combination of methods used to manage a company`s business processes is BPM. Processes can be structured and repeatable or unstructured and variable. Though not required, enabling technologies are often used with BPM.

Exam Probability: **Medium**

3. *Answer choices:*

(see index for correct answer)

- a. Quick response manufacturing
- b. Fall guy
- c. Wireless informatics
- d. Process Management

Guidance: level 1

:: Payment systems ::

A _________ is a bond of the redeemable transaction type which is worth a certain monetary value and which may be spent only for specific reasons or on specific goods. Examples include housing, travel, and food _________ s. The term _________ is also a synonym for receipt and is often used to refer to receipts used as evidence of, for example, the declaration that a service has been performed or that an expenditure has been made. _________ is a tourist guide for using services with a guarantee of payment by the agency.

Exam Probability: **Low**

4. *Answer choices:*

(see index for correct answer)

- a. Certified check
- b. Voucher
- c. Automated teller
- d. PAN truncation

Guidance: level 1

:: Generally Accepted Accounting Principles ::

Paid-in capital is capital that is contributed to a corporation by investors by purchase of stock from the corporation, the primary market, not by purchase of stock in the open market from other stockholders . It includes share capital as well as additional paid-in capital.

Exam Probability: **Medium**

5. *Answer choices:*

(see index for correct answer)

- a. Operating statement
- b. Expense
- c. Generally accepted accounting principles
- d. Contributed capital

Guidance: level 1

:: Budgets ::

A _________ is a financial plan for a defined period, often one year. It may also include planned sales volumes and revenues, resource quantities, costs and expenses, assets, liabilities and cash flows. Companies, governments, families and other organizations use it to express strategic plans of activities or events in measurable terms.

Exam Probability: **Low**

6. *Answer choices:*

(see index for correct answer)

- a. Participatory budgeting
- b. Budget
- c. Link budget
- d. Public budgeting

Guidance: level 1

:: Free accounting software ::

A _________ is the principal book or computer file for recording and totaling economic transactions measured in terms of a monetary unit of account by account type, with debits and credits in separate columns and a beginning monetary balance and ending monetary balance for each account.

Exam Probability: **High**

7. *Answer choices:*

(see index for correct answer)

- a. Grisbi
- b. Ofuz
- c. GnuCash
- d. SQL-Ledger

Guidance: level 1

:: Accounting software ::

_________ is any item or verifiable record that is generally accepted as payment for goods and services and repayment of debts, such as taxes, in a particular country or socio-economic context. The main functions of _________ are distinguished as: a medium of exchange, a unit of account, a store of value and sometimes, a standard of deferred payment. Any item or verifiable record that fulfils these functions can be considered as _________ .

Exam Probability: **High**

8. *Answer choices:*

(see index for correct answer)

- a. Money
- b. National Software
- c. Moneydance
- d. Chrysler Comprehensive Compensation System

Guidance: level 1

:: Budgets ::

_________ is a method of budgeting in which all expenses must be justified and approved for each new period. Developed by Peter Pyhrr in the 1970s, _________ starts from a "zero base" at the beginning of every budget period, analyzing needs and costs of every function within an organization and allocating funds accordingly, regardless of how much money has previously been budgeted to any given line item.

Exam Probability: **High**

9. *Answer choices:*

(see index for correct answer)

- a. Performance-based budgeting
- b. Operating budget
- c. Zero-based budgeting
- d. Zero budget

Guidance: level 1

:: Management accounting ::

_________ accounting is a traditional cost accounting method introduced in the 1920s, as an alternative for the traditional cost accounting method based on historical costs.

Exam Probability: **High**

10. *Answer choices:*

(see index for correct answer)

- a. Standard cost
- b. Owner earnings
- c. Entity-level controls
- d. Profit center

Guidance: level 1

:: Economics terminology ::

A corporation`s share capital or _________ is the portion of a corporation`s equity that has been obtained by the issue of shares in the corporation to a shareholder, usually for cash. "Share capital" may also denote the number and types of shares that compose a corporation`s share structure.

Exam Probability: **High**

11. *Answer choices:*

(see index for correct answer)

- a. Profit motive
- b. Normal profit
- c. Capital stock
- d. economic profit

Guidance: level 1

:: Generally Accepted Accounting Principles ::

__________ , or non-current liabilities, are liabilities that are due beyond a year or the normal operation period of the company. The normal operation period is the amount of time it takes for a company to turn inventory into cash. On a classified balance sheet, liabilities are separated between current and __________ to help users assess the company`s financial standing in short-term and long-term periods. __________ give users more information about the long-term prosperity of the company, while current liabilities inform the user of debt that the company owes in the current period. On a balance sheet, accounts are listed in order of liquidity, so __________ come after current liabilities. In addition, the specific long-term liability accounts are listed on the balance sheet in order of liquidity. Therefore, an account due within eighteen months would be listed before an account due within twenty-four months. Examples of __________ are bonds payable, long-term loans, capital leases, pension liabilities, post-retirement healthcare liabilities, deferred compensation, deferred revenues, deferred income taxes, and derivative liabilities.

Exam Probability: **Low**

12. *Answer choices:*

(see index for correct answer)

- a. Depreciation
- b. Goodwill
- c. Generally Accepted Accounting Practice
- d. Cash method of accounting

Guidance: level 1

:: ::

The __________ or just chief executive , is the most senior corporate, executive, or administrative officer in charge of managing an organization especially an independent legal entity such as a company or nonprofit institution. CEOs lead a range of organizations, including public and private corporations, non-profit organizations and even some government organizations . The CEO of a corporation or company typically reports to the board of directors and is charged with maximizing the value of the entity, which may include maximizing the share price, market share, revenues or another element. In the non-profit and government sector, CEOs typically aim at achieving outcomes related to the organization`s mission, such as reducing poverty, increasing literacy, etc.

Exam Probability: **Low**

13. *Answer choices:*

(see index for correct answer)

- a. Chief executive officer
- b. Character
- c. levels of analysis
- d. information systems assessment

Guidance: level 1

:: Mathematical finance ::

In economics and finance, _________ , also known as present discounted value, is the value of an expected income stream determined as of the date of valuation. The _________ is always less than or equal to the future value because money has interest-earning potential, a characteristic referred to as the time value of money, except during times of negative interest rates, when the _________ will be more than the future value. Time value can be described with the simplified phrase, "A dollar today is worth more than a dollar tomorrow". Here, 'worth more' means that its value is greater. A dollar today is worth more than a dollar tomorrow because the dollar can be invested and earn a day's worth of interest, making the total accumulate to a value more than a dollar by tomorrow. Interest can be compared to rent. Just as rent is paid to a landlord by a tenant without the ownership of the asset being transferred, interest is paid to a lender by a borrower who gains access to the money for a time before paying it back. By letting the borrower have access to the money, the lender has sacrificed the exchange value of this money, and is compensated for it in the form of interest. The initial amount of the borrowed funds is less than the total amount of money paid to the lender.

Exam Probability: **Medium**

14. *Answer choices:*

(see index for correct answer)

- a. AZFinText
- b. Earnings response coefficient
- c. Present value
- d. Quantitative investing

Guidance: level 1

:: Accounting in the United States ::

_________ is the title of qualified accountants in numerous countries in the English-speaking world. In the United States, the CPA is a license to provide accounting services to the public. It is awarded by each of the 50 states for practice in that state. Additionally, almost every state has passed mobility laws to allow CPAs from other states to practice in their state. State licensing requirements vary, but the minimum standard requirements include passing the Uniform _________ Examination, 150 semester units of college education, and one year of accounting related experience.

Exam Probability: **Medium**

15. *Answer choices:*

(see index for correct answer)

- a. Financial Accounting Foundation
- b. Certified Public Accountant
- c. Cotton Plantation Record and Account Book
- d. Statements on Auditing Procedure

Guidance: level 1

:: Tax credits ::

A __________ is a tax incentive which allows certain taxpayers to subtract the amount of the credit they have accrued from the total they owe the state. It may also be a credit granted in recognition of taxes already paid or, as in the United Kingdom, a form of state support.

Exam Probability: **Low**

16. *Answer choices:*

(see index for correct answer)

- a. Business Energy Investment Tax Credit
- b. Hope credit
- c. New Jobs tax credit
- d. Pennsylvania Film Production Tax Credit

Guidance: level 1

:: Accounting journals and ledgers ::

The subledger, or __________, provides details behind entries in the general ledger used in accounting. The subledger shows detail for part of the accounting records such as property and equipment, prepaid expenses, etc. The detail would include such items as date the item was purchased or expense incurred, a description of the item, the original balance, and the net book value. The total of the subledger would match the line item amount on the general ledger. This corresponding line item in the general ledger is referred to as the controlling account. The __________ balance is compared with its controlling account balance as part of the process of preparing a trial balance.

Exam Probability: **Low**

17. *Answer choices:*

(see index for correct answer)

- a. Check register
- b. Cash receipts journal
- c. Subsidiary ledger
- d. Journal entry

Guidance: level 1

:: Inventory ::

__________ is the maximum amount of goods, or inventory, that a company can possibly sell during this fiscal year. It has the formula.

Exam Probability: **High**

18. *Answer choices:*

(see index for correct answer)

- a. Cost of goods available for sale
- b. Stock-taking
- c. Inventory optimization
- d. Stock obsolescence

Guidance: level 1

:: Management accounting ::

An __________ is a classification used for business units within an enterprise.The essential element of an __________ is that it is treated as a unit which is measured against its use of capital, as opposed to a cost or profit center, which are measured against raw costs or profits.

Exam Probability: **High**

19. *Answer choices:*

(see index for correct answer)

- a. Responsibility center
- b. Investment center
- c. Customer profitability
- d. Variable cost

Guidance: level 1

:: Generally Accepted Accounting Principles ::

_________ is a small amount of discretionary funds in the form of cash used for expenditures where it is not sensible to make any disbursement by cheque, because of the inconvenience and costs of writing, signing, and then cashing the cheque.

Exam Probability: **Low**

20. *Answer choices:*

(see index for correct answer)

- a. Deprival value
- b. Petty cash
- c. Net profit
- d. Consolidation

Guidance: level 1

:: Taxation in the United States ::

The Modified Accelerated Cost Recovery System is the current tax depreciation system in the United States. Under this system, the capitalized cost of tangible property is recovered over a specified life by annual deductions for depreciation. The lives are specified broadly in the Internal Revenue Code. The Internal Revenue Service publishes detailed tables of lives by classes of assets. The deduction for depreciation is computed under one of two methods at the election of the taxpayer, with limitations. See IRS Publication 946 for a 120-page guide to _________ .

Exam Probability: **Low**

21. *Answer choices:*

(see index for correct answer)

- a. Above-the-line deduction
- b. Income tax audit
- c. Endowment tax
- d. Half-year convention

Guidance: level 1

:: Quality control tools ::

A _________ is a type of diagram that represents an algorithm, workflow or process. _________ can also be defined as a diagramatic representation of an algorithm .

Exam Probability: **Low**

22. *Answer choices:*

(see index for correct answer)

- a. Flowchart
- b. Multi-vari chart
- c. CUSUM
- d. X-bar chart

Guidance: level 1

:: Taxation and efficiency ::

_________ is the legal usage of the tax regime in a single territory to one`s own advantage to reduce the amount of tax that is payable by means that are within the law. Tax sheltering is very similar, although unlike _________ tax sheltering is not necessarily legal. Tax havens are jurisdictions which facilitate reduced taxes.

Exam Probability: **Medium**

23. *Answer choices:*

(see index for correct answer)

- a. Tax advantage
- b. Tax avoidance
- c. Capital flight
- d. Tax exporting

Guidance: level 1

:: ::

A __________ is an individual or institution that legally owns one or more shares of stock in a public or private corporation. __________ s may be referred to as members of a corporation. Legally, a person is not a __________ in a corporation until their name and other details are entered in the corporation`s register of __________ s or members.

Exam Probability: **High**

24. *Answer choices:*

(see index for correct answer)

- a. cultural
- b. Shareholder
- c. Character
- d. levels of analysis

Guidance: level 1

:: Accounting terminology ::

__________ are liabilities that reflect expenses that have not yet been paid or logged under accounts payable during an accounting period; in other words, a company`s obligation to pay for goods and services that have been provided for which invoices have not yet been received. Examples would include accrued wages payable, accrued sales tax payable, and accrued rent payable.

Exam Probability: **High**

25. *Answer choices:*

(see index for correct answer)

- a. Impairment cost
- b. profit and loss statement
- c. Accrued liabilities
- d. Enterprise liquidity

Guidance: level 1

:: Management accounting ::

A __________ is an organizational unit headed by a manager, who is responsible for its activities and results. In responsibility accounting, revenues and cost information are collected and reported on by __________ s.

Exam Probability: **Medium**

26. *Answer choices:*

(see index for correct answer)

- a. Responsibility center
- b. Backflush accounting
- c. Variable cost
- d. Standard cost

Guidance: level 1

:: Financial accounting ::

A __________ is an ownership interest in a corporation with enough voting stock shares to prevail in any stockholders` motion. A majority of voting shares is always a __________. When a party holds less than the majority of the voting shares, other present circumstances can be considered to determine whether that party is still considered to hold a controlling ownership interest.

Exam Probability: **Medium**

27. *Answer choices:*

(see index for correct answer)

- a. Money measurement
- b. Associate company
- c. Controlling interest
- d. Asset recovery

Guidance: level 1

:: Notes (finance) ::

A _________ , sometimes referred to as a note payable, is a legal instrument , in which one party promises in writing to pay a determinate sum of money to the other , either at a fixed or determinable future time or on demand of the payee, under specific terms.

Exam Probability: **High**

28. *Answer choices:*

(see index for correct answer)

- a. Equity-linked note
- b. A notes
- c. Capital note
- d. Promissory note

Guidance: level 1

:: Financial ratios ::

The _________ or dividend-price ratio of a share is the dividend per share, divided by the price per share. It is also a company's total annual dividend payments divided by its market capitalization, assuming the number of shares is constant. It is often expressed as a percentage.

Exam Probability: **High**

29. *Answer choices:*

(see index for correct answer)

- a. Dividend yield
- b. Average accounting return
- c. Accounting rate of return
- d. Average collection period

Guidance: level 1

:: Management accounting ::

_________ is a professional business study of Accounts and management in which we learn importance of accounts in our management system.

Exam Probability: **Low**

30. *Answer choices:*

(see index for correct answer)

- a. Profit center
- b. Average per-bit delivery cost
- c. Accounting management
- d. Cost accounting

Guidance: level 1

:: Value theory ::

Within philosophy, it can be known as ethics or axiology. Early philosophical investigations sought to understand good and evil and the concept of "the good". Today, much of _________ aspires to the scientifically empirical, recording what people do value and attempting to understand why they value it in the context of psychology, sociology, and economics.

Exam Probability: **High**

31. *Answer choices:*

(see index for correct answer)

- a. Value theory
- b. Marginalism
- c. Theory of value
- d. Paradox of value

Guidance: level 1

:: Generally Accepted Accounting Principles ::

A _________ is a reduction of the recognized value of something. In accounting, this is a recognition of the reduced or zero value of an asset. In income tax statements, this is a reduction of taxable income, as a recognition of certain expenses required to produce the income.

Exam Probability: **Medium**

32. *Answer choices:*

(see index for correct answer)

- a. Deprival value
- b. Earnings before interest, taxes, depreciation, and amortization
- c. Fin 48
- d. Write-off

Guidance: level 1

:: Payment systems ::

A _________ or cheque, also called an image cash letter , clearing replacement document , or image replacement document , is a negotiable instrument used in electronic banking systems to represent a physical paper cheque . It may be wholly digital from payment initiation to clearing and settlement or it may be a digital reproduction of an original paper check.

Exam Probability: **Low**

33. *Answer choices:*

(see index for correct answer)

- a. Euronet Pakistan
- b. CNG Processing A/S
- c. Payzone
- d. Sleekpay

Guidance: level 1

:: Land value taxation ::

_________ , sometimes referred to as dry _________ , is the solid surface of Earth that is not permanently covered by water. The vast majority of human activity throughout history has occurred in _________ areas that support agriculture, habitat, and various natural resources. Some life forms have developed from predecessor species that lived in bodies of water.

Exam Probability: **Medium**

34. *Answer choices:*

(see index for correct answer)

- a. Physiocracy
- b. Land value tax
- c. Henry George
- d. Land

Guidance: level 1

:: Finance ::

_________ is a notional asset or liability to reflect corporate income taxation on a basis that is the same or more similar to recognition of profits than the taxation treatment. _________ liabilities can arise as a result of corporate taxation treatment of capital expenditure being more rapid than the accounting depreciation treatment. _________ assets can arise due to net loss carry-overs, which are only recorded as asset if it is deemed more likely than not that the asset will be used in future fiscal periods. Different countries may also allow or require discounting of the assets or particularly liabilities. There are often disclosure requirements for potential liabilities and assets that are not actually recognised as an asset or liability.

Exam Probability: **Medium**

35. *Answer choices:*

(see index for correct answer)

- a. Clawback
- b. Creative industries
- c. Mohatra contract
- d. Strategic financial management

Guidance: level 1

:: Investment ::

In economics, _________ is spending which increases the availability of fixed capital goods or means of production and goods inventories. It is the total spending on newly produced physical capital and on inventories —that is, gross investment—minus replacement investment, which simply replaces depreciated capital goods. It is productive capital formation plus net additions to the stock of housing and the stock of inventories.

Exam Probability: **Medium**

36. *Answer choices:*

(see index for correct answer)

- a. Net investment
- b. Dispersion
- c. Pre-emerging markets
- d. Qirad

Guidance: level 1

:: Management accounting ::

__________ , or dollar contribution per unit, is the selling price per unit minus the variable cost per unit. "Contribution" represents the portion of sales revenue that is not consumed by variable costs and so contributes to the coverage of fixed costs. This concept is one of the key building blocks of break-even analysis.

Exam Probability: **Low**

37. *Answer choices:*
(see index for correct answer)

- a. Accounting management
- b. Fixed cost
- c. Backflush accounting
- d. Management control system

Guidance: level 1

:: ::

A work order is usually a task or a job for a customer, that can be scheduled or assigned to someone. Such an order may be from a customer request or created internally within the organization. Work orders may also be created as follow ups to Inspections or Audits. A work order may be for products or services.

Exam Probability: **Low**

38. *Answer choices:*
(see index for correct answer)

- a. similarity-attraction theory
- b. hierarchical
- c. Job order
- d. surface-level diversity

Guidance: level 1

:: Basic financial concepts ::

In finance, maturity or _________ refers to the final payment date of a loan or other financial instrument, at which point the principal is due to be paid.

Exam Probability: **Low**

39. *Answer choices:*

(see index for correct answer)

- a. Maturity date
- b. Lodgement
- c. Forward guidance
- d. Leverage cycle

Guidance: level 1

:: Password authentication ::

A _________ , or sometimes redundantly a PIN number, is a numeric or alpha-numeric password used in the process of authenticating a user accessing a system.

Exam Probability: **High**

40. *Answer choices:*

(see index for correct answer)

- a. Secure Remote Password protocol
- b. S/KEY
- c. OTPW
- d. Personal identification number

Guidance: level 1

:: Organizational theory ::

Decentralisation is the process by which the activities of an organization, particularly those regarding planning and decision making, are distributed or delegated away from a central, authoritative location or group. Concepts of _________ have been applied to group dynamics and management science in private businesses and organizations, political science, law and public administration, economics, money and technology.

Exam Probability: **High**

41. *Answer choices:*

(see index for correct answer)

- a. Linking pin model
- b. Decentralization
- c. Smart city
- d. Resource dependence theory

Guidance: level 1

:: United States federal income tax ::

Under United States tax law, the _________ is a dollar amount that non-itemizers may subtract from their income before income tax is applied. Taxpayers may choose either itemized deductions or the _________, but usually choose whichever results in the lesser amount of tax payable. The _________ is available to US citizens and aliens who are resident for tax purposes and who are individuals, married persons, and heads of household. The _________ is based on filing status and typically increases each year. It is not available to nonresident aliens residing in the United States . Additional amounts are available for persons who are blind and/or are at least 65 years of age.

Exam Probability: **Low**

42. *Answer choices:*

(see index for correct answer)

- a. Presidential election campaign fund checkoff
- b. Foreign housing exclusion
- c. Foreign earned income exclusion
- d. Standard deduction

Guidance: level 1

:: Management accounting ::

In business, a _________ is a division that gains revenue from product sales or service provided. The manager in _________ is accountable for revenue only.

Exam Probability: **High**

43. *Answer choices:*

(see index for correct answer)

- a. Management accounting in supply chains
- b. Revenue center
- c. Certified Management Accountants of Canada
- d. Resource consumption accounting

Guidance: level 1

:: Management accounting ::

A _________ is a cost that differs between alternatives being considered. In order for a cost to be a _________ it must be.

Exam Probability: **High**

44. *Answer choices:*

(see index for correct answer)

- a. Relevant cost
- b. Constraints accounting
- c. Chartered Cost Accountant
- d. Pre-determined overhead rate

Guidance: level 1

:: Expense ::

An _________, operating expenditure, operational expense, operational expenditure or opex is an ongoing cost for running a product, business, or system. Its counterpart, a capital expenditure , is the cost of developing or providing non-consumable parts for the product or system. For example, the purchase of a photocopier involves capex, and the annual paper, toner, power and maintenance costs represents opex. For larger systems like businesses, opex may also include the cost of workers and facility expenses such as rent and utilities.

Exam Probability: **Low**

45. *Answer choices:*

(see index for correct answer)

- a. Operating expense
- b. Expense account

- c. Momentem
- d. Stock option expensing

Guidance: level 1

:: ::

Accounts _________ is a legally enforceable claim for payment held by a business for goods supplied and/or services rendered that customers/clients have ordered but not paid for. These are generally in the form of invoices raised by a business and delivered to the customer for payment within an agreed time frame. Accounts _________ is shown in a balance sheet as an asset. It is one of a series of accounting transactions dealing with the billing of a customer for goods and services that the customer has ordered. These may be distinguished from notes _________ , which are debts created through formal legal instruments called promissory notes.

Exam Probability: **Low**

46. *Answer choices:*

(see index for correct answer)

- a. interpersonal communication
- b. Receivable
- c. Character
- d. personal values

Guidance: level 1

:: Commerce ::

A _________ , is a document acknowledging that a person has received money or property in payment following a sale or other transfer of goods or provision of a service. All _________ s must have the date of purchase on them. If the recipient of the payment is legally required to collect sales tax or VAT from the customer, the amount would be added to the _________ and the collection would be deemed to have been on behalf of the relevant tax authority. In many countries, a retailer is required to include the sales tax or VAT in the displayed price of goods sold, from which the tax amount would be calculated at point of sale and remitted to the tax authorities in due course. Similarly, amounts may be deducted from amounts payable, as in the case of wage withholding taxes. On the other hand, tips or other gratuities given by a customer, for example in a restaurant, would not form part of the payment amount or appear on the _________ .

Exam Probability: **High**

47. *Answer choices:*

(see index for correct answer)

- a. Grain trade
- b. Receipt
- c. Sales quote
- d. Bill of sale

Guidance: level 1

:: Management accounting ::

_________ is a professional certification credential in the management accounting and financial management fields. The certification signifies that the person possesses knowledge in the areas of financial planning, analysis, control, decision support, and professional ethics. The CMA is a U.S.-based, globally recognized certification offered by the Institute of Management Accountants.

Exam Probability: **Medium**

48. *Answer choices:*

(see index for correct answer)

- a. Direct material usage variance
- b. Institute of Cost and Management Accountants of Bangladesh
- c. RCA open-source application

- d. Relevant cost

Guidance: level 1

:: Generally Accepted Accounting Principles ::

__________ is, in accrual accounting, money received for goods or services which have not yet been delivered. According to the revenue recognition principle, it is recorded as a liability until delivery is made, at which time it is converted into revenue.

Exam Probability: **Low**

49. *Answer choices:*

(see index for correct answer)

- a. Standard Business Reporting
- b. Fixed investment
- c. Financial position of the United States
- d. Deferred income

Guidance: level 1

:: Accounting terminology ::

A __________ contains all the accounts for recording transactions relating to a company`s assets, liabilities, owners` equity, revenue, and expenses. In modern accounting software or ERP, the __________ works as a central repository for accounting data transferred from all subledgers or modules like accounts payable, accounts receivable, cash management, fixed assets, purchasing and projects. The __________ is the backbone of any accounting system which holds financial and non-financial data for an organization. The collection of all accounts is known as the __________. Each account is known as a ledger account. In a manual or non-computerized system this may be a large book.The statement of financial position and the statement of income and comprehensive income are both derived from the __________. Each account in the __________ consists of one or more pages. The __________ is where posting to the accounts occurs. Posting is the process of recording amounts as credits , and amounts as debits , in the pages of the __________. Additional columns to the right hold a running activity total .

Exam Probability: **Medium**

50. *Answer choices:*

(see index for correct answer)

- a. Accounts payable
- b. Impairment cost
- c. Accrued liabilities
- d. Chart of accounts

Guidance: level 1

:: Accounting source documents ::

A __________ is a commercial document and first official offer issued by a buyer to a seller indicating types, quantities, and agreed prices for products or services. It is used to control the purchasing of products and services from external suppliers. __________ s can be an essential part of enterprise resource planning system orders.

Exam Probability: **High**

51. *Answer choices:*

(see index for correct answer)

- a. Credit memo
- b. Credit memorandum
- c. Parcel audit
- d. Invoice

Guidance: level 1

:: Financial economics ::

A __________ is defined to include property of any kind held by an assessee, whether connected with their business or profession or not connected with their business or profession. It includes all kinds of property, movable or immovable, tangible or intangible, fixed or circulating. Thus, land and building, plant and machinery, motorcar, furniture, jewellery, route permits, goodwill, tenancy rights, patents, trademarks, shares, debentures, securities, units, mutual funds, zero-coupon bonds etc. are __________ s.

Exam Probability: **Medium**

52. *Answer choices:*

(see index for correct answer)

- a. Forward rate
- b. Capital asset
- c. International finance
- d. Covered interest arbitrage

Guidance: level 1

:: Types of accounting ::

Various _________ systems are used by various public sector entities. In the United States, for instance, there are two levels of government which follow different accounting standards set forth by independent, private sector boards. At the federal level, the Federal Accounting Standards Advisory Board sets forth the accounting standards to follow. Similarly, there is the _________ Standards Board for state and local level government.

Exam Probability: **Low**

53. *Answer choices:*

(see index for correct answer)

- a. Personal environmental impact accounting
- b. Governmental accounting
- c. Product control

Guidance: level 1

:: Stock market ::

_________ is a form of stock which may have any combination of features not possessed by common stock including properties of both an equity and a debt instrument, and is generally considered a hybrid instrument. _________ s are senior to common stock, but subordinate to bonds in terms of claim and may have priority over common stock in the payment of dividends and upon liquidation. Terms of the _________ are described in the issuing company`s articles of association or articles of incorporation.

Exam Probability: **High**

54. *Answer choices:*

(see index for correct answer)

- a. Delivery versus payment
- b. Follow-on offering

- c. Preferred stock
- d. Wealth management

Guidance: level 1

:: Financial ratios ::

_________ or interest coverage ratio is a measure of a company`s ability to honor its debt payments. It may be calculated as either EBIT or EBITDA divided by the total interest payable.

Exam Probability: **Low**

55. *Answer choices:*

(see index for correct answer)

- a. AlphaIC
- b. Times interest earned
- c. Savings ratio
- d. Bid-to-cover ratio

Guidance: level 1

:: Insurance terms ::

A _________ in the broadest sense is a natural person or other legal entity who receives money or other benefits from a benefactor. For example, the _________ of a life insurance policy is the person who receives the payment of the amount of insurance after the death of the insured.

Exam Probability: **Low**

56. *Answer choices:*

(see index for correct answer)

- a. Replacement value
- b. Home warranty
- c. Uninsured motorist clause
- d. Double indemnity

Guidance: level 1

:: Management accounting ::

__________ is the profit the firm makes from serving a customer or customer group over a specified period of time, specifically the difference between the revenues earned from and the costs associated with the customer relationship in a specified period. According to Philip Kotler,"a profitable customer is a person, household or a company that overtime, yields a revenue stream that exceeds by an acceptable amount the company`s cost stream of attracting, selling and servicing the customer."

Exam Probability: **Medium**

57. *Answer choices:*

(see index for correct answer)

- a. Invested capital
- b. Direct material usage variance
- c. Backflush accounting
- d. Entity-level controls

Guidance: level 1

:: Accounting source documents ::

A __________ or account statement is a summary of financial transactions which have occurred over a given period on a bank account held by a person or business with a financial institution.

Exam Probability: **Medium**

58. *Answer choices:*

(see index for correct answer)

- a. Air waybill
- b. Invoice
- c. Remittance advice
- d. Bank statement

Guidance: level 1

:: Corporate crime ::

__________ LLP, based in Chicago, was an American holding company. Formerly one of the "Big Five" accounting firms , the firm had provided auditing, tax, and consulting services to large corporations. By 2001, it had become one of the world`s largest multinational companies.

Exam Probability: **Low**

59. *Answer choices:*

(see index for correct answer)

- a. Corporate manslaughter
- b. New England Compounding Center
- c. Walter Forbes
- d. General Development Corporation

Guidance: level 1

INDEX: Correct Answers

Foundations of Business

1. : Pattern

2. c: Availability

3. a: Innovation

4. : Market share

5. b: Inflation

6. : Entrepreneur

7. a: Duty

8. b: Human resources

9. c: American Express

10. : Insurance

11. a: Supply chain

12. d: INDEX

13. b: Arbitration

14. a: Raw material

15. b: SWOT analysis

16. c: Diagram

17. b: Privacy

18. d: Preference

19. : Fraud

20. d: Loan

21. d: Net income

22. c: Outsourcing

23. a: Career

24. a: Social responsibility

25. b: Patent

26. a: Organizational culture

27. d: Copyright

28. : Protection

29. a: Cash flow

30. d: Initiative

31. : Economic growth

32. d: Cooperative

33. d: Schedule

34. d: Market segmentation

35. d: Credit card

36. a: Energies

37. a: Six Sigma

38. : Crisis

39. a: Cash

40. c: Health

41. d: Number

42. b: Price

43. c: Competitor

44. : Meeting

45. c: Competition

46. d: Stock market

47. a: Project

48. c: Logistics

49. b: Restructuring

50. : Return on investment

51. : Present value

52. d: Marketing mix

53. : Exercise

54. : Policy

55. : Finance

56. b: Building

57. c: Comparative advantage

58. : Project management

59. d: Tool

Management

1. : Organizational commitment

2. a: Goal

3. a: Transformational leadership

4. b: Business plan

5. a: Reputation

6. b: Entrepreneur

7. a: Offshoring

8. d: Quality management

9. b: Learning organization

10. : Argument

11. d: Logistics

12. c: Question

13. b: Labor force

14. : Individualism

15. d: Checklist

16. : Expert

17. c: Information

18. c: Assembly line

19. : Product design

20. b: Return on investment

21. a: Intranet

22. a: Corporation

23. a: Business process

24. b: Delegation

25. : Entrepreneurship

26. b: Discipline

27. d: Leadership style

28. a: Interaction

29. c: Referent power

30. d: Benchmarking

31. a: Political risk

32. d: Integrity

33. c: Time management

34. c: Bureaucracy

35. b: Evaluation

36. d: Trade

37. c: Statistic

38. : Decentralization

39. d: Human resource management

40. : Procurement

41. d: Consultant

42. : Job analysis

43. a: Authority

44. a: Skill

45. c: Competitive advantage

46. b: SWOT analysis

47. b: Interview

48. d: Facilitator

49. c: Bottom line

50. d: Market share

51. d: Empowerment

52. b: Standard deviation

53. b: Asset

54. d: Restructuring

55. c: Management by objectives

56. c: Decision tree

57. b: Utility

58. : Industry

59. : Reason

Business law

1. a: Oral contract

2. a: Insolvency

3. : Consumer Good

4. b: Internal Revenue Service

5. b: Statutory Law

6. b: General partnership

7. b: Directed verdict

8. c: Warranty

9. c: Mens rea

10. c: Holder in due course

11. a: Preference

12. : Authority

13. c: False imprisonment

14. : Delegation

15. b: Restraint of trade

16. c: Property

17. : Cause of action

18. a: Product liability

19. b: Appeal

20. a: Bailee

21. : Money laundering

22. : Incentive

23. a: Uniform Commercial Code

24. : Intellectual property

25. b: Treaty

26. b: Judicial review

27. d: Berne Convention

28. c: Consumer credit

29. c: Writ

30. b: Board of directors

31. b: Uniform Electronic Transactions Act

32. b: Arbitration clause

33. d: Relevant market

34. d: Security agreement

35. a: Industry

36. c: Investment

37. d: Commerce Clause

38. c: Sexual harassment

39. b: Marketing

40. d: Real property

41. a: Surety

42. b: Supreme Court

43. d: Broker

44. d: Unconscionability

45. d: Independent contractor

46. a: Health insurance

47. d: Stock

48. d: Respondeat superior

49. : Utility

50. : Sherman Antitrust

51. : Substantive law

52. d: Service mark

53. c: Purchasing

54. b: Partnership

55. b: Operating agreement

56. a: Cyberspace

57. : Apparent authority

58. a: Commercial Paper

59. a: Committee

Finance

1. d: Financial crisis

2. c: Return on assets

3. d: Credit

4. : Subsidiary ledger

5. b: Incentive

6. a: Futures contract

7. c: Preferred stock

8. d: Comprehensive income

9. b: Bankruptcy

10. d: Fixed cost

11. d: Fraud

12. a: Limited liability

13. : S corporation

14. b: Trial balance

15. b: Put option

16. d: Choice

17. c: Balance sheet

18. b: Accountant

19. c: Current asset

20. : Relevance

21. c: Purchasing

22. : Financial accounting

23. : Accrued interest

24. b: Ending inventory

25. : Debtor

26. a: Face

27. b: Asset turnover

28. d: Monetary policy

29. b: Utility

30. c: Tax expense

31. c: Coupon

32. a: Price

33. b: Compound interest

34. c: Mutual fund

35. b: Chart of accounts

36. d: Pricing

37. c: Financial management

38. a: Creditor

39. b: Buyer

40. c: Variable Costing

41. c: Petty cash

42. b: Financial risk

43. b: Capital asset pricing model

44. b: Bank account

45. : Sole proprietorship

46. d: Opportunity cost

47. b: Absorption costing

48. c: Shares

49. c: Operating lease

50. d: Internal Revenue Service

51. a: Secondary market

52. : Interest rate risk

53. b: Interest rate

54. a: Goldman Sachs

55. c: Payment

56. c: Long-term liabilities

57. : Cost accounting

58. c: Internal control

59. d: Competition

Human resource management

1. d: Talent management

2. d: Census

3. b: Right to work

4. : Restructuring

5. a: Balanced scorecard

6. c: Knowledge management

7. a: Cost leadership

8. b: Rating scale

9. c: Balance sheet

10. b: Human resource management

11. b: Reasonable person

12. : Conformity

13. d: Organizational justice

14. d: Minimum wage

15. : Online assessment

16. c: Adaptive

17. b: Family violence

18. : Social networking

19. c: Recession

20. d: Job security

21. a: Goal setting

22. : Evaluation

23. : Peter Principle

24. c: Psychological contract

25. d: Globalization

26. : Fair Labor Standards Act

27. d: Eustress

28. c: Kaizen

29. c: Strategic management

30. d: Outplacement

31. a: Phantom stock

32. : Training and development

33. a: Control group

34. d: Layoff

35. : Restricted stock

36. d: Hazard

37. a: Workforce

38. d: Performance measurement

39. a: Whistleblower

40. a: Prevailing wage

41. : Survey research

42. a: Overlearning

43. b: Love contract

44. a: Job rotation

45. d: Delayering

46. : Internal consistency

47. d: Closed shop

48. a: Job analysis

49. b: Organizational structure

50. c: Aptitude

51. c: Person Analysis

52. b: National Institute for Occupational Safety and Health

53. d: Case interview

54. a: Externship

55. c: Authoritarianism

56. : Union shop

57. b: Asbestos

58. : Pregnancy discrimination

59. d: Meritor Savings Bank v. Vinson

Information systems

1. b: Interoperability

2. : Picasa

3. b: Semantic Web

4. d: System software

5. b: Artificial intelligence

6. b: Total cost

7. b: Strategic planning

8. d: Debit card

9. : Folksonomy

10. c: Positioning system

11. b: Intranet

12. c: Balanced scorecard

13. b: Star

14. b: Government-to-business

15. : Application software

16. a: Gmail

17. c: Code

18. a: Google Docs

19. : Tacit knowledge

20. a: Groupware

21. d: Domain name

22. a: Click-through

23. a: Relational database

24. b: Sustainable

25. d: Strategic information system

26. d: ICANN

27. a: Entity-relationship

28. c: Digital rights management

29. d: Porter five forces analysis

30. d: Business intelligence

31. : Web content

32. c: Information flow

33. a: Geographic information system

34. b: Virtual team

35. c: BitTorrent

36. : World Wide Web

37. d: Data link

38. : Unstructured data

39. b: Interactivity

40. c: Packet switching

41. a: Data model

42. c: Data aggregator

43. c: First mover advantage

44. b: System

45. d: Monopoly

46. a: Data governance

47. d: Drill down

48. a: Business process

49. b: Content management system

50. : Analytics

51. b: Blogger

52. : Mass customization

53. b: Metadata

54. : Consumer-to-business

55. b: Big data

56. b: Operational system

57. : Local Area Network

58. a: Click fraud

59. : Accessibility

Marketing

1. a: Complexity

2. c: Selling

3. b: Business marketing

4. : Testimonial

5. c: Code

6. b: Primary data

7. d: Reinforcement

8. c: Data warehouse

9. c: Security

10. b: Consultant

11. c: Auction

12. b: Exploratory research

13. b: Quantitative research

14. d: Sherman Antitrust Act

15. b: Data analysis

16. a: Logistics

17. : Star

18. a: Partnership

19. : American Express

20. d: Audit

21. a: Distribution channel

22. c: Marketing plan

23. c: Customer service

24. a: Patent

25. b: Qualitative research

26. a: Marketing channel

27. d: Secondary data

28. a: Competitive intelligence

29. : Organizational structure

30. a: Brand

31. a: Shopping

32. d: Statistic

33. a: Customer satisfaction

34. d: Reseller

35. a: Public

36. : Revenue

37. : Inflation

38. : Mobile marketing

39. d: Sales management

40. b: Market segments

41. c: Shares

42. a: Consideration

43. : Mass media

44. c: Hearing

45. d: Infomercial

46. a: Feedback

47. d: Regulation

48. b: Franchising

49. d: Accounting

50. d: Respondent

51. a: Interview

52. c: Mass marketing

53. a: Perception

54. : Nonprofit

55. : Marketing communications

56. d: Organizational culture

57. : Database

58. a: Market segmentation

59. c: Google

Manufacturing

1. c: Synergy

2. d: Management process

3. : Ishikawa diagram

4. : Steering committee

5. c: Design of experiments

6. a: Turbine

7. c: Poka-yoke

8. a: New product development

9. d: Supply chain risk management

10. a: Economies of scope

11. c: Cost

12. a: Sputnik

13. a: Value engineering

14. b: Quality Engineering

15. a: Service level

16. c: Purchasing

17. c: Sony

18. d: Manufacturing

19. : Thomas Register

20. c: Authority

21. : Control chart

22. a: Supply chain management

23. : Quality costs

24. d: Global sourcing

25. : Ball

26. a: Supply chain

27. b: Sharing

28. : Request for proposal

29. a: Zero Defects

30. d: Opportunity cost

31. c: Project manager

32. a: Transaction cost

33. c: Waste

34. : Control limits

35. d: Change management

36. a: Reorder point

37. c: Bill of materials

38. : Quality function deployment

39. c: Risk management

40. b: Concurrent engineering

41. b: Downtime

42. c: Flowchart

43. d: Retail

44. a: Malcolm Baldrige National Quality Award

45. b: Aggregate planning

46. b: Cash register

47. : Catalyst

48. a: Furnace

49. c: Pareto analysis

50. b: Performance

51. : Resource management

52. c: Quality policy

53. d: Statistical process control

54. c: Total quality management

55. d: Licensed production

56. c: Service quality

57. : Time management

58. c: Cost driver

59. : Strategic planning

Commerce

1. : Project

2. b: Statutory law

3. b: Initiative

4. b: Logo

5. b: Forward auction

6. b: Enabling

7. b: Complaint

8. : Cooperative

9. c: Merger

10. b: Inventory control

11. c: Basket

12. c: Product line

13. d: General manager

14. b: Anticipation

15. b: Loyalty

16. : Vendor

17. c: Jury

18. : Total cost

19. d: Shares

20. c: Webvan

21. : Accounting

22. c: Customs

23. b: American Express

24. a: Americans with Disabilities Act

25. d: Microsoft

26. d: Market share

27. d: Credit card

28. b: Organizational structure

29. b: Trial

30. : Pizza Hut

31. a: Inventory

32. : Bank

33. b: Game

34. d: Payment system

35. b: Consumer-to-consumer

36. d: Strategic plan

37. : Minimum wage

38. d: Supervisor

39. d: Trade

40. a: Market structure

41. d: Short run

42. : Negotiation

43. d: Variable cost

44. c: Electronic funds transfer

45. d: Audit

46. : Consignee

47. : Real estate

48. a: Stock

49. d: Yield management

50. d: Vickrey auction

51. b: Long run

52. a: Joint venture

53. d: Quality assurance

54. : Strategic alliance

55. : Liquidation

56. b: Marginal cost

57. c: Board of directors

58. a: Front office

59. a: Staff position

Business ethics

1. a: Micromanagement

2. c: Perception

3. b: Greenpeace

4. b: Consumer Protection

5. : Stanford Financial Group

6. a: Utilitarianism

7. b: Organizational culture

8. a: Planet

9. c: Volcker Rule

10. c: Accounting

11. d: Lead

12. c: Nonprofit

13. a: Risk assessment

14. : Urban sprawl

15. : Cause-related marketing

16. b: Recovery Act

17. b: Marketing

18. a: Feedback

19. d: Organizational structure

20. d: Biofuel

21. b: Madoff

22. d: Oil spill

23. d: Communist Manifesto

24. : Chamber of Commerce

25. d: Corporate social responsibility

26. a: Clayton Act

27. a: Executive compensation

28. a: Planned obsolescence

29. : Occupational Safety and Health Administration

30. b: Corporate governance

31. : New Deal

32. : Pyramid scheme

33. d: Sexual harassment

34. b: Lawsuit

35. a: Living wage

36. d: Forest Stewardship Council

37. b: Coal

38. : Layoff

39. d: Medicaid

40. a: Endangered Species Act

41. d: Ethical leadership

42. c: Real estate

43. c: Building

44. d: Disclaimer

45. b: Cultural relativism

46. b: Employee Polygraph Protection Act

47. d: Pollution Prevention

48. b: ExxonMobil

49. a: Sustainable

50. a: Partnership

51. d: Aristotle

52. : Insider trading

53. a: Vigilance committee

54. : Public relations

55. c: United Farm Workers

56. c: Green marketing

57. c: Charles Ponzi

58. : Corporate structure

59. b: European Commission

Accounting

1. : Controversy

2. b: Tax reform

3. d: Process Management

4. b: Voucher

5. d: Contributed capital

6. b: Budget

7. : Ledger

8. a: Money

9. c: Zero-based budgeting

10. a: Standard cost

11. c: Capital stock

12. : Long-term liabilities

13. a: Chief executive officer

14. c: Present value

15. b: Certified Public Accountant

16. : Tax credit

17. c: Subsidiary ledger

18. a: Cost of goods available for sale

19. b: Investment center

20. b: Petty cash

21. : MACRS

22. a: Flowchart

23. b: Tax avoidance

24. b: Shareholder

25. c: Accrued liabilities

26. a: Responsibility center

27. c: Controlling interest

28. d: Promissory note

29. a: Dividend yield

30. c: Accounting management

31. a: Value theory

32. d: Write-off

33. : Substitute check

34. d: Land

35. : Deferred tax

36. a: Net investment

37. : Contribution margin

38. c: Job order

39. a: Maturity date

40. d: Personal identification number

41. b: Decentralization

42. d: Standard deduction

43. b: Revenue center

44. a: Relevant cost

45. a: Operating expense

46. b: Receivable

47. b: Receipt

48. : Certified Management Accountant

49. d: Deferred income

50. : General ledger

51. : Purchase order

52. b: Capital asset

53. b: Governmental accounting

54. c: Preferred stock

55. b: Times interest earned

56. : Beneficiary

57. : Customer profitability

58. d: Bank statement

59. : Arthur Andersen

CPSIA information can be obtained
at www.ICGtesting.com
Printed in the USA
LVHW041329301019
635717LV00008B/999/P

9 781538 863527